Advance Praise

"Joy isn't some extra sprinkle on leadership; it's the whole cake. In *Joyosity*, Jenn Whitmer reminds us that people don't follow spreadsheets; they follow joy-filled leaders. This book is an invitation with an instruction manual that is equal parts story, science, and strategy. If you've ever rolled your eyes at joy, Jenn will change your mind and your leadership."

—**Bob Goff,** Four-time *New York Times* bestselling author

"With humor, heart, and a knack for turning conflict into connection, Jenn Whitmer shows leaders how to transform stress into joy and build teams that thrive as much as they achieve."

—**Will Guidara,** *New York Times* bestselling author of *Unreasonable Hospitality,* co-producer of FX's *The Bear,* host of The Welcome Conference

"As the CEO of the American Negotiation Institute and host of the world's number-one negotiation podcast with over 1,600 episodes, I've had the privilege of learning from some of the best. Jenn Whitmer is one of the rare guests I've invited back multiple times—because she brings something different. While many focus on tactics and scripts, Jenn goes deeper, shining a light on the often-overlooked drivers of joy, connection, and humanity. Her work is a refreshing and necessary reminder that success in life and leadership isn't just about strategy—it's about the courage to create spaces of joy where people can truly thrive."

—**Kwame Christian Esq.,** MA, Bestselling author, podcaster, founder and CEO of American Negotiation Institute

"*Joyosity* isn't another book about chasing happiness. It's a smart, research-based road map for leaders. With stories that resonate and tools you can actually use, Jenn makes the case that joy is not a luxury; it's the foundation for cultures where people flourish and deliver extraordinary business results."

—**Dr. Tasha Eurich,** *New York Times* bestselling author of *Shatterproof, Insight,* and *Bankable Leadership*

"Leadership is everyday negotiation. In *Joyosity*, Jenn Whitmer shows how curiosity and joy transform conflict into connection. Not fluff—practical and tactical strategies that make workplaces less exhausting and more collaborative."

—**S. Lucia Kanter St. Amour,** Attorney, VP for UN Women, and author of *For the Forces of Good*

"*Joyosity* is the book we ALL need! This is a brilliant blend of unforgettable stories, rock-solid science, and strategies you can use right away. This isn't leadership fantasy. It's the perfect playbook for real leaders in real life. I couldn't stop reading, and I kept thinking: Leaders need this NOW. Bonus? You'll laugh out loud while you learn. Jenn Whitmer shows joy as the science and the strategy for leaders who actually want to thrive."

—**Jenny Evans,** Speaker, author, and executive coach on resilience and performance

"*Joyosity* is a road map for brave leaders with the audacity to create cultures where humanity and high performance finally live in harmony—where roots bear fruit and the fire within is free to fly."

—**Judi Holler,** *USA Today* bestselling author, speaker, and self-expressionist

"If there's anyone I'd take notes from on how to bring and create more joy at work (and in life), it'd be Jenn Whitmer. *Joyosity* brings wisdom, research, and story together in a way that feels both deeply human and entirely practical. This book is a refreshing call for leaders to embrace joy, not as a luxury, but as a force for trust, performance, and connection. If you lead others—or even yourself—this book will help you do so with more courage, clarity, and heart."

—**Stephen "Shed" Shedletzky,** Leadership speaker, coach, and author of *Speak-Up Culture*

"In a world where culture is a competitive advantage, joy is the secret ingredient to success, and *Joyosity* is the guide. Jenn Whitmer provides research-backed tools and practices to help leaders overcome challenges—from burnout to business metrics—to create joyful environments that get results."

—**Kindra Hall,** *Wall Street Journal* bestselling author and keynote speaker

"*Joyosity* is a much-needed guide for leaders committed to creating workplaces where people flourish. Jenn Whitmer shows that joy isn't fluff—it's a deeply rooted and powerful fuel for productivity, connection, and lasting impact."

—**Lauren Ready,** Six-time Emmy winner, owner and principal storyteller at Forever Ready Productions, and author of *Ask Like a Leader*

"Jenn Whitmer reminds us that joy isn't a luxury in leadership—it's a necessity. *Joyosity* is honest, practical, and deeply human, showing leaders how to fuel both people and performance through joy."

—**Lisa Nichols,** CEO and cofounder of Technology Partners, speaker, author, and host of the *Something Extra* podcast

"*Joyosity* isn't about pretending everything's fine or putting on a happy face—it's about leading well from the mess of a Monday morning through the demands of a Friday afternoon, and every moment in between. With wisdom grounded in the Enneagram, experience, and research, Jenn Whitmer shows leaders how joy and curiosity can help people flourish and organizations thrive."

—**Scott Allender,** Author of *The Enneagram of Emotional Intelligence*

"We've been conditioned to believe that joy doesn't belong in the workplace—that work is supposed to be serious and hard. With wisdom, clarity, and practical insight, *Joyosity* is a powerful invitation to rethink what we've been taught and to embrace the idea that joy at work isn't a luxury but a necessity for thriving organizations and people."

—**Amy Shaw,** President and CEO of Nine PBS

"Meeting Jenn was the silver lining to my COVID clouds, building up my self-confidence at a point when I really needed it. By sharing her wisdom through writing *Joyosity,* many others can benefit as I did. There can be a lot of toxicity in modern life, often the consequence of poor leadership, which Jenn draws out and then provides the antidote—joy to counteract the stress and anxiety we invariably encounter. *Joyosity* is a robust resource for you and to recommend to others!"

—**Steve J. Smith,** Business advisor and author of *The Power of Baked Alaska*

"Forget toxic positivity. This is joyful leadership with teeth (and a smile). Backed by research and packed with tools, *Joyosity* turns joy into your secret weapon. Stop surviving and start leading (and reading)."

—**Ron Tite,** Bestselling author of *Think. Do. Say.* and *The Purpose of Purpose*

"Joy is more than a commodity . . . it's the foundation upon which we build a meaningful life. And we're losing it. *Joyosity* is essential reading for employees, entrepreneurs, and everyone in between."

—**Rebecca Tolbert,** LICSW, ADHD specialist

"As a creative leader who has always believed that we were never made to suffer our way to greatness, I have learned that real brilliance flows when joy fuels the making—when teams create, collaborate, and innovate with life in the process, not just in the outcome. *Joyosity* is a playbook for that kind of work and Jenn Whitmer shows us that joy isn't just the reward—it's the way."

—**Ken Black,** Former Nike creative director and chief creative officer at GMR Marketing

"*Joyosity* is the leadership book I didn't know I was waiting for. Unlike most you-can-do-it leadership books, Jenn doesn't just talk theory; she hands you stories, research, and tools you can actually use today. This read gives you a road map to create teams that perform, belong, and thrive."

—**Kim Kaupe,** Entrepreneur, speaker, and cofounder of Bright Ideas Only

"I was the first to preorder *Joyosity* because I knew Jenn would deliver the truth about joy at work and why it matters. I once built success that looked great from the outside but left me burned out inside. This book is deeply researched, wildly relatable, and packed with tools that help leaders create success that actually feels like success with JOY."

—**Erika Biddix,** Speaker and entrepreneurial strategist

"Work without joy is toil—and Jenn Whitmer refuses to let us languish."

—**Liane Davey,** PhD, The Teamwork Doctor and *NYT* bestselling author

"*Joyosity* is so much more than a typical leadership book—it's a celebration of what makes us human. I absolutely loved every page! This book recognizes the beautiful complexity within each of us and addresses the whole person, not just the leader. The insights are profound, the information is invaluable, and the practical to-dos are incredibly helpful. I found myself inspired and energized, and I'll be ordering copies for my entire leadership team. If you want to foster authentic, joyful leadership, this is the book you need!"

—**Angela Quinn,** Esq., COO of Husch Blackwell

"Jenn Whitmer's *Joyosity* is the ultimate playbook on leading yourself and translating it into leading others. She gives you the human-centered skills to become the kind of person who leads with curiosity, emotional intelligence, and authentic joy. It's leadership from the inside out."

—**Kevin B. Jennings,** Business coach and personal brand strategist

Joyosity

Joyosity

How to Cultivate
Intense Happiness
in Work & Life

(Even If Things Are What They Are)

Jenn Whitmer

WASHINGTON, DC

IDEAPRESS
PUBLISHING

Copyright © 2025 by Jenn Whitmer

All rights reserved. No part of this book may be reproduced, stored, or transmitted by any means—whether auditory, graphic, mechanical, or electronic—without written permission of both publisher and author, except in the case of brief excerpts used in critical articles and reviews. Unauthorized reproduction of any part of this work is illegal and is punishable by law.

Ideapress Publishing | www.ideapresspublishing.com

All trademarks are the property of their respective companies.

Cover Design: Catherine Casalino

Interior Design: Jessica Angerstein

Author Photo: Jeff Brown

Cataloging-in-Publication Data is on file with the Library of Congress.

Hardcover ISBN: 978-1-64687-285-5

Special Sales

Ideapress books are available at a special discount for bulk purchases for sales promotions and premiums, or for use in corporate training programs. Special editions, including personalized covers, a custom foreword, corporate imprints, and bonus content, are also available.

1 2 3 4 5 6 7 8 9 10

In memory of Grandma Jane, who brought joy in darkness and magic to messes.

We need joy as we need air. We need love as we need water.
We need each other as we need the earth we share.

—attributed to Maya Angelou

People are entitled to joy at work.

—W. Edwards Deming

Tell me, what is it you plan to do
with your one wild and precious life?

—Mary Oliver, "The Summer Day," *House of Light*

Contents

Your Printed Invitation xiii

Chapter One: Has Anyone Seen Joy?
Why You Care Right Now 1

Chapter Two: Languishing in Leadership:
Call in the Joy Ratio 15

Part I: Explore
Same You. New Truth.

Chapter Three: Don't Let Your Personality Drive the Bus:
Steer with Self-Awareness 43

Chapter Four: Cut! Rewrite! Action!
Lead with Better Stories 73

Chapter Five: Eagles on Posters Don't Fly:
Make Values Actionable 95

Part II: Engage
Complex People. Power Skills.

Chapter Six: Feelings at the Table:
Lead with Emotional Intelligence 117

Chapter Seven: Clean It Up: Better Communication Now 141

Chapter Eight: Conflict Is Opportunity: Lead with Curiosity 163

Chapter Nine: The Wisdom of Tomatoes:
Decision-Making Under Pressure 185

Part III: Experience
Stop Rehearsing. Live in Joy.

Chapter Ten: Your Inbox Isn't a Hippo:
Practice Your Way out of Stress 219

Chapter Eleven: Wipe Out the Fuzz:
Practices That Protect Joy 243

Chapter Twelve: Three-Layer Biscuits:
Steady Structures That Sustain Joy 271

Chapter Thirteen: The Serious Business of Play:
Productivity and Performance Through Play 303

Your RSVP to Joyosity:
The Choice That Changes Everything 331

Extra! Extra!

The Joyosity Resource Lounge 347

Stories, Study Stacks, and Citations 353

High-Fives, Hugs, and Hallelujahs 379

About Jenn, Your Joy-Bringing Host 385

Your Printed Invitation

Welcome, Doubters, Devotees, and the Joy-Curious,

We're literally dying without joy at work. To the tune of 120,000 deaths a year.[1]

On top of the tragic loss of life, the pain of dysfunctional workplaces pours past our interactions with coworkers, clients, and customers. It follows us home. Three in four people who experience work-related anxiety and stress report that it significantly impacts their home life.[2*]

Joy is what will save us.

Leaders who work at creating joy consistently develop high-performing teams, loyal customers, and trust-based cultures that outperform the market average by nearly four times.[3**] Research also shows that those same positive relational skills flow through your personal relationships and literally help you live longer.[4]

You're holding a guide for leaders like you to cultivate more joy in work and in the rest of life, even when you can't change the circumstances. These pages show you how to create and maintain joy through the moments that stop you—like what to do when you get *that* email. You know, the one that makes you feel like a cartoon

---

* So you don't have to flip to the notes yet: *Zippia's 40+ Worrisome Workplace Stress Statistics 2023.*

** "Best Places to Work" from *Great Place to Work 2024.*

character with steam billowing out of your ears. Or when the hospital calls, and you're plunged into a new reality.

And, yes, I know the subtitle says, "Work and Life," but let's not pretend they exist in separate bubbles. What happens in one flows into the other, because wherever you go, there you are. Your self-awareness, the way you engage with other people, and how you structure your days don't log off at five or stay outside the office door. They all come with you. You are a whole person, living one whole life.

Substantial research provides the foundation for this book, and real-life experiences of leaders connect the theory to your too-long to-do list and the complexity of your actual life.* Use *Joyosity* as a robust resource you'll reach for to buoy yourself and share with others.

I've lived through the slow poison of a great place becoming great pain. I promise to tell you the truth—from my own hard-won wisdom and other leaders who've walked it—so you can use it in your actual, walking-around life.

I invite you to:

 Engage your curiosity. When you feel cynicism or despair creeping in, let curiosity keep flipping to the next page.

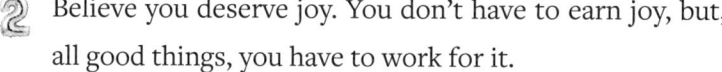 Believe you deserve joy. You don't have to earn joy, but, like all good things, you have to work for it.

Let's go.

Jenn

---

* There are about 350 citations and notes in the back, just in case you're curious.

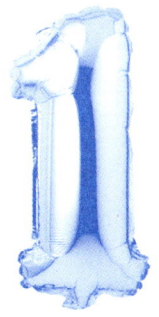

Has Anyone Seen Joy?

Why You Care Right Now

Joy is an act of resistance.

—Toi Derricotte, "The Telly Cycle," *The Undertaker's Daughter*

"I'm eliminating your position," my boss said. His words slapped me, clean and cold. I didn't know it yet, but my journey to joy at work had just begun.

Before we get to what happened next, let's start seven years earlier, when my leadership intersected with a third grader named Maisie.

I was the new director of assessment and feedback in a small private elementary school with about 300 students, including my four kids. Not only did I get to shape how the school approached student success, but I worked with the fiercely dedicated educators and administrators.

This community operated with a collaborative growth mindset. I led the work of aligning classroom assessments to standards, utilizing standardized assessments, administrating report cards and parent-teacher conferences . . .

Did you shudder a little? Don't worry. Most people have that response. And so did Maisie, as most kids did when I started at the school. TESTING WAS SERIOUS. Accreditation, funding, enrollment—oh, and actual educational work—all depended on accurate assessments. But I knew there had to be a better way to get clear results that didn't stress out the teachers, families, and students. By third grade, Maisie had heard the horror stories and felt the intense anxiety that permeated the school every spring, and now it was her turn.

One afternoon, I sat in my tiny office as the recess sounds of voices squealing, balls bouncing, and children laughing floated through the window. *Could I make testing feel like that? Could I at least start with joy?* I pitched the idea, and we took the risk.

Instead of the traditional end-of-year testing frenzy, we moved the tests to January. We spread them out to avoid overload. I even sent home kits filled with bouncy balls, bubbles, and encouragement to approach testing with curiosity and ease.

As the testing season ended that first January, Maisie's mom, Jessi, strolled into my office and plopped a bright purple gift bag on my desk. I peeled back the tissue paper to reveal a colorful desk plaque that read: *Jennifer Whitmer, Director of Good Moods.*

"Jessi! What is this for?"

Jessi launched into a hilarious impression of her nine-year-old: "Mom! Testing is the best. We get animal crackers and cheese sticks. We play a game before we start and get EXTRA recess. And all I have to do is the stuff we already learn in school!"

The first part of our experiment had succeeded. We could bring joy into testing.

When Jessi came into my office, I'd already seen the score reports. Our school had scored in the top 25th percentile, and many students had scored even higher. A few years later, the US Department of Education designated our school as a Blue Ribbon School, which is the highest government honor for a school. Awarded to only fifty private schools each year, the Department choses schools based on test scores and culture.

We brought joy to the center of the workiest work—to the very place where most people lean into austerity and anxiety.

Maisie's experience confirmed part one of my theory: We could reduce stress with joy. Our scores and awards confirmed part two: Joy produced better results.

When Joy Leaves the Building

How did I go from accepting the highest academic honor on stage with the US Secretary of Education, to sitting on the white couch in the head of school's office feeling shocked, yet not surprised?

In the years between changing testing and receiving the Blue Ribbon, we transitioned to a new leader. The new leader drifted from the student- and joy-centered approach to appeasing various stakeholders, constantly changing internal systems, and appealing to donors for a building fund. When we replaced joy as the center of our culture, communication fractured. Gossip increased. Decisions felt erratic. Gaslighting brought confusion. Shame became the primary motivator, and we existed in a fake peace.

Whenever I share this story from the stage during a keynote, I always pause at this point. Without fail, people in the audience stare back at me with wide eyes and nodding heads of recognition. I originally thought I was the only one, but unfortunately, this experience is far too common. Depending on the source, 50 to 75 percent of workers label their workplace as dysfunctional, with up to one in four experiencing a toxic environment.[1]

Do you recognize dysfunction and pain where you've worked or where you are now?

In our organization, in addition to the steadily rising toxicity, we spent so much time solving communication issues, muddling through personality clashes, and revisiting decisions that productivity inevitably plummeted. Everyone was working harder, but not seeing the same results we had experienced only a few years earlier.

In casual conversations, regular meetings, and formal documentation, I and others on the admin team brought these concerns to our leader. He dismissed those concerns, insisting we were overreacting or didn't really get it.

The Moment of Unwelcome Truth

One April morning, after a disastrous presentation to an outside accreditation agency, a fellow director came to my office and pulled up a chair next to my desk.

"Jenn, this is toxic. And we have to recognize it."

I dropped back in my chair, blown away. I found myself stammering, words of resistance building on my tongue. Somehow, I summoned the wisdom to stay silent for a moment.

Our leader had again shirked responsibilities, deflected, and blamed, while gaslighting us that "this was the plan all along." He had siloed communication and pitted one group against another.

Stuck in this cycle of crazy-making behavior, I had such little mental space left that I was missing deadlines and poorly supporting the faculty. I had an unexplained knee injury that wouldn't go away. I wasn't sleeping. My weight was skyrocketing, even though nothing about my diet or exercise had changed. I couldn't even read to my kids at night without being filled with thoughts of work.

I was doing what a lot of leaders do—pretend I could get through it by staying the course. I just needed to persevere! Resilience in the face of adversity! *Once we get through accreditation, it will get better.*

Leaning back in that chair, I finally began to see we had floated our way into the deep end of a leadership crisis that was demolishing our culture, devastating our people, and derailing us from our mission.

My friend was right. The situation was toxic, a slow poison destroying everything.

And still! I didn't want to admit it. I didn't want to use the word *toxic* or *trauma*. I didn't want to be that person in that place. Yet, I already *was* that person in that place. Denying the reality didn't magically make me the exception. I was another burned-out leader pretending everything was fine, while being complicit in it all.

I wish I could tell you I got up from that bungee chair and fixed it all like Wonder Woman with my golden lasso. The situation deteriorated more, but that was the moment I realized truly how far we had drifted from joy.

Three months later, I sat on that ridiculous white couch with a quiet scream behind my ribs: *It doesn't have to be this way!* We had years of healthy, flourishing leadership. What created that culture? How did we maintain it? How did we lose it?

Your Leadership Casts a Long Shadow

Research shows most people don't leave a job—they leave a boss. Your direct manager has more influence on your mental health than your partner, doctor, or therapist.[2] And that means you as a leader hold a weighty responsibility.

Before we go any further: **You are a leader.** You picked up this book. You got out of bed today. You brushed your teeth (right?). Regardless of the position or title you hold, you have to lead yourself first. You are CEO of your own life.

The leader directly influences the day-to-day work experience, including workload, resources, time off, communication, and much more.[*] When you dig deeper into the causes of low engagement, attrition, and low productivity, the research raises consistent red flags:

---

[*] Reminder: that means you as a leader also have this level of influence in your own life.

poor communication, unreasonable expectations, meaningless tasks, insufficient recognition, and disjointed direction. Many of these fall under the responsibility of you as the leader—for you and your team.

What you want at work looks like what everyone else wants: purposeful work that makes a difference, a sense of belonging to a group, Goldilocks workloads that aren't boring but aren't absurd, systems and resources that support your work, and respect for your humanity.

Most leadership advice begins with questions like, How do we solve productivity? How do we increase engagement? How do we retain talent? And while those are good questions, they bring a scattershot approach to solving our workplace problems and creating the culture I described. If you're going to be the leader that is effective without destroying yourself and others, you need to start with a bigger question.

The question to begin with is this: Where is joy?

Joyosity Is the Way: Lead Without Losing Yourself

I define joy as *intense happiness from a feeling of profound connection and appreciation, experiencing something greater than yourself.* Joy is the profound contentment rooted in deep connections to yourself, others, and purpose—with the intense appreciation of what you do and how you get to do it—plus the embodied experience of something that is greater than just you in the moment.

Does that sound like a place you want to be? I mean, me too!

Joy doesn't merely show up. You've got to chase it down, tackle it, and actively cultivate it. That's where Joyosity comes to the rescue.

Joyosity actively pursues joy with curiosity through connection, leading to that place where you are flourishing, experiencing overall peace, wholeheartedness, and well-being, content with yourself and relationships, and engaged in meaningful work that brings life to you and your community. That is the work of Joyosity—where joy is sustained by curiosity and connection.

No biggie, right? I know. It's far from easy.

The Joyosity Overture

The first time you hear the Bom, bom, bum-bum-bum bahhhh dahhhh of the *Star Wars* main theme in *Episode IV: A New Hope*, you lean in. John Williams's brass fanfare serves a bigger purpose than hooking you into the main title sequence. The overture of a musical or movie score gives you a snippet of the significant musical motifs coming in the show. It's enough to excite you, provide the comfort of recognition later, and indicate some direction without overwhelming you.

Welcome to the Joyosity Overture!

We're going to start with what languishing in leadership looks like today: the reasons the pervasive problems in workplaces leave you stuck, ineffective, and exhausted in your whole life. Then, you'll get a new picture of joy and your introduction to the Joy Ratio.

Next up are the three sections from the Joyosity Compass.

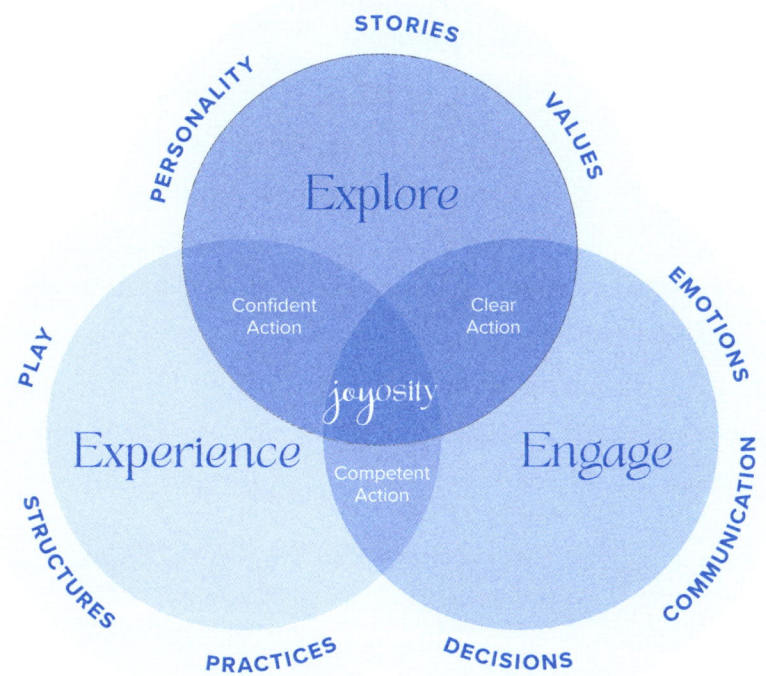

Part One: Exploring Joy from the Inside Out

You can't lead anyone else until you lead yourself. So joy begins with exploring your self. Chapter three breaks down the power of self-awareness as a foundational leadership skill and introduces you to the Johari Window and the Enneagram as the tools you'll use throughout the book. Chapter four addresses how leadership mindset and internal stories create the results in your life—intended and unintended. Chapter five lays out your values alignment that creates ease and success.

Part Two: Engaging Authentically with People-Power Skills

Self-awareness is the foundation. But self-awareness alone won't make you a joyful leader; you need to engage with people-power skills. In chapter six, you'll learn why there is no sustainable leadership without emotional intelligence. Chapter seven helps strengthen the primary engagement skill you must master as a leader—healthy communication. Chapter eight takes you to the next level through managing conflict. Chapter nine will transform your decision-making skills. Woven through the Engage section, you'll learn your Enneagram conflict and leadership styles, and how to apply that style to cultivate joy.

Part Three: Experiencing Joy in Your One, Whole Life

You don't live your entire life at the pinnacle of success. You have to build an experience that sustains joy, even when things are what they are. Chapter ten provides use-them-right-now practices to navigate stress. Chapter eleven gives you a menu of practices and connects them to your Enneagram group so you sustain joy. Chapter twelve shows you how to build steady structures that hold you up under the pressures of life. Lucky chapter thirteen shows you the serious benefit of play as an essential tool of leadership, including how to use your play persona for problem-solving, productivity, and expertise.

We'll wrap up with real-life stories of transformation, unpacking the stages of growth and the keys to sustaining change, so you are inspired and equipped to cultivate joy in your one, whole life.

Each chapter closes with Joy Work to give you immediate ways to apply the content of the chapter. And in the back, you've also got the Joyosity Resource Lounge (the Lounge) with Stories, Study Stacks, and Citations, which are notes, references, and bonus materials for you. If you're ready to go deeper, grab the *Joyosity Works Playbook* (the *Playbook*), a robust collection of exercises, frameworks, reflection prompts, and practical tactics to deepen joy in your one, whole life.

Read This Before You Start the Show

My husband, Michael, and our oldest daughter, Sabrina, spoil books for everyone else. Our youngest, Annalise, and I like surprises and mystery and all the context of the story unfolding. Michael and Sabrina do not. They flip around, read the end, and unless I'm waving my arms like a frantic traffic cop, they'll ruin the story for me. Our oldest son, Chase, will read every footnote and check every citation.[*] And our son Stuart wants the action: "Just tell me what to do now."

So I've structured this book to keep us *all* happy.

The Joyosity Compass isn't linear. It's more like a spiraling Slinky—flexible, looping, and interconnected. You'll wind through all the sections continuously as you face new challenges and successes. Although I believe the linear order here provides the best path, you may face a pressing need today in your leadership that's in a later chapter. Go there. Choose your own adventure.

Here's what I recommend:

First, you need to understand the principles in chapter two: the depth of the problem, why we haven't changed it yet, a new image of joy, and the Joy Ratio.

Next, head to chapter three. Every successful and meaningful leadership approach begins with understanding yourself first.

---

[*] "That's what they're there for. Of course."—Chase Whitmer

You'll want to choose your Enneagram personality type.* If you just thought *Ennea-whatsit?*, no problem. The Enneagram is a personality framework that shows you *why* you feel, think, and act the way you do. Throughout the book, I connect strategies back to specific Enneagram types. With that understanding, you'll be more effective in cultivating joy.

Then, after chapters two and three, you can skip around. (As much as I've tailored each word, I know you're already skimming.) *Get what you need when you need it.* Once you've read the remaining chapters, go for the conclusion. If you're like Michael and Sabrina and you've already read it, promise me (and yourself) that you'll go back to pick up the actual tools and practices that cultivate joy.

Finally, mark this baby up. This is the book you'll pull off the shelf when everything changes. Because here's an inconvenient truth: *The struggles circle back.*

Circumstances will change and the same issues will reappear, especially when you level up in leadership or experience personal shake-ups. Because when you, your team, and the world changes, you need both the foundations *and* different tools for different circumstances.

To be a dog-eared, reached-for guide, I've loaded this book with a Cheesecake Factory menu of resources, thoughtfully categorized and surprisingly delightful. What we're not doing? Shame. Take what you need now and come back when life inevitably twists again.

So cue the orchestra. Grab your lightsaber (or pen). The joy-filled rebellion for a new hope in leadership starts now.

---

* Even if you know your type, subtype, and Tritype, read this chapter. You *will* learn something new, and I want us to be speaking the same Enneagram language. I teach the Enneagram differently than others, so *Let's get together, yeah yeah yeah.*

Real joy has deep roots. Roots form in the dark.

Languishing in Leadership

Call in the Joy Ratio

> I am not merely an economic unit.
> I am human . . . I need a new money.
>
> —**Andy Grammer, "I Need a New Money"**

Takebayashi Katsuyoshi collapsed of a hemorrhage on December 12, 1969, on the floor of the Asahi Newspaper Company in Osaka, Japan. After working intense hours each month, at twenty-nine years old, he died of a stroke. Mr. Katsuyoshi became the first documented case of *karoshi*, death by overwork. Tragically, many others followed.[1]

Miss Yoshida, a twenty-two-year-old nurse, suffered a fatal heart attack after working thirty-four-hour shifts five times a month. With a three-and-a-half-hour commute plus working over seventy hours a week at an advertising agency, Mr. Yagi also died from a heart attack. He was forty-three. Matsuri Takahashi slept barely ten hours a week because of her workload and died at the age of twenty-four in December 2015.

Despite workplace reforms, the phenomenon continues. Many workers develop severe fatigue, back pain, stomach ulcers, and asthma, as well as critically high blood pressure and deadly heart problems.

Do you recognize even a hint of this in your own life? These physical symptoms of overwhelm and overwork don't simply hang out in Japan. They are rampant in global workplaces at every level.

The Current State of Stress

"This stress is so much, but everyone else is stressed too."
"I have to just keep going until XYZ. Then it will be better."
"I feel so stuck and lost. But what else am I going to do?"
"This is ridiculous. I just don't know why my work matters."
"I'm exhausted. The pressure won't let up."

I hear phrases like this from leaders regularly. Any like you? Leaders across the world face this epidemic. Study after study shows the rising challenge of workplace stress and its impact on people, performance, productivity, and profitability.

Here's a small sample of US data:

- In 2022, fifty million people left their jobs, setting a record-high attrition rate.[2]
- Gallup reported that workplace engagement hit an eleven-year low in April 2024.[3]

- Workforce State of Mind 2024 published that work stress has negatively impacted the physical health of 77 percent of employees.[4]
- Zippia's 2023 research found more than 65 percent of employees find it difficult to concentrate because of their work environment, compared to 46 percent in 2018.[5]

The research roundup concluded with this sobering fact: "Work-related stress causes 120,000 deaths and results in $190 billion in health care costs" each year.[6]

Wait, I thought this was a book about joy? It is. We're literally dying from lack of joy.

The majority of stress and anxiety in and out of the workplace comes from *how* we work together, not *what* our work is. How we work and flow together—that's where the struggle bus parks.

On the *Joyosity* podcast, culture expert Moe Carrick told me culture is simply "the way we do things here," and the leader has the most influence on the day-to-day experience of the way we do things.[7] Can't you just hear Bill Lumbergh from *Office Space*? "Ummm, I'm gonna need you to go ahead and . . . "

So we must start with you, the leader. What if you are inching toward *karoshi* yourself? What if you're falling back on old models of leadership? According to statistics from Gallop, you probably got tossed into leadership without much more than a thirty-minute HR training.[8] DDI's 2023 Global Leadership Forecast said only 40 percent of leaders see the quality of leadership in their organization as very good or excellent.[9]

We've got some work to do.

Based on the numbers—and that you're holding this book—I'm guessing you're just as concerned, while also feeling the smoosh of trying to lead the "right way."

Leaders are supposed to be authentic but nonemotional. Care about people but put the bottom line at the top. Have work-life balance but also be available all the time. Be collaborative but decisive. It's no wonder, according to DDI's forecast, 72 percent of leaders are burnt out.[10]

We need to look at the deeper question: Why is joy absent from work?

Roadblocks to Joy

It's been one hundred years since leadership expert Elton Mayo introduced the idea that people at work are not interchangeable widgets (groundbreaking and yet obvious!). Since then, W. Edwards Deming, Rosabeth Moss Kanter, Brené Brown, Adam Grant, Michael C. Bush, Simon Sinek, and countless others have advocated that a human-centered approach to business sustains successful business.

And yet, old habits die hard. Transactional management practices that fit with the more command-and-control leadership style of the early twentieth century, when most corporate culture and structures were established, linger everywhere. Economists like Milton Friedman and Thomas Sowell advocated for profit-centered cultures. Those voices say, yes, positive culture is great, but that's not what we're doing in business. We maximize profits.

That feels a lot like greed. And I don't think that's who you are. I don't think that's who we are.

It's the bill of goods that's a bunch of empty promises. The message is that unless you're only focused on ever-increasing profit, you will fail. Then the insecurity creeps in. Organizations live in a quicksand of fear, clinging to outdated ways of thinking that are slowly killing us. All of this makes joy, at best, nice to have and, at worst, unattainable.

This shows up on the news alert, the business bro podcasts, and your annual all-hands meeting. It has seeped into our vocabulary: "monetize your hobby" or "the side hustle." And it's costing us our humanity.

We don't actually have to live this way. We can have profitable businesses and design the entirety of our lives for joy. But to do it, we need to live in a new, human-centered paradigm.

What if we see business and work as a way to solve problems for people? To solve problems well, you have to be curious, stay connected to people, and have a clear purpose. If we do this successfully, it results in profit.

Remember the definition of joy: intense happiness from a feeling of profound connection and appreciation, experiencing something greater than yourself. Everything about joy puts people in the center.

This is why joy is the heartbeat of a healthy leader and a healthy organization. Joy is the center of how we get all the things we need at work. Not only does it reduce all those terrible health statistics, but it also increases engagement, excellence, innovation, and, as a result, profit.

If we're going to create a new paradigm with joy as the center, we need to name the fallacies getting in the way.

The Myth of Measurement

Many leaders avoid the topic of joy, positive culture, and people-power skills (if you call them soft skills, I will challenge you like Inigo Montoya) because they feel squishy and theoretical. Western workplace culture is obsessed with metrics and measurements. There are three main origins of the zealous idolization of measurement:

1. *If you can't measure it, you can't manage it.* This lie spews from the mouths of too many management experts. Often attributed to W. Edwards Deming, the idea is in order to effectively lead and manage, there must be a quantitative metric by which to judge growth. But Deming never said this. In fact, he wrote, in *The New Economics*, "It is wrong to suppose that if you can't measure it, you can't manage it—a costly myth." The Deming Institute provided more clarification in 2015, saying, "[Deming] also knew that just measuring things and looking at data wasn't close to enough. There are many things that cannot be measured and still must be managed. And there are many things that cannot be measured, and managers must still make decisions about."[11]

2. *Objectivity is the holy grail of wisdom.* A long holdover from the Age of Enlightenment in the eighteenth century, objectivity supposedly removes bias and emotions from clouding our judgment by basing reason in observable facts. The problem with this is humans are going to be human. Bias and emotions will always have a presence in decision-making (we'll get to this in chapters six and nine), and facts without context are meaningless. When you lead, there must be some objectivity and ways to manage biases as well as healthy emotional reg-

ulation. However, leading will always be subjective because humans are subjects to study, not objects to control.

3. *Checklists, metrics, KPIs, and measurements require less effort.* Humans, well, we're going to run from struggle. You know that feel-good dopamine hit you get when you cross everything off your list? It's easy for leaders to confuse leading effectively with a completed checklist. Dealing with complex human nature (including your own) *requires* a different skill set and level of effort. So many leaders, and therefore companies and cultures, grab for the five surefire ways to be the best leader, check off those measurements, and feel good about the work without actually considering the rest of the human element of work.

Do we need measurement and metrics? Absolutely. But these alone are simply insufficient to create the business outcomes leaders want, and woefully short of helping you design a life with joy. As a leader, you need more than metrics to create a thriving culture that gets you all the measurements you want for a healthy workplace and joyful life.

Tradition, TRADITION!

"Why do you cut off the end of the ham?" the husband asked his wife.

"This is the way you do it. It's the way my mom always did it," she replied.

At the next family dinner, the husband asked his mother-in-law, "Your daughter says she cuts the end of the ham because that's what you do. Why do you cut off the end?"

"Well, that's what my mom did too. So that's how I learned it," the mother replied.

At the holidays, Grandma was resting in the living room, and the husband saw his chance. "Your granddaughter and daughter both say they cut off the end of the ham because that's how you always prepared it. Why did you cut off the end of the ham?"

Grandma covered her mouth, giggled, and wiggled her eyebrows, "Well, that's easy. My pan was too small."

Argumentum ad antiquitatem is the logical fallacy that claims, "This way is the right way because we've always done it this way." As Grandma's small pan/large ham issue shows, the "way it's always been" doesn't always match the current need.

When I began teaching in the late '90s, my lesson plan book, student papers, and my own Post-it collection of ideas filled my messenger bag I schlepped to and fro. Around 2002, our district overhauled its technology infrastructure, giving every teacher a fruit-colored iMac on their desk with wireless internet. Each building also received a set of colorful iBooks (the predecessor of the MacBook) teachers could check out and take home.[*]

Suddenly, the work I took home wasn't only the lessons and grading I chose to do on my own time. I was now tethered (literally, by an ethernet cable) to all the parents, colleagues, and administrators wanting information, asking questions, or reminding me to bring bread pudding to the all-staff party.

Today, you may be reading this book on a computer you hold in your hand that you call a phone. Clients text you at 7 a.m. The soccer coach sends a GroupMe message at lunch. Your boss fires out Teams

---

[*] It sounds like the Dark Ages! How fast it's changed.

messages on Sunday. Your team member emails the report you need to edit, and you open it while you wait in the carpool line.

The way we flow together has changed. In the early days of *karoshi*, you had to be at a physical place to overwork. We now have the privilege of technology letting us overwork with ease, at a swim meet on a Saturday morning or the dining room table at midnight.

The runaway acceleration of technology intensifies the pressure, demanding us to sacrifice more of ourselves because we're applying the traditional way of working only at work to everywhere we go all the time. The *way* we work is nearly unrecognizable compared to sixty years ago. "We've always done it this way" is stealing our joy.

It's Not That Bad. Everything's Fine.

My family didn't rent crutches and slings—we owned them. I broke or sprained a limb every year. I got so used to being on crutches, I could nearly beat a healthy walking person in a foot race. I would convince myself broken bones and sprains were totally fine. *It's not that bad. Look at what I can still do!*

Yet, that didn't mean I should have walked on fractures just to prove I could.

When I experienced the toxic workplace environment I described in the first chapter, I told myself the same story: *It's not that bad. We're still doing good things!* At the time, I didn't recognize the hidden signs of toxic environments:

- Saying one thing but doing another
- A growing lack of trust
- Lack of respect for boundaries, especially the amount of

work time expected
- Mission drift
- Improvements or requests shot down in favor of the (broken) status quo

I got so accustomed to those not-so-obvious signs that I didn't bat an eye when blatant dysfunctional and toxic behaviors became the norm:

- Gaslighting
- Blame shifting
- Using shame as a motivator
- Siloing people and forbidding communication
- Saying one thing behind closed doors and another to the public
- Passive-aggressive behavior, and shirking responsibilities and hard decisions

After a LinkedIn post about the problem of toxic workplaces and sharing some of my story, I received a DM from a leader that basically said, "Suck it up. It's not that bad. You should have just been grateful to have a job." The narrative of *It's not that bad* has changed our expectations of what a healthy workplace is, while idolizing unhealthy behaviors we once used to survive. We're living with broken bones and believing that's the way it's supposed to be.

Work Before Play

In second grade, spelling homework filled me with rage. At eight years old, I would actively fume while sitting at my ivory desk with gold trim. The mimeographed pages of ten words to rewrite, define, and *WRITE IN A SENTENCE*—for the love of all that's holy—blocked my path to after-school fun. There was no playing outside or resting until I finished my spelling assignment *every day*. I lived in a prison.

A bit dramatic? Maybe a little.

Although I did learn great things from my jail cell, I carried an unhelpful lesson into adulthood: Rest must be earned, and joy is extra.

Because of the centering of profit, the culture values productivity over humanity. We relentlessly measure output so much that we fraction people—some people are .75 FTE (full-time employee) based on productivity. You accrue (meaning, *earn*) PTO (paid time off) based on how much you have worked.

And we've internalized it. Do you ever think:

"I can't relax until this job is done."

"Taking a break means I'm lazy."

"I'll rest when I achieve the goal."

It's no wonder we're exhausted. DDI's 2023 Global Leadership Forecast showed burnout rates are up 12 percent since 2021.[12] If you have to earn rest, when is it enough? How do you measure "enough" when the to-do list never ends? If work always comes before joy, you will always be in the same prison of work before play. Rest and joy aren't earned after productivity—they fuel it.

"We're Not Worthy"

Two guys. One camera. A cable-access show of random thoughts, cringy interviews, and a lot of "party time . . . excellent." "Wayne's World" sketches on *Saturday Night Live* are TikTok's awkward Gen X uncle.

In the *Wayne's World* movie, after headbanging through an Alice Cooper concert, Wayne and Garth head to the green room to meet their idol in the flesh. Contrary to his bad-boy persona, Cooper is intelligent and friendly. They gawk as Cooper talks Milwaukee history with the band.

As the boys stammer awkward thank-yous and goodbyes, Cooper interrupts and says, "No, no, no. Stick around. Hang out with us."

Wayne and Garth drop to their knees, repeatedly bowing with their faces to the floor—as in the now widespread gif—saying, "We're not worthy. We're not worthy."[13]

We approach joy like Wayne and Garth approach Alice Cooper. Unattainable. And if we do get close to joy, we believe we're not allowed to exist in its presence.

The reasons we operate in this belief system are layered and complex. We don't see joy modeled. Possibly, someone said to you, with out-loud words, "The world doesn't owe you anything"—including happiness.

Mostly, I think it's because we're afraid and unpracticed at joy. "Joy isn't a beginner's virtue; it comes as the culmination. They say its opposite is not sadness, but fear," says Anne Robertson, Methodist pastor and writer.[14]

Joy is vulnerable, exposing. If you've ever been chastised by a teenager for expressing excitement that goes beyond a slight nod of approval, you know the feeling. In the *Journal of Positive Psychology*, researcher Matthew Kuan Johnson published a review of the literature on joy. He quotes philosophers Hubert Dreyfus and Sean Kelly: "Joy makes you more intensely you."[15] Basically, we're afraid to be seen.

From the research, joy appears to be the most connected emotion humans experience. And we exist in a workplace culture constantly telling us to disconnect from ourselves and just do the job. But what if joy, that deeply connected and vulnerable experience, provides the very way to cultivate not merely a successful career, but a whole, flourishing life?

The Wild Resilience of Joy

Ah, but joy feels fleeting and theoretical. Cultivating joy when things are messy seems like an abstract concept. Let's make it more concrete.

Every year, my husband, Michael, counts down the days to the Great Forest Park Balloon Race—his favorite St. Louis tradition. We started going with friends when we first moved to St. Louis and continued the tradition with our kids (the ones who are now in their teens and twenties). He will go alone, if we can't join him. He has swag he wears year-round. The man *loves* balloons.

On Friday night before the race, all of the balloons spread out across the Central Field of Forest Park. More than 100,0000 people flock to the park with picnic baskets, blankets, bikes, and strollers. People pack the field, buzzing with excitement. Just after dusk, the crowds wander among the balloons, delighting in the magic of fire filling the enormous globes of silk.

One year, all six of us piled in the van, stopped at Schnucks for our picnic fixings, and drove to Forest Park. We promptly got stuck in traffic. One hundred thousand people plus only two roads in and out? Gridlock.

Our kids' excitement disappeared as we inched along.

Their whining increased as we finally found a parking spot and loaded the wagon with our folding chairs, blankets, and food.

Michael's irritation steadily grew.

Joyosity

I was trying my best to keep them engaged and encouraged but failing miserably.

By the time we trudged down the crowded slope as the sun had dipped below the hill, every single member of my family radiated the same dark mood: cranky and sullen. Delusional, I clung to the sheer force of positive vibes, desperate to salvage the experience. Then, out of the haze, a woman toting her own picnic basket collided with our wagon. We stared as she faceplanted into the grass. No one moved. No one spoke.

Her stumble drove the dagger in it all. Not even the majestic balloons could withstand the crushing pressure and deep disappointment of that moment. We trudged back up the hill and headed home.

Positive vibes and excitement aren't enough to sustain joy. Circumstances, work, and people are all too complex, too unpredictable to survive on such fragile things. It's a good thing joy has dirt on its face and fire in its eyes, showing up with unflinching strength, unafraid of the messiness of this life.

The Roots

As gorgeous as giant hot-air balloons are, they provide a weak picture of joy. So do cotton candy and rainbows. I want you to replace these common images of joy with lavender.

Lavender resists drought, spreading easily where other plants simply die. It flourishes in rocky, hilly soil with a bite of acid to it. A deep, complex root system allows the plant above the soil to grow both wide and tall. Even planted in rows, lavender refuses to lose its wild streak.

Cotton candy dissolves on the tongue. Rainbows burn off in the heat. Balloons float away, deflate, or pop. But lavender roots deepen, resilient.

That's the genuine joy you're building—the intense happiness that sustains you, even when life bites you with acid and you're parched for hope.

Real joy has deep roots, and roots form in the dark.

Intense happiness doesn't mean every moment of every day. You cultivate this joy by being connected deeply, appreciating what you're doing, and experiencing something greater than yourself in this one moment in time.

Can you find a moment when you experienced this type of joy? Go back to that moment. Close your eyes. Feel it in your body.

You didn't arrive at that moment struggle-free. When I do this exercise in my keynotes, every single time, I see a sea of smiles in the audience. I'm imagining yours right now. That feeling? That's lavender.

Hold onto that feeling as we look at the impact joy has in the workplace and the rest of your life.

Joy Versus Toil

You'll spend a third of your life at work. Before the "business metrics," consider if you're ready to resign that much of your life stripped of joy. Also, you can't compartmentalize joy. A third of your life without joy impacts the entirety of your life.

Let's look at the data. Joy at work is:

- *Productive*: Inspired employees who experience joy at work are 143 percent more productive than disengaged employees, according to Michael Mankins of Bain & Company.[16]
- *Profitable*: Companies with healthy cultures (meaning high levels of trust with engaged, joyful employees) are more profitable and have higher stock market returns. According to research from FTSE Russell, organizations with positive cultures outperform the market by a factor of 3.36.[17]
- *Viral*: Joyful employees improve the group performance by 25 percent and are three and a half times more likely to help others, according to Gitnux Market Data Report 2024.[18]

When Jessi walked in with the "Director of Good Moods" plaque, I experienced joy. When I saw test scores that accurately showed our students' progress, again that was joy. Now, when I get messages from clients like, "We are communicating so much better. The friction is disappearing," that's joy.

So if joy is intense happiness from a feeling of deep connection and appreciation, experiencing something greater than ourselves, what's the opposite?

The opposite of joy is toil. Toil is overtaxing work that is outside of your expertise, skills, resources, interest, and enjoyment. It's meaningless and boring.

For me that's working on a spreadsheet, creating invoices, meeting unrealistic deadlines, analyzing website data, and cleaning out the cat box. Everyone is different.

Regardless of what your toil is, toil left unchecked turns into toxicity. Too much toil and toxicity cost you.

- A toxic employee costs your organization more than twice as much as the contribution of the best performer, according to Harvard Business School.[19]
- Toxicity is ten times more important than compensation when people think about leaving a job.[20]
- Increased levels of toil are linked to impaired cognitive function, diminished memory, a reduced ability to learn, and reduced engagement.[21]

Let's imagine you're adopting a new process or system. Choose your team: Team Joy or Team Toil.

On Team Joy, people are more productive, get through training, and start implementing faster. As you're working, and even after the go-live date, they help each other out with the system. When bugs happen (as they always do), the joy group flexes and solves problems.

Those on Team Toil don't have the brain space for anything new, so learning is glacial. The team has difficulty concentrating, and they can't remember details well. With the extra training needed and the lack of progress, the go-live date gets pushed back. Throughout the entire process, people have a hard *lean out* approach to everything.

So team captain, who ya picking to be on your team? I know I'm choosing Team Joy every time. They get the job done and have fun doing it. As for Team Toil? They can have their eye rolls, delays, and bad attitudes. Hard. Pass.

The Joy Ratio

You might be thinking, *OK, am I supposed to just love what I do every moment?*

Joyosity

Absolutely not. That's entirely unrealistic. You have responsibilities you don't like. Everyone does. You must do the necessary tasks that keep life going, the things no one wants to do.

Is there a formula that cultivates those positive outcomes all while mitigating the negative ones? Why, yes. Yes, there is. When it comes to joy at work and the rest life, you want to be in the Joy Ratio of 35–10–55.[22]

Joy's Magic Third

To experience the benefits of joy at work, you want 35 percent of your time and tasks spent on doing work you love. This is the Magic Third. Work that you're skilled to do, with the appropriate time to do it, still might be challenging or difficult. But the work connects to purpose, you feel fortunate to do it, and other people benefit from it too.

Signals you're experiencing joy in your work:

1. You feel favored or fortunate, not by comparison. It's almost as if you're scared that it feels this good. It's like, *Do people know I get to do this?*
2. You feel connected to more than just yourself. In this moment, you know you're not alone. You have a quiet certainty that you belong, you're seen, and you're woven in with others.
3. Your work impacts other people. Your work solves a problem for real humans—from nano improvements to global change.

Looking for these signals means exploring self-awareness: assessing how you see the world, cultivating your strengths, understanding your blind spots, and remembering what play feels like. You need to own your mindset, values, and purpose. (Good news, you'll learn how to do this in part one, and learn more in the *Playbook*. You can start now with the Joyosity Explorer Map in the Lounge.)

These make the root system and core of the lavender plant—the sturdy branches, the wild beauty, the foundation of flourishing.

Toil's Tiny Ten

You will have work that depletes you. Even if you do it well, some work requires extraordinary effort, and you're relieved when it's over. Some tasks feel like meaningless busywork that accomplishes nothing. The work doesn't interest you, or you don't have the skills or resources to enjoy it if it does. It could be the work you used to love, but don't anymore. I wish I could take those away in the Wizard of Oz's hot-air balloon, but alas, toil's going to happen.

Aim to keep the toil to less than 10 percent of your time and tasks. Creep above the Tiny Ten, and toil starts to eat away at the Magic Third of joy. Too much toil is like too much acid or too many rocks in the soil. Sure, you can take more, but you'll suffer if you do.

The Messy Middle

The other 55 percent is the Messy Middle. This is the commonplace, the skill-building, and the daily practice and systems. This includes engaging with other people who aren't as easy as you would like. It's practicing emotional intelligence, working through your mindset, processing decisions, and crafting the experience of your day-to-day life. The Messy Middle is sneaky. We're so used to it, it can feel unimportant.

But this is where life happens; where your leadership is shaped, your habits take root, and you cultivate—or crush—your joy.

We'll spend much of this book working on what you need in the Messy Middle—because when you don't tend it well, the middle mess quietly turns to toil.

The good news? In the Joy Ratio, all the goodness of the 35 percent makes even the middle magical and the toil tolerable.

When that poor woman bit the dust over our wagon, our ratio of joy to toil was out of whack, mostly because we were depending on something on the outside to float joy our way rather than digging within ourselves. We gave up. We packed the car, shut the trunk, and left the balloons behind. Because when you outsource joy, it dissolves the moment things fall apart.

From Languishing to Flourishing— By Design, Not Default

No one wakes up and thinks, *I really hope I suffer debilitating anxiety when I read my email today.* No one sits at their desk and puts all their focus on being a lousy leader. You wander onto the path of least resistance, allowing the roadblocks to quietly, but steadily, detour you from your humanity. You slip into the tide of toil, into languishing.

Here's the truth: You don't have to live that way. You can design the entirety of your life in the Joy Ratio.

We're moving into a new paradigm of wholeheartedness and joy. But this is not "positive vibes only" or denying the reality of difficult circumstances.

Sometimes, life can almost break you. Joyosity doesn't deny the complexity of what it means to be human or what it means to lead a profitable business. With Joyosity, you're building a flourishing life that creates the success you wanted, but thought you had to sacrifice your soul for. You don't have to languish. You can cultivate joy.

The Gist

Leaders aren't merely drowning in stress; they're dying from it. This isn't sustainable, and the research shows the way we're doing work doesn't work.

You don't have to live this way. To bring joy into work and all of your life, you need to reject sterile, profit-and-productivity blocks to joy and create success with the 35–10–55 Joy Ratio. You can have joy without sacrificing your life.

Real joy has deep roots. Roots form in the dark.

—Jenn Whitmer

Connection

What teachers, friends, or leaders in your life have been your favorite and produced great results? How did they help you?

What connections can you see between their impact and what you do today?

. . . .

Curiosity

Which of the five roadblocks trips you up the most?

1. Myth of Measurement
2. Tradition, TRADITION!
3. Work Before Play
4. It's Not That Bad. Everything's Fine.
5. "We're Not Worthy."

What new idea do you need to break through that roadblock?

. . . .

Joy

When you were a kid, what was fun for you? What type of activities brought you joy? Who were you with? What did you love to study?

Get your Joyosity Explorer Map in the Lounge. You're going to want it for the rest of the journey.

Part 1

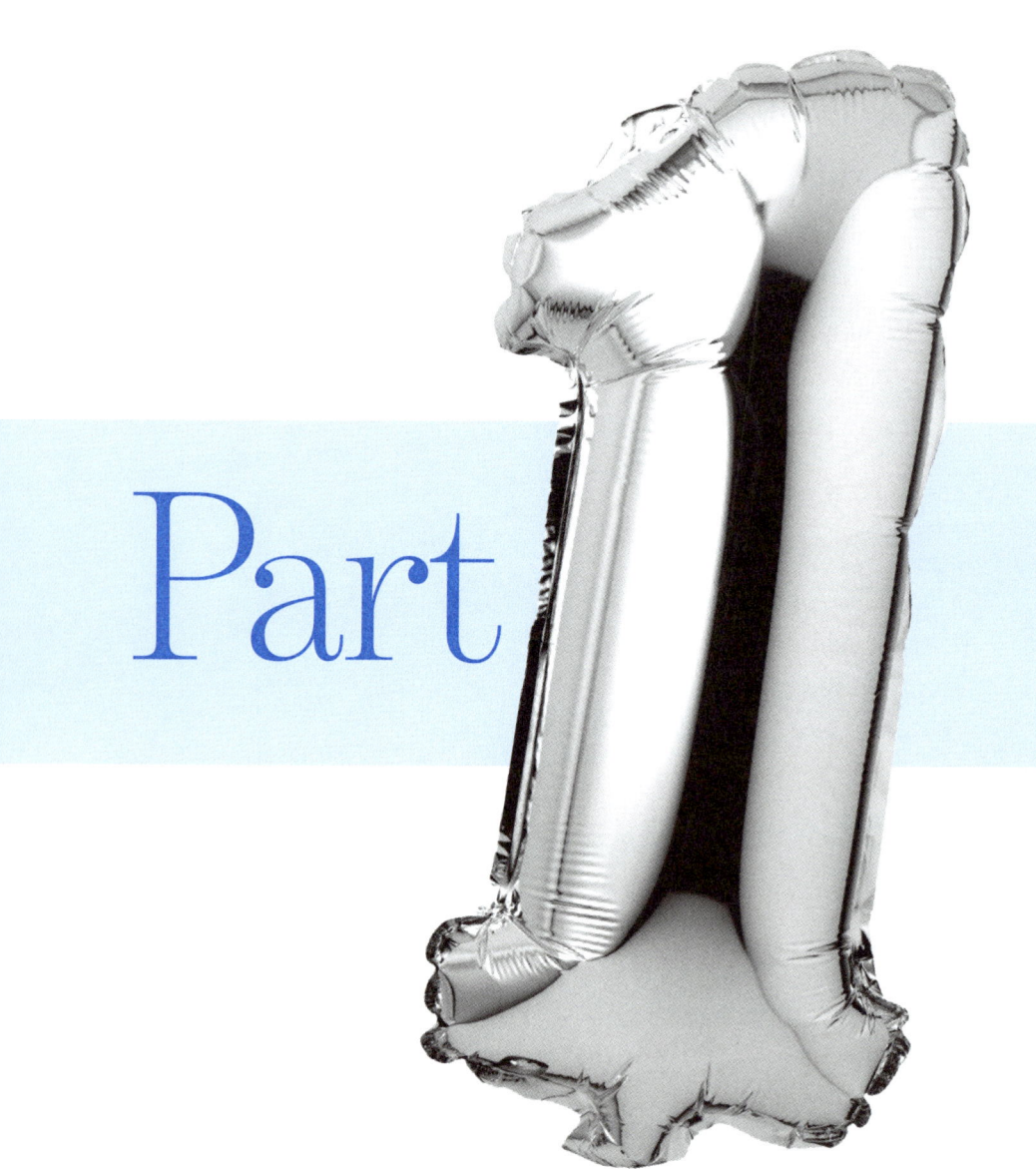

To know yourself, you must sacrifice
the illusion that you already do.

—Vironika Tugaleva

Explore

Same You. New Truth.

As a Girl Scout, I couldn't wait to earn the Finding Your Way badge. I can still feel the shiny compass in my palm and the slick, laminated map our troop leader gave us at the trailhead one spring Saturday.

We were checking off the final activity to earn the badge: use a map and compass to complete a wilderness trail. The golden forsythia had hardly just started fading to green, and baby shoots of leaves covered the trees. The entire trail had a vernal haze.

Oh this will be a piece of cake. We won't even need the map, I thought, with all the hubris of a Junior Girl Scout on a trail she'd navigated before.

I tucked the map away, and my buddy and I set off. Not ten minutes later, we were lost, digging through the backpack for the map, trying to figure out the way back to the trailhead. What my eleven-year-old self didn't consider? Seasons. I'd only been on the trail in the fall. And though the actual geography remained the same, the change of seasons created an entirely new experience we had to navigate. (Which we did, learning more than a few orienteering skills!)

This is what it will feel like in this Explore section. There are core parts of you that do not change. Personality structures, old narratives, and values will always be a part of how you walk through the world. Yet, there will always be exploration as you grow, your circumstances shift, and the people around you move in and out of your life.

Curiosity provides the foundation of this exploration. So please learn from that Junior Girl Scout with a sash full of badges. Just because you've been here before doesn't mean you know your way around. Keep exploring.

Leadership requires ruthless self-honesty and radical self-compassion.

Don't Let Your Personality Drive the Bus

Steer with Self-Awareness

> It is not only the most difficult thing to know oneself, but the most inconvenient one, too.
>
> **—Josh Billings**

"How in the world is she doing that?" I stage-whispered to my college friends as we all stared at a woman doing a handstand on the edge of the rocks. Her gray hair dangled off the overhang as she curved her legs back over her head in what seemed like effortless balance, all while gripping the ragged edge.

We were climbing at Elephant Rocks State Park where large rock outcroppings form cliffs and drops in the middle of the Black River. Dozens of other people climbed over the rocks around this woman as she did this scorpion-handstand-yoga move in baggy, faded jeans as if she were alone in the studio.

I obsessed about this woman for days. I'd ask my friends, "How did she get to that level of confidence? How did she trust herself so well? How did she know she wouldn't topple down the precipice into the shallow water below?"

To balance on that rock, she had to know herself completely and honestly; she needed accurate self-awareness. This is also the number-one predictor of success as a leader and the first step in staying in the Joy Ratio.

The Self-Awareness Advantage

Organizational psychologist A. H. Church, PhD, and other researchers continue to show that people with high levels of self-awareness are better workers who get more promotions. Self-aware leaders are more effective and have more committed and engaged team members. Oh, and they run more profitable companies.[1]

The Stanford Graduate School of Business Advisory Council rated self-awareness as the most important competency for leaders to develop.[2] Self-awareness is the foundational skill you need as a leader, because communication, imagination, vision-casting, and decision-making all build upon it—including your joy.

It's easy to believe you know yourself. And yet, Tasha Eurich, PhD, found only 10 to 15 percent of us demonstrate accurate self-awareness.[3] Ouch.

So when you work at cultivating joy, you must begin with understanding and developing an accurate sense of yourself. Self-awareness helps you hone your strengths, navigate your predictable pitfalls, and improve how you work with others.

Meet Johari: The Window to You

The Johari Window describes the four areas of self-awareness. Each quadrant holds different information that you need to holistically understand yourself. If a section is missing, your joy isn't rooted in reality.[4]

	Known to Self	Hidden from Self
Known to Others	Open	Blind Spot
Hidden from Others	Façade	Unknown

Johari Window

The Open

Open is the space of self-awareness where what you think is true about you aligns with what others think is true about you. It's the space of alignment and growth. For example, I have a client who speaks softly and mumbles at times. This pattern causes frequent miscommunication. He knows he does this. I know he does this. Because we're both aware, we're in the Open space.

Open is the space of creating change. In this example, my client is practicing slowing down and speaking slightly louder when he's talking in a meeting. When using self-awareness as a leadership skill and way to joy, you want to get to Open in the Johari Window.

The Façade

I have what my friend Jeff calls a "resting interested face." So, most of the time, I'm smiling, and my eyes are open, often with a slight head tilt.

When I'm confused, my eyebrows knit together, I squint my eyes, and my lips form more of a straight line. In many difficult conversations, people have said to me, "You're clearly angry. Are you even listening?" I've learned to preempt this with, "I know my face looks angry. I'm not angry. I'm confused, and I want to understand."

In the Façade, you know something about yourself that others can't see. The path from Façade to Open is self-disclosure.

When something is behind the Façade, others will fill in their own stories about what they see (more about stories in chapter four). Those assumptions prevent clear communication, healthy problem-solving, and clear decision-making.

Here, Façade does not mean fake or deceitful. The front of a building is the façade. The front isn't a sneaky way to hide your living room—it simply protects the inside. Not everyone needs every part of you. You don't disclose every internal whim. But if you want to build trust, have better communication, and combat assumptions, you must have the self-awareness to see that other people can't read your mind.

Self-awareness without self-disclosure is just self-centeredness. That disconnection will always steal your joy.

The Blind Spot

Not long after I started as a new director, I needed help. The faculty weren't following through on their responsibilities in a pilot program.

I paced and peppered my leader, Josh, with questions: "What can I do? What am I missing? Am I not being clear? Are my expectations unreasonable? Can you help me with this?"

Josh listened calmly, fingers steepled under his chin. He folded his hands flat on the table and leaned forward. "It's your laughter."

I stopped and grabbed the chair. "My laughter?"

He proceeded to assure me my directions were clear, and the expectations and timeline were reasonable. But when I gave directions, I'd giggle at the end.

"That giggle undermines your authority. They don't know if you're serious or not."

I plopped down in the chair, surprised. I was aware I had an easy laugh, but I had no idea I was giggling after giving directions, let alone its negative impact on the authority of my message.

What a gift. I couldn't see it in my Blind Spot.

In the Blind Spot, others see something about you that you can't see about yourself. The road from Blind Spot to Open is feedback.

Useful feedback acts as the mirror you need so you can see what's hanging out where you can't see. *Both your magic and your mischief hang out in your Blind Spot.* When you have an accurate mirror, you can move to Open, resolving the mischief and multiplying your magic. Self-awareness, and therefore your joy, needs to see what's in the Blind Spot.

Not all feedback is the same. You want feedback from trusted peers, mentors, and leaders, as well as from other tools such as assessments, audits, and reflection questions. The key to this type of self-awareness is *accuracy*, not a funhouse mirror that distorts the positive or the negative.

After Josh gifted me an accurate picture of what was wreaking havoc in my Blind Spot, we were operating in the Open space. I felt uncomfortable directing seasoned educators. We brainstormed a few ideas to solve for my discomfort and established a signal for when I slipped into "giggle as defense against discomfort." Over time, I stopped the giggle, and amazingly, the teachers began to follow through and even bring better ideas.

The Unknown

In the Unknown, you don't recognize something about yourself, and others can't see it either. Well, damn it, what do we do here? You need a new tool to dig with.

In the Unknown, you need to consider broader patterns of human behavior, thought processes, and emotions. You need a tool to help you name an internal experience, to identify what's going on in this unconscious space. Without finding what's happening in the Unknown, you'll have all the assumptions of the Façade and the mischief of the Blind Spot stealing your joy.

To paraphrase famed psychologist Carl Jung: Until you make the unconscious conscious, it will direct your life, and you will call it fate.[5]

So how do you dig out of the Unknown so you can cultivate joy? Personality work is the spade.

What's Lurking Under "Normal"

Here's the scene: A 400-square-foot apartment in married-student housing. A tiny kitchen with a half sink, a two-burner range, and four cupboards. Two newlyweds are fixing to have a fight—about flour.

I'm Italian. My grandparents owned a restaurant. Because I cook to show love, twenty-one-year-old me baked from scratch.

When I needed to refill the flour jar, I couldn't find the five-pound bag in the cupboard. I'd look all over, repeatedly finding it in the freezer. This made no sense to me, but I'd return the bag of flour to the cupboard and move on.

Once after a trip to Hy-Vee, I saw my new husband putting the flour in the freezer.

I ever-so-calmly asked him, "What the hell are you doing?" (OK, maybe not so calm.)

He looked at me incredulously. "Putting the flour away."

"That's not where the flour goes."

"Yes, it is."

We stood in the kitchenette-ette, bickering about where the flour goes.

We finally discovered the disconnect. Michael's grandma grew up on a farm in Arkansas where weevils in the flour were a real problem. Solution? Flour in the freezer.

My mom grew up on a dairy farm in Connecticut where they needed easy access for all-day use but not the mess of the entire bag. Solution? A container on the counter and the flour bag in the pantry.

Both locations logically solved a problem. Neither was bad. We simply grew up with different views. And we weren't aware that they were different because we called them "normal."

Where you put the flour isn't a personality trait. But your personality hides from you in the same way, hanging out in the Unknown because it's your normal.

Personality is an unconscious, organizing story you use to solve problems. Personality is how you make sense of the world and process it quickly so you can have love, safety, and belonging.

Imagine personality as translucent colored glasses you always have on—mine are pink-tinted flamingos, and yours are yellow-tinted pineapples. We look at a white wall, but I see pink, and you see yellow. Without awareness of the color of your personality lens, you'll spin in useless arguments, repeat the same mistakes, and stay stuck in the Unknown where joy doesn't grow.

Suzanne Stabile, known as the Enneagram Godmother, says, "You can't change the way you see. But you can change what you do with the way you see."[6] You'll grow joy when you know which color glasses you have so you aren't a victim of your unconscious directing your life.

The Enneagram Answers What Other Tools Can't

Most people love a good self-assessment quiz. The first quizzes appeared in women's magazines in the mid-twentieth century, and BuzzFeed built an empire on "Which Character Are You?" quizzes. But the concept of understanding yourself and personality types is as old as the ancient philosophers Cicero and Hippocrates, who explored how humans craft a sense of self around 370 BCE.[7]

Personality tools help you observe yourself—MBTI, DISC, Kolbe, Strengths, Working Genius, to name a few. Most personality tools show us *what* or *how* we behave, and that is valuable. But the personality tool I've found that brings the deepest insights and most dynamic view of personality is the Enneagram. (Download your "Leadership Personality Dashboard" from the Lounge to see how different personality tools work together with the Enneagram, revealing your unique personality portrait from the most common tools.)

The Enneagram framework shows nine different personality types (named One to Nine) that tell you *why* you feel, think, and act the way you do. If you only know *what* or *how* you do something, you're fixing something externally that rarely lasts (and often comes out sideways with unintended consequences). When you know *why*, you can leave behind the spiraling in Unknown, and you have the freedom to choose differently. And that freedom is where joy begins, when you curiously observe yourself, how you interact with others, and how you react to difficulty.

The Ground Rules for Exploration

"Some people are concerned about using personality as part of our professional development," my corporate client shared in a prep call before our event.

"Tell me more," I said. (My all-time favorite conversation-continuer is "tell me more.")

"Well, some of our staff who came from another agency had DISC profiles displayed, and their personality profiles were used against them in performance reviews."

Flames, flames. On the side of my face.[8]

If you've had a bad experience with any personality tool, I would bet all the money in my pockets that your training and implementation inflated your personality to more than what it is. To prevent misuse of the tool, I have a few rules of the road:

- **1** **Curiosity is the foundation.** You may have an inner, "Nu-uh!" come up as we go through these types. Or you may feel attacked because you feel a little too seen for your liking. When you experience that, channel curiosity. Even if you just say to yourself, "What if I were curious about this?" you will stay in the work.

2. **Start with yourself.** "There are three things that are extremely hard: steel, a diamond, and to know one's self," wrote Benjamin Franklin.[9] Because it's hard, we instead want to label and talk about other people. "My wife is just like that." "This is totally my boss." Here's the deal: You can never know if they don't tell you. Motivations live behind the Façade. If your mind wanders to other people, make a note for later, and bring it back to you.

3. **No swords or shields.** Swords attack based on type: "She's so mean. She's such an Eight." "Of course he won. He's a Three." Shields excuse bad behavior or a refusal to change: "Oh, they're just like that, never deciding. They're a Nine." "Oh, I can't do that. I'm a Four." We're not doing either of these here in *Joyosity*. It's like an online cookies agreement. By continuing to read, you're agreeing to terms.

Say Hello to the Nine Enneagram Types

Jim simply wanted to do something nice for Pam, and Dwight kept being, well, Dwight.

In this episode of *The Office*, Dwight closed the office and put the entire office staff in a temporary workspace: the Work Bus. Jim begs Dwight to take them to Laverne's Pie Shack, so this isn't the "worst day ever." With the entire bus chanting "Pie, Pie, Pie," Dwight shouts, "Everybody, hang on!" as he shoves the bus into first gear.

The tires screech out of the parking lot, and at the first haphazard turn, chaos ensues. Nothing is getting in Dwight's way. He's getting pie before Laverne shutters the shack for the day.[10]

Your personality is a lot like the Work Bus. The motivations of all nine Enneagram types ride on your bus. One of them barrels to the driver's seat and will speed off with all the mayhem of Dwight downshifting to get pie. Figure out which one is driving, pry its hands off the steering wheel, and be the driver of your life.

Treat your personality as a knee-jerk reaction, a reflex trying to keep you safe. It's not you shining—it's you surviving. These descriptions use patterns and defaults as a way for you to understand yourself and others better. Ask yourself, "How much is this like me?" and rate yourself on a scale of one to five. *One*: This is nothing like me. I don't even understand how someone operates like that. *Five*: This is me to my very core. How have you seen into the depths of my soul?

As you read a description, you may feel suddenly exposed, a heat rise in your body, or an urge to throw this book across the room. You may feel a gut punch of anger, shame, or fear. That type is very likely your core Enneagram type.

Self-awareness as a practice of leadership requires ruthless self-honesty and radical self-compassion.

If you can't decide immediately what your type is, that's OK. Consider this as a test drive that you'll use as you go through the rest of the chapters. (If you want deeper descriptions and more, grab the *Playbook*.)

The Five Unconscious Motivations

Every personality type has five strings directing it. These five strings are the deep *whys* that shape every first feeling, initial thought, and gut reaction. The Five Unconscious Motivations are:

Trusted Tactic: "Here's how I get it done."
Your brain uses a consistent strategy to protect you and get your needs met. It's your go-to that is so natural you don't even question it.

Fundamental Fear: "Whatever you do, don't do that!"
This fear looms larger than the monster under your bed. It's what your personality believes will be the absolute end of you—the very worst, most destructive thing that could happen. You're always running away from it because you want to prevent that fear from coming true.

Driving Desire: "I want to be where the people are . . . "
This is the "I Want" song of your life (Think Ariel singing "Part of Your World" on that rock). It's the flip side of the core fear. Your personality perpetually strives for this goal. It believes that if you get this, you will have the love, safety, and belonging that solves everything.

Persistent Pattern: "Why do I keep doing this?"
This is the consistent tendency you face throughout your life. Sometimes it's amazing, and other times it's problematic because the best parts of us are also the worst parts of us. This pattern comes around again and again, like a Ferris wheel. The goal is to recognize the gondola when it shows up, so you don't get smacked off the platform with the worst of you and instead choose to ride with the best of you.

Don't Let Your Personality Drive the Bus

Lasting Longing: *"Oh, please let that be true."*
This is the deep message your heart wants to hear. You looked for it around every corner as a child and into adulthood (yes, it follows you into work). It's the message you are desperate to believe is true. Because if it is, you're safe, you belong, and you are loved.

These five unconscious motivation strings come together like DNA strands. Each is its own thread, weaving to form your personality. And each Enneagram type has its own unique set of five.

Each type also grounds itself into one of three groups: the Body Group, Heart Group, and Head Group. Each group shares a core emotional struggle and common desires. We start with the first in the Body Group: Eights.

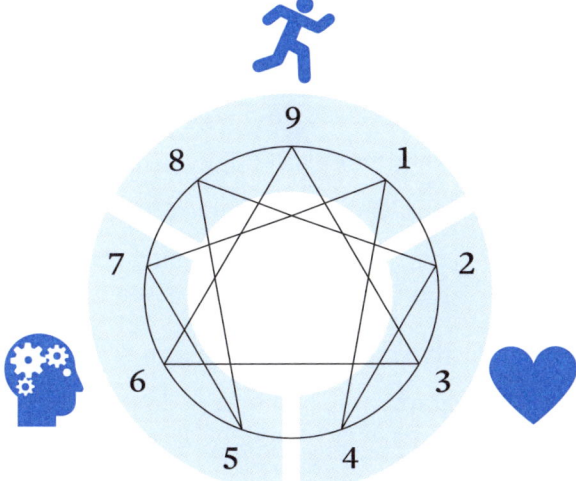

The Body Group

This group struggles with anger, and most desire justice, respect, and belonging. They take in information first through their physical body or gut instinct. The Body Group's strength is a connected groundedness, an invitation to presence, and embodied belonging. When they misuse or overuse these strengths, it leads to control, impulsivity, or inertia.

Enneagram Eight: The Protective Challenger

Trusted Tactic	Protect
Fundamental Fear	Being vulnerable, powerless, weak, controlled, or manipulated
Driving Desire	To protect yourself and those closest to you
Persistent Pattern	Excess and intensity
Lasting Longing	"You will not be betrayed."

Strong and protective, Enneagram Eights don't show weakness, fearing someone may control or manipulate them if they do. Rather than risk someone playing them like a puppet—or worse, betraying them—they snip the strings and take charge themselves. For an Eight, protecting themselves and those they allow inside their castle always takes priority. If there's a leadership vacuum, an Eight will stride forward to fill it and manage that scene. In taking charge, Eights don't end up powerless.

The Eight intensity can hit like a tsunami. They have the most energy of any Enneagram type, and others don't always know what to do with that intensity, tagging them as "bitches and bullies." For the Eight, they simply believe they're the only ones who take responsibility or say the hard truth directly. They trust their gut and their ability to see the entire system to solve problems quickly, often before others have even processed the situation. If they trust someone else's authority, Eights will follow, and even be relieved to not always be the strong one. But at a whiff of weakness or manipulation, Eights will rush right back into the driver's seat. Eights want belonging, but they'll settle for power.

At their best, Eights lower their bar required to trust others and use their strength to care for people in a genuine, tender way. Eights have a melty center of compassion hidden by a rougher exterior. Ultimately, Eights remind us that real power doesn't come from dominating others. They show us how to create belonging by standing firm for what's right and shielding those who need protection. When they harness their fierce energy for good, Eights become unstoppable champions of justice and loyalty.

Enneagram Nine: The Harmonious Peacemaker

Trusted Tactic	Withdraw
Fundamental Fear	Loss of connection and belonging, conflict, being overlooked
Driving Desire	Internal and external harmony, stability, and peace
Persistent Pattern	Disengagement
Lasting Longing	"Your presence matters."

Easygoing and accommodating, Enneagram Nines desire both internal and external harmony. If folks around them don't respond with a similar vibe, Nines will merge with what others want, just to keep the peace. They believe their deepest fear is conflict, but underneath, it's loss of connection. Nines believe if they assert their independence and autonomy, they'll lose belonging. Instead of voicing their own ideas and feelings, they fall into patterns of indecision, procrastination, and disengagement. Broom in hand, sweeping difficulties right under that rug, often sounds like, "Whatever you think. I don't know."

Sometimes, it looks like daydreaming or escaping to numbing activities (Netflix and a cozy blanket, anyone?).

To manage the compulsion to maintain peace and an even-tempered image, Nines avoid disagreement. Preserving external harmony leaves them disconnected from their own wants, needs, and sense of worth, creating a deep lack of harmony within themselves. Surprisingly, Nines are the most stubborn of the Enneagram type structures. Because they want to maintain that easygoing image, they find subtle ways to resist rather than offer an outright no. One of their go-tos? Adjusting the pace. Push a Nine to hurry, and they will find a lower gear you didn't know existed. No conflict to see here, just a slowdown. Nines want to be connected, but they'll settle for keeping the peace.

At their best, Nines build consensus, employing their ability to see all sides of an issue. They show up to the table ready to contribute thoughtfully and confidently while smoothly incorporating what others bring, cultivating belonging. In this space, Nines show us that real connection isn't keeping the peace—it's making peace by valuing everyone in the process, including themselves.

Enneagram One: The Reforming Perfectionist

Trusted Tactic	Perfect
Fundamental Fear	Being bad or wrong, unredeemable, misaligned, rude, or corrupt
Driving Desire	Goodness and rightness
Persistent Pattern	Resentment
Lasting Longing	"You are good."

Principled and ever-improving, Enneagram Ones strive to make everything and everyone better—no detail too small, no spreadsheet too color-coded. Fueled by a deep desire to be good all the way through, Ones fear any hint of flaws or wrongdoing because they believe that negates their goodness. Enter the ever-present inner critic, barking orders like the middle school queen bee who dangles belonging and then changes the rules. "Yes, you finished that project, but you should have done more." This internal scorekeeper keeps them locked into perfection mode.

All that drive for precision simmers into frustration when the world refuses to meet their standards, leaving Ones feeling like they're the only adults in the room. To others, it can feel like Ones must always be right, but really Ones want to be in "rightness," aligned to the external rules (and whatever the queen is berating them about in the moment). Inside they wrestle with overthinking, shame spirals, and never-ending to-do lists. Over time, that internal pressure morphs into resentment—a mixing bowl of anger, envy, and judgment. Others seem far too lax about, well, everything. Ones want to be good, but they'll settle for being right.

At their best, Ones relax their perfectionism and release resentment. Chris Heuertz, Enneagram expert, writes that they realize the "nuance between the binaries of right and wrong, good and bad, or perfection and imperfection."[11] When Ones lower their shoulders and unclench their jaws, they invite their natural power of creating order out of chaos. With flexibility, they become inspiring problem-solvers, empathetic motivators, and compassionate advocates for fairness and belonging. Ultimately, Ones remind us that true integrity shines brightest when we balance high standards with a willingness to let life (and ourselves) be delightfully imperfect.

The Heart Group

This group struggles with shame or grief, and most desire significance, identity, validation, and love. They take in information first through emotions. The Heart Group's strength is a high level of empathy and emotional intelligence. When they misuse or overuse these strengths, it leads to insensitivity, oversensitivity, or emotional manipulation.

Enneagram Two: The Considerate Giver

Trusted Tactic	Help
Fundamental Fear	Being rejected, dispensable, needy, or unworthy
Driving Desire	To be needed and wanted
Persistent Pattern	Pride
Lasting Longing	"You are wanted."

Warm, welcoming, and always ready to lend a hand, Enneagram Twos thrive on genuine relationships, but they believe they have to earn that love by helping others. Twos make themselves indispensable, jumping headfirst into helping before anyone even asks. In their eyes, helping guarantees their place in a relationship, dodging rejection and proving their worth. The trouble is, this easily slips into manipulation: "If I make myself indispensable, you wouldn't possibly toss me aside." While Twos generally aren't scheming villains, they do need to watch out for that little voice urging them to do more, give more, be more, just so they'll feel loved.

Ironically, the Two's persistent pattern of pride looks like humility personified ("Oh, it's no trouble at all, I'm happy to help!"). When Twos slip into toxic self-sacrifice, they deny their needs, convinced they exist above the realm of normal human requirements. They also have a knack for believing they know exactly what others need. This well-intentioned, but presumptive, approach leads to unsolicited advice and unnecessary activities. When others don't appreciate their efforts, the Two feels rejected anyway. Twos want love, but they'll settle for appreciation.

At their best, Twos learn to identify "What is mine to do?" and set healthy boundaries. In this balanced state, Twos become empathetic mentors who foster genuine connection and develop the people around them. They still anticipate needs, but they don't assume everything falls to them, or that they have to sacrifice themselves to have significance. Twos show us all how to give fully to others and give the same love and acceptance to ourselves.

Enneagram Three: The Successful Inventor

Trusted Tactic	Achieve
Fundamental Fear	Failure or being worthless
Driving Desire	Being valued
Persistent Pattern	Vainglory
Lasting Longing	"You are worthy simply by being you."

Living, breathing motivational posters, Enneagram Threes crush the goal, seize the opportunity, and reinvent themselves for that next big win. Behind the natural-winner façade, they're desperately trying to manage shame by proving their worth through efficiency and achievement. To add to the trouble, the achievement metrics are external: "Will this make me look good to others?" Threes read the room and adapt—often at lightning speed—to keep that curated "I'm killing it" image. With every new invention, they move further from their authentic selves.

Three's hustling for their worth is exhausting and requires suppressing those pesky emotions that slow you down. Block a Three's path to success or fail to keep up, and the shame-fueled frustration comes out swinging (emails at 3 a.m. or a polite-but-icy "I'll handle it myself"). Because anything less than 110 percent is unacceptable. An Enneagram Three client texted me, "It's baffling that mediocrity could ever be OK." Yet deep down, they want to be able to give less effort and still be seen as valuable. Threes want to be worthy without the work, but they'll settle for a chart of gold stars.

At their best, Threes know they are a human being, not a human doing. They reconnect with their true, authentic identity and define success for themselves rather than chase empty glories that never satisfy. The compulsion to gather all the gold stars eases, and they accept that failure is a part of the process of winning. They also open that dusty box of emotions on the shelf and allow themselves (and others) a little extra space to feel. They still inspire us to achieve but stop tying their worth to accomplishments. Threes show us that being what everyone else wants is a losing game, and winning means accepting the limits of our ever-worthy humanity.

Enneagram Four: The Romantic Individualist

Trusted Tactic	Create
Fundamental Fear	Being insignificant, typical, or flawed, lacking unique identity
Driving Desire	Be authentically yourself
Persistent Pattern	Envy
Lasting Longing	"You are seen for who you are."

Dwelling within a rich internal landscape of feelings, beauty, and imagination, Enneagram Fours long to be fully known. They fear they have a tragic flaw, a missing piece that others seem to possess. Whether it's creating vivid designs, penning heartfelt words, or cultivating an intangible atmosphere, Fours imbue life with depth and intensity. Behind the scenes, the creative expressions come from deep pain and melancholy. Never wanting to be ordinary, they imagine an ideal that they can never quite reach while at the same time believing other people can't really see their suffering or true selves. And everyone else seems to be able to just enjoy it all so easily.

Fours despise small talk and welcome complexities and paradoxes. And they lean in, amplifying emotions to feel truly alive, pulling friends into swirling seas of memory or imagination. Whatever the emotion, Fours want it more intensely because that feels like the path to authenticity: not angry, livid; not happy, elated; not sad, morose. But having feelings, then thoughts about the feelings, then more feelings about the thoughts about the feelings, leaves Fours stuck in cycles of longing rather than action. Both craving and shunning external validation, Fours often resist practical solutions that feel too "everyone does that." Fours want to be known, but they'll settle for being noticed.

At their best, Enneagram Fours usher the world into authenticity, deep beauty, and powerful insights. When they recognize they already are inherently special (no grand display required), they channel their capacity for beauty and authenticity into meaningful action. They bring us back to the values we say we want to live by. Fours remind us how to be fully human, revealing the unique gifts of the most ordinary moments.

The Head Group

This group struggles with fear and isolation, and most desire security and safety.* They take in information first through their minds and intellect. The Head Group's strength is to connect complex ideas, create creative options, and offer wise counsel that provides psychologically safety. When they misuse or overuse these strengths, it leads to cynicism, intellectual superiority, or decision paralysis.

Enneagram Five: The Curious Specialist

Trusted Tactic	Intellectualize
Fundamental Fear	Being incompetent, ignorant, or helpless
Driving Desire	To be capable and competent
Persistent Pattern	Avarice
Lasting Longing	"Your needs are not a problem."

Reserved, private, and curious, Enneagram Fives believe competence and capability will keep them safe in the unknown. If they can master the facts—researching, analyzing, and synthesizing data and related information—then maybe they'll stave off any threat of internal depletion. Believing it's not OK to be too comfortable, Fives see their own needs as an intellectual exercise in solving a problem statement. From the constant inquiry, analysis, and questioning, Fives require a significant amount of energy management. Think of a Five as starting each day at 60 percent battery, and that's what they've got for the rest of the day. They work meticulously to preserve their energy and avoid unwanted demands.

Fives can get stuck in planning mode. They can fall down a research rabbit hole—Reddit thread, data drive, library session—convinced

---
* Aren't we having fun? Anger! Shame! Fear!

they don't yet have enough information to decide. But once they've mapped out a detailed solution, they've effectively solved the problem. Oh wait, they didn't actually take action to complete the plan. Meanwhile, their fear of depletion can lead to hoarding time, resources, and knowledge—a tendency known as avarice. Interaction with the outside world feels like it drains their internal battery even faster, so they keep to themselves to protect their mental reserves. Fives want to be safe in the unknown, but they'll settle for being the competent expert.

At their best, Fives offer specialized expertise, bringing invaluable data, context, and institutional memory to the table. (And usually a witty comment that surprises everyone.) They begin to balance curiosity and investigation with experimental doing, trusting they already have enough insight to act. Additionally, they believe asking for help doesn't equate to incompetence. Five's careful observations and thorough thinking become indispensable assets for teams and projects. Ultimately, Fives remind the world that curiosity safely navigates us all through the mysteries of living.

Enneagram Six: The Loyal Skeptic

Trusted Tactic	Prepare
Fundamental Fear	Lacking support or guidance, or being blamed or abandoned
Driving Desire	To be secure and have guidance and support
Persistent Pattern	Angst
Lasting Longing	"You are safe."

Enneagram Sixes live in a world of potential pitfalls, ever on guard for what might go wrong. Afraid they'll be blamed and abandoned, they prepare for every eventuality for themselves and others as if they are writing the worst-case scenario guidebook. Sixes have an internal conference room hosting a committee of competing voices: "Have we considered this angle? What if that happens? Are we sure we can trust this person?" Have you made decisions by committee? Exhausting. All the internal debate erodes trust in their ability to make decisions in the face of a world that feels extremely insecure. Hence, they prepare for it all.

Sixes flow along a continuum, from compliance and rule-following to oppositional scrutiny, testing whether leaders and systems are actually worthy of their loyalty. Individual Sixes seesaw on the continuum depending on the committee report.

The elaborate scenario building leads to indecision, self-doubt, and the constant companion of low-grade angst. Sixes second-guess themselves and others, worried someone's overlooking a crucial detail. Craving security, they barrage others with questions, unintentionally appearing resistant or parental, maybe hearing a mumbled, "Killjoy." Frequently the truth is they want to ensure they've poked enough holes to help an idea succeed. Sixes want to have security, but they'll settle for being the ever-ready supporter.

At their best, Sixes transform "what-if" worries into pragmatic plans. Because nobody sees the hidden snags and potential crises like a Six, their questions spot risks, leading to robust strategies. When they trust their own judgment (and tell the internal committee to sit it on down), they discover they may not be fearless, but they can trust themselves. In an unpredictable world, Sixes remind us that solid plans (and maybe a few backup plans) go a long way, and courage means feeling the fear and doing it anyway.

Enneagram Seven: The Enthusiastic Visionary

Trusted Tactic	Reframe
Fundamental Fear	Experiencing pain, feeling trapped or limited
Driving Desire	To be fully content and satisfied
Persistent Pattern	Voracity
Lasting Longing	"You will be taken care of."

Excitable and deeply optimistic, Enneagram Sevens strive for the next thing that will satisfy the discontentment they keep hidden. Beneath brainstorming options and finding the silver side of that raincloud, Sevens desperately want to avoid pain. Believing others won't come through for them, Sevens learn to find multiple options to keep themselves safe from pain. Others see days filled with group chats, airplane tickets, creative endeavors, and the latest innovation. Sevens are managing a deep fear of missing out, being trapped in disappointment, or—heaven forbid—dealing with the low-level anxiety creeping around in the basement of their minds.

Because limits, micromanagement, or boredom feel painful, Sevens keep themselves preoccupied and switch-tasking—reading multiple books at once, juggling disparate projects, or dreaming about the next destination while wading in the ocean on their current vacation. They'll grab for "Well, at least . . . " or "It's not a crisis, it's an adventure!" And when Sevens drop to neutral, people are disappointed because they want the Chief Optimist. That pressure makes it all the more confusing when unchecked reframing swells into toxic positivity, leaving others hurt and exhausted. FOMO might be the motivator, but ironically, the bigger fear is being left alone to deal with the messy feelings that they've been sidestepping with all that fun. Sevens want enduring contentment, but they'll settle for thrills.

At their best, Sevens lead with hopeful visions and deep empathy. They're masters of turning challenges into opportunities and sparking creative solutions. When they learn it's OK to not be OK, they begin to trust that life won't implode if they pause long enough to feel uncomfortable emotions. Their natural optimism matures into genuine resilience and commitment. Sevens remind all of us that we have endless imagination *and* limits are good. We don't need every waking minute jammed with novelty to feel safe.

Lead with a Clearer View

As you go through the rest of the book, explore how your Enneagram type shows up in different contexts. If you find the one you've chosen right now doesn't fit, come back here and test drive another.

Remember, these are thumbnail sketches of a complex personality structure. No one fits perfectly into three paragraphs. Resist the urge to head to the internet to take a test (I know you may have already done that!). Identifying your Enneagram type *is* self-awareness, digging out of the Unknown. Don't abdicate that to a multiple-choice test, expecting it to give you the deepest motivations of your soul.

The Enneagram is a shiny lens but not the goal itself. Use the Enneagram to keep from repeating patterns without knowing why. The more clearly you see yourself, the more choices you have in how you respond to the slings and arrows life throws your way. And that's where the roots of joy begin.

Balancing on the Rock

Many days, trying to stay in the Joy Ratio feels like balancing on the edge of the rocks, keeping yourself and other people safe on an uneven surface. It's easy to see a woman on the edge of the cliff doing a handstand and think, "I can't do that, so I'm not as good." That's just a story you tell yourself. (Good thing that's up next!)

The temptation to compare is human, but indulging it will keep you ineffective at best. Comparisonitis will slowly destroy you, increase your toil, and steal your joy. At this moment, there is no way on God's green Earth I can do a scorpion handstand, let alone perform that on a rocky outcropping. But I do know I can do a solid Warrior III. Not because I'm a yoga expert, but because I accurately see and accept myself.

Your greatest joy and power as a leader don't come from being like anyone else. Your joy grows from knowing yourself fully and completely, and being that human every day.

The Gist

Leadership without accurate self-awareness is a liability. So you need to understand yourself, including what's underneath the surface. The Enneagram reveals the unconscious motivations steering your behavior so you can stop reacting and begin leading yourself toward real joy.

> Leadership requires ruthless self-honesty and radical self-compassion.
>
> —Jenn Whitmer

Connection

Who are the people who consistently provide you with helpful, honest feedback? What area of your leadership do you want to ask them to help with so you can see your Blind Spot? Send an email or text (before you forget or avoid it).

Where do you need to practice self-disclosure? What do you think people know about you, but you want to make clear?

. . . .

Curiosity

Which Enneagram type do you identify with?

What light bulbs flicked on as you were reading this chapter?

Which type made you deeply uncomfortable? Why?

. . . .

Joy

How does knowing your Five Unconscious Motivations help you see your way to more compassion for yourself and empathy for others?

Download your Leadership Personality Dashboard and start inputting your results.

Live in the story that creates joy.

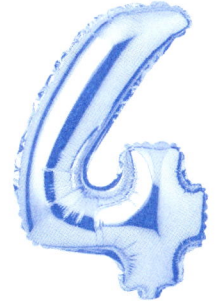

Cut! Rewrite! Action!

Lead with Better Stories

To make a change at work, tell yourself a different story.

—Scott Galloway, founder of Prophet and
RedEnvelope, and business expert

"I wish" turned into "happy ever after" and descended into absolute chaos.

Act II of Stephen Sondheim's *Into the Woods* rips apart the happy-ever-after stories of your favorite fairy tales.[1] Everything is falling apart, and all the stories tragically overlap. Jack is on the run from the Giant's Wife who has come down the beanstalk to avenge her husband. Little Red Riding Hood has become a knife-wielding vigilante. Cinderella, Rapunzel, and even the Narrator get tangled in the plot.

In the story, the Witch sends the Baker and his Wife on a quest. They divide and conquer. Counting her steps into the woods, the Baker's Wife smacks right into Cinderella's wayward prince.

In full regalia, he questions, "Why are you *alone* in the woods?"

She, in her peasant garb, stammers, "I came with my husband, we, uh . . . it's a long story," she bobs a curtsey and walks away, counting her steps.

The Prince turns from curious amusement to seduction and kisses the Baker's Wife (it's a fairy tale, remember?).

She begins to melt into the affection, but breaks away, exclaiming, "What am I doing here? I'm in the wrong story."

The Prince leaves, and the Baker's Wife stands alone in the woods, unsure of who she is and confused about what to do next. She walks in the wrong direction, and the Giant's Wife crushes her beneath her enormous boot.

Life and leading feel like the story of the Baker's Wife sometimes. You live with imposter feelings, unsure of your identity, and confused about the next right step to take. The wish to create a vibrant and flourishing life feels like it's under the boots of the giants of life. You may not live with main character energy every day, but you do live in a story. Most stories appear without your permission or direction—much as Cinderella's prince did for the hapless Baker's Wife—hanging out in the Unknown quadrant of the Johari Window, whispered by your personality.

The stories in your mind will always determine your results. And joy will elude you until you can reliably change your internal narrative.

This isn't toxic positivity or absurd affirmations. Exploring the way you create meaning from the events at the office, on the highway, and in your kitchen means understanding where stories originate, identifying the types of stories you tell yourself, and then learning to rewrite stories with truth.

Why Your Brain Runs on Story

I grew up a dandelion farmer. I'd gather all those white fluffy balls and blow them all around the back corner of our yard. Then, I'd harvest the yellow bright spots and create soup for my Barbies. And I was so good at farming, more white fluffy balls and bright yellow flowers appeared all over the rest of my yard too. I created an entire identity story to explain why the green grass was covered with dandelions.

Every day—even as an adult—you're still creating narratives to make meaning about the world. Without examination, your stories will fall prey to your brain's negativity bias too. Miss an action item in that email? "I'm such a failure. I should have seen that." Your team member is late for a meeting (again)? "They are so irresponsible." That car with a dent on the left bumper pulls out in front of you in traffic? "Come on, jerk! Clearly, you're a terrible driver."

All day, every day, you're creating stories to make sense of the world. And you started young. Clinical psychologist Mary Clare Champion, PhD, writes that children around age three "begin to organize their thoughts and experiences into spoken narratives."[2] This world is confusing, and stories are how we make sense of why Jamie swipes your favorite LEGO or why Felicia won't leave the Zoom call. Developmental psychologist Robert Kegan, PhD, observes: "Human being is meaning making."[3]

With unconscious abandon, you craft stories to answer questions: *What does this mean about me? Who am I? Who are you? How do we fit to-*

gether? Your cognitive structure of meaning-making is your biological advantage.[4] In other words, your ability to create a narrative to make sense of the world is one of the greatest strengths of your humanity.

In psychology, these meanings are called "lay theories." A story you write doesn't follow the linear steps of the scientific method to test a theory. Your mind automatically creates connections into a narrative structure without bothering to assess its validity.[5] Instead of a meticulous scientist, your brain cooks like Grandma: Throw it all together and live with what comes out of the oven.

There isn't just one story. You have a sweeping generational epic of interconnected stories. You create these stories, and you also receive stories. Stories come from your personality, your family of origin, your first work experience, the majority culture, your ethnic culture, your generation, and on and on.

The way you create meaning directly impacts the way you experience any situation. You have essentially no control over what happens to you. But you do get to decide the *meaning* you make and what you *do* when something happens. Which is why stories impact your results that impact your joy.

Outcomes Follow the Story You Tell

Do you remember the summer before you went to college? So many stories come in with the plastic bins of dorm bedding. The gut-churning anxiety of *Will I make friends?* and the chest-squeezing dread of *I'm sure I'm going to fail College Algebra. I'm doomed to fail; I should just go live in a box under a bridge.*

A group of educators and researchers were curious if changing the narrative improved college success rates, so they tested the power of stories to change outcomes for historically disadvantaged students. Over three different experiments at both public and private universities, the "lay theory interventions"—meaning they helped students change the stories they told themselves—consistently improved the indicators of success in college. Full-time enrollment went up. Students increased their grade point averages. Social connections expanded. Those story rewrites helped students who often don't graduate stay in school and decreased how many disadvantaged students ended up at the bottom of their class.[6]

The story you tell determines your results. Here's how the "meaning-making machine" works.

1. Something happens.
2. You create a story to make meaning from that "something."
3. You take action based on that meaning.
4. Your actions determine your results.

Too often, leaders skip identifying the story and making meaning.* You spiral around the action steps or the results, and then you're frustrated because it doesn't change the way you want it to. If you've skipped choosing the meaning, you are at the whims of whatever nonsense your negativity bias throws your way.

---

* For more, see "Stories Shape Results" in "Stories That Didn't Fit" in Stories, Study Stacks, and Citations.

Joyosity

You can ignore your stories, fall into negativity bias, or you can create a story that makes sense for joy. So how do you name it as sense or nonsense? Back to the Baker's Wife . . . how do you know if you're living in a story that is going to get you crushed by a giant?

Spotting the Story You're Living

Does It Feel Like Middle School?

"Miss Dellario, you are first," the judge announced. I walked to the microphone.

It was 1988, and I was the sixth-grade spelling champion representing my elementary school at the district spelling bee. I wiggled my toes in my pale pink ballet flats waiting for the judge to give me the first word of the competition.

"Hungry," she read. "Are you hungry for lunch yet? Hungry."

Without even taking a breath, I said, "H-U-N-G-E-R-Y." Immediately, my stomach dropped. I scrunched my eyes closed. What had I done?

"I'm sorry. That is incorrect. Miss Dellario, you are eliminated. Mr. Carlisle, you are next."

As Jim strutted up to the mic, I shuffled back to my blue plastic chair. Not down in the audience, ON. THE. STAGE. I disassociated. I couldn't tell you who went down next, or who won to go on to the regional competition.

I am so stupid. And hungry? *I* misspelled hungry? *Forever, every time I walk into the cafeteria, people will cackle and point.*

Those stories hung around and sprouted new stories. Before that spring day, I thought I was a good speller. But from that day on, I would say, "Oh, I'm a terrible speller." Or if someone didn't say hi to me between classes, I would think it was because they thought I was stupid.

Isn't the middle school brain hilarious? Most people don't want to return to middle school, but it feels that way when you get that full-body awkward cringe. Your face gets hot, and you just want to melt into the floor. Does this happen to you? You fumble in a meeting, and then you're quiet for the rest of the quarter. You second-guess your outfit. You spiral because you weren't on the calendar invite. You overcompensate by being *the* expert. Or the universal issue: You interpret someone's tone in an email—*that period felt aggressive*.

When you feel teleported back to middle school in your mind, there's a good chance you're living in a nonsensical, unhealthy, or unhelpful story that will cost you joy.

Silent Scripts

The other reliable way to identify an unhelpful story is the Silent Script your personality believes. The Silent Scripts feel universally true at your core, but they're a lie most of the time. Your personality developed these formative falsehoods so early, they are just part of the fabric of your unconscious.

Why create a new meaning every time when I can rely on the old meaning that kept me safe before? I've got a script for that! Your personality tries to run the meaning-making structure of your brain like a fast-talking producer shouting, "Get to the meaning. Make it snappy."

THE SILENT SCRIPTS
[SCENE: Enneagram personalities on the work bus. A typical day.]

EIGHT PERSONALITY
[Hands on hips, EIGHT stands tall.]
It's not OK to be vulnerable or trust anyone.
I'm the strong one. If I totally take care of myself, I won't get hurt. I'm the protector, and if I don't protect, I won't belong. I'm tough, and if you reject me, I'll just get tougher. FAFO.

NINE PERSONALITY
[NINE on the couch with a blanket.]
It's not OK to assert myself.
I am the harmonious one. If I don't make waves, then everything will be OK. If other people are fighting, I just slip away and think happy thoughts. If I share my own needs and feelings, I will lose my connection and place of belonging with others. It's just easier to say, "Whatever you want."

ONE PERSONALITY
[ONE is busy sorting papers and organizing the desk.]
It's not OK to make mistakes.
I am the one who's right, because I have to follow all the rules. I must always be responsible and reasonable, even when others aren't. I must catch any mistake before people see it, so I make more rules than they have. By making things perfect, I will be good and always belong.

TWO PERSONALITY
[Carrying boxes from the swag closet, TWO stops.]
It's not OK for me to have my own needs.

I am helpful. I have to always be generous and selfless so I can earn love. If I show my own needs, then I would be too needy for others to love me. In fact, just to make sure, I will help them before they even ask for it.

THREE PERSONALITY
[Texting on one phone, THREE has a second phone to their ear.]
It's not OK to have my own feelings or identity.
I am successful. By winning, I hide my fear that I'm not worthy if I don't accomplish anything. I give 110 percent at all times because it's shameful to lose or fail. I want the gold star in your eyes, so my own identity and true self just stay tucked under the cupboard displaying all my trophies.

FOUR PERSONALITY
[Staring into the middle distance, FOUR wipes away a tear.]
It's not OK to be too functional or too happy.
I am authentic. I have to be, because it's not OK to be too much or not enough. No one really sees me, so why hide? But, if they don't see me, how can they love me? [deep sigh] So, I will lean into my feelings and express them, even if others don't like my melancholy or loneliness.

FIVE PERSONALITY
[FIVE looks up from a book.]
It's not OK to be too comfortable.
I am competent. I have to be an expert in a subject because I cannot let my guard down. As long as I am capable and intellectually competent, I will be safe. I operate like this: "Don't ask too much of

me, and I won't ask too much of you." It's just better to isolate myself.

SIX PERSONALITY

[SIX checks the weather app and puts their bag on one shoulder and their extra bag on the other. Opens the traffic app.]
It's not OK to trust myself.
I am loyal. If I prepare for anything that could happen, then I won't be blamed, rejected, or abandoned. I must ask questions, so I have the guidance of others because I second-guess myself. Then I'm ready for anything and anyone, and I will be safe.

SEVEN PERSONALITY

[One AirPod in, SEVEN listens to a podcast. The news blares on TV. SEVEN is looking at flights.]
It's not OK to depend on anyone to take care of me. I am fun and perfectly happy. I've always got to be doing so I don't have to deal with any kind of fear or discomfort. If I start down that path . . . well, I'd be trapped in pain forever. And really, who wants to be a Debbie Downer? Wah wah. It's so much safer to—look at that balloon—distract myself. I can take care of myself. Isn't that great? I'm totally fine.

[END SCENE]

Your personality developed the Silent Script from a singular experience and elevated it to a universal truth that will rule your life, keep you stuck, and steal your joy if you allow it.

It's time to rewrite the story.

The Leader's Story Edit: SNAP

I loved my first career. I taught vocal music to kindergarten through eighth grade students. The process of music literacy begins much like learning to read. It starts with hearing the same song repeatedly. My literal job was singing songs and chanting rhymes *designed* to get stuck in your head.

I'd tap the steering wheel singing *"Ain't she rock candy"* while driving down the interstate or *"Hey, Ho, Nobody Home"* while stirring supper. *Wee Sing* became the soundtrack of my life!

What's the song that always gets stuck in your head and it finally just drives you bananas?* You can't just say to yourself, *Stop singing that song*. Stories are the same. Like a soundtrack, the story spins in the back of your mind. You can't just say to yourself, *Stop thinking that*. Your brain can't perform a negative. Once you bring attention to it, that's all you see.

Just like an annoying earworm, unhelpful stories steal your confidence, clarity, and connection. Cultivating joy requires intentionally replacing the old story with a new helpful story. And since that producer in your head is shouting, "Make it snappy!" you're going to snap right back.

The Story Transformation Process is **SNAP—Stop. Notice. Ask. Pivot.** Think of it as "snap out of it." Below is a quick how-to, but there is more for you in the *Playbook*. Throughout the book you'll see times we refer back to this reliable process to change your story and your mindset.

---

* The best song to sing to get a song out of your head is the US national anthem, "The Star-Spangled Banner." It's a bear to sing, and few people know all the words. So you stop singing both songs. Earworm, gone.

Stop

Literally, stop. Or at least pause. When you feel like you're in middle school again or you're just feeling activated and uncomfortable, pause what you're doing. Breathe for at least thirty seconds. (Chapter ten has more on practices like this.)

Notice

Next, notice what's happening without adding any story. Imagine you are a CCTV or a court reporter. You can only add what is observable without judgment. Stick with answering *who*, *what*, *when*, and *where*, not *why* or *how*. If you find yourself adding subjective adjectives (such as *idiotic*, *bizarre*, or *ridiculous*), you're adding story.

Then, identify your emotions, such as angry, confused, deflated, afraid, proud, guilty, or suspicious. Don't judge your emotions either. Just observe them as key data points. (In chapter six, you'll learn the Name-Rate-Find tool that you can use here.)

Ask

This is the real work of the SNAP process. Ask yourself these three questions:

1. What story am I believing right now?
2. Is it true?
3. What could happen if I believed a different story?

Allow yourself to brainstorm options that are positive and helpful but also rooted in reality. With your natural negativity bias, it will take some practice to find other options that are both positive and possible.

If your story determines your actions and those actions determine your results, this is where you choose the action that creates the flourishing and freedom you want.

Pivot

In a new story, you have a new set of actions to choose from. Pivot is taking the new action.

When you SNAP to a new story, you choose how to respond. Not only does this determine your results—it affects your joy. Especially when things are what they are, the meaning you make *matters*. Choosing the story you tell yourself keeps you in possibility (not lost in toxic positivity) and shifts how you actually experience your life—physically, emotionally, even neurologically. So let me tell you a story.

A Saturday Story

"I am . . . " Scrub, scrub, scrub. "The only one . . . " Spray. Spray. Spray. "Who does anything around here." Scrub, scrub, scrub.

The counters had smears of jam and egg yolk, and the crumbs of 6.2 million Goldfish crackers clustered around the trash can. The kitchen table held papers, sixteen half-full glasses of milk, a piano book, friendship beads, a used tissue, and—oh, is that . . . yes—a muddy sock. Exasperated and surrounded by the detritus of a family of six, I wanted to pitch everything out onto the deck.

"Do other people who live here not have eyes?" I shout as I grab the broom and slam the garage door. "I can't depend on anyone to help me at all."

Ever been there? The kitchen floor, the office copy room, or the shared drive? You've created a meaning and story.

Here's how I used the Story Transformation process:

As I pinched the muddy sock between my fingertips trying to decide between the sink or the trash, I remembered, SNAP.

Stop and breathe (and drop the sock in the sink to deal with later).

Notice. I'm cleaning up. I'm grumbling about the mess. I feel disregarded and unappreciated. This is *not fun*!

Ask myself, What's the story?

I'm telling myself the story that I can't depend on anyone else. Hello, Enneagram Seven Silent Script!

Is it true?

The sinking feeling of foolishness began. Michael has always been a partner in our shared lives. At that *very moment*, Michael was out with all four kids for a grocery run and then soccer games so I could have a quiet morning alone. Clearly, no, my story wasn't true.

What else could be true?

Michael sees different problems than I do. There wasn't time to clean the kitchen before the soccer games. Our elementary school-aged children still need reminders and training.

What could happen if I believed a different story?

If I believe the story that I have help, I feel safe and supported. (Even though I don't want to deal with that muddy sock.) I can express my gratitude to Michael for being such a great partner and dad. My children can gain the life skill of "pick up after yourself."

Pivot.

When my family arrived home, the kitchen wasn't clean yet. We put away groceries together while reliving the soccer games. I thanked Michael for the time alone and showed the kids their things to put away. The child with the muddy sock was thrilled to find the match to his favorite pair and put it in the laundry.

Changing the story led me to different actions that transformed my results from a sour morning and potentially a yelling fit to a connected, more joyful Saturday.

That Saturday situation isn't unique at home or work. You've gotten that email that sends you to the roof, banging out "per my last email" while thinking, *I'm the only one who can do this*. You've sat in the conference room chair, wanting to melt into the floor, telling yourself, *I don't belong here*.

When you rewrite an internal story, you can't ignore reality. That's just spinning another fairy tale that will crush your confidence and steal your joy. How do you find the truth beneath the make-believe?

Rewriting with Truth

Don't turn metacognition, this thinking about your thinking, into nonsense when you rewrite stories. I'm a 5′3″ Italian American. No amount of story rewriting will transform me into Yao Ming, the 7′6″ Chinese basketball player, the first-round NBA draft pick in 2002. You can't change certain aspects of yourself, and if you try, your brain calls BS. Psychologists call this *self-discrepancy*.[7] If the gap between who you are now and the new story is too great, your mind rejects the discrepancy and stays stuck in the old story. You must rewrite in the "latitudes of acceptance": the new story has to be close enough to where you are now to be effective.[8]

You need self-efficacy to rewrite with truth. Self-efficacy is your ability to believe you have the desired capacity or capability. It's specific, targeted at helping you believe you have the agency to achieve what you want.⁹ Self-efficacy gives you reality-based options for your rewrite: your previous experience, vicarious experience from others, visualization and imagined experience, and coaching and feedback. When you are rewriting, use one or a mix of these components to reduce the discrepancy and increase your brain's acceptance of the new story. (More in the *Playbook*.)

Sustaining Stories to Replace the Silent Scripts

Over time, you'll start to notice some of the same stories come up again and again, and many are the Enneagram Silent Scripts. When you notice a Silent Script, use your corresponding Enneagram Sustaining Story to replace it.

You're probably going to read these and scoff, *That cannot be true.* But I promise, they are. When you use your Sustaining Story consistently, you'll have experiences that *prove* them to be true. So, your brain starts to *believe* them. That's when they become your new reality.

Your old Silent Script will try to follow you to work as well. But it won't have the same hold on you anymore, because you've rewritten it into something that sustains you and your joy. These are anchoring affirmations you can repeat and reflect. Let them become true in your life as a leader.

Eight	Nine	One
Silent Script: It's not OK to trust anyone.	*Silent Script*: It's not OK to assert myself.	*Silent Script*: It's not OK to make mistakes.
Sustaining Story: I am wise enough to trust the right people who won't betray me. I do not have to fight for my belonging. It's OK to be vulnerable.	*Sustaining Story*: My presence matters. People want to hear what I have to say. I still belong when I engage with others, even when I assert myself.	*Sustaining Story*: I am good, even in imperfection. If someone else catches my mistake, I still have respect and belonging in the group.

Cut! Rewrite! Action!

Two	Three	Four
Silent Script: It's not OK for me to have my own needs.	*Silent Script*: It's not OK to have my own feelings or identity.	*Silent Script*: It's not OK to be too functional or too happy.
Sustaining Story: I am wanted. My emotional and physical needs are part of my humanity, and I can put them first. People will still love me when I express my needs.	*Sustaining Story*: I am loved for just being me. My accomplishments don't determine my value. I can share my feelings and still have worth.	*Sustaining Story*: I am seen for who I am. I am not too much. I am enough. It's OK for me to find joy in the world and take care of myself.

Five	Six	Seven
Silent Script: It's not OK to be comfortable in the world.	*Silent Script*: It's not OK to trust yourself.	*Silent Script*: It's not OK to depend on anyone for anything.
Sustaining Story: My needs are not a problem to solve. It's OK for me to be comfortable with people and take care of my body. I am safe to ask for help from other people and when I act before I've gathered all the information.	*Sustaining Story*: I can trust my judgments. I am safe. I can rest and let life unfold, knowing I can handle whatever comes my way.	*Sustaining Story*: I will be taken care of. I can experience discomfort or pain without distractions. I can experience difficulty and still be safe.

As you rewrite the stories, you will experience less toil because you find better meanings, keeping you in the Joy Ratio.

The Possibility Question

In 1991, Dave Chappelle arrived in New York City, with dreams of pursuing a career in comedy. Late nights, smokey venues, beer-stained microphones, he kept going. Finally making it to the rite of passage that was the Apollo Theater, the audience booed him off the stage.

You might not have been booed off the stage, but you've had a moment that felt like that. The presentation fell flat. The feedback conversation exploded. In that moment, what story did you tell yourself? *I'm so terrible, I should quit.* Chappelle thought a similar story: "The idea of bombing was horrifying. Nobody wants to bomb. Nobody." He'd never really bombed, let alone been run off the stage.

But he didn't stay in that story.

He said, "When I failed so far beyond my wildest nightmares of failing, it was like, 'Hey . . . this is not that bad.'"

His new story: *I can fail and still be successful. Failure isn't the end. I can move beyond a bad night.* Now he views that experience differently, "That night was liberating. After that, I was fearless."[10]

That fearlessness led him to the comedic dream. Just two years later, he made his film debut in Mel Brooks's parody *Robin Hood: Men in Tights*. He continued to make successful moves in TV, film, and the standup circuit for the next three decades.

Change the story. Change the results. Cultivate your joy.

What if Chappelle had stayed in the story that bombing the Apollo meant he was done in comedy? What happens if you stay stuck in the wrong story, unsure of your identity, paralyzed to take the next step, getting crushed by giants every day?

Your mind is a forest of stories. Some of them are fresh and new. Others are old and dark and deep. And in order to be a healthy leader —and to experience *joy*—you're going to have to rewrite those stories. You're going to have to go into those woods.

At the end of *Into the Woods*, the Witch delivers this haunting truth: "Be careful the tales you tell. That is the spell."

Whatever the story you tell yourself, that story shapes your life. It casts the spell over how you see the world, how you lead, and how you live. So rewrite with truth and tell the story that brings the most *freedom* and *joy*.

The Gist

The stories you tell yourself are either strengthening the roots of your joy or chopping them off. You have outdated Silent Scripts from your personality you need to rewrite. To build a life of meaning, connection, and results, use SNAP to rewrite a story that sustains joy.

Live in the story that creates joy.

—Jenn Whitmer

Connection

What internal stories do you have about your team, your boss, or your family? How can you use SNAP to connect or rewrite as a group?

· ·

Curiosity

Find a situation that keeps irritating you. Get curious about the story there. Use SNAP to identify a new story.

Write your Silent Script and Sustaining Story on a Post-it note and tally every time you notice your Silent Script come up.

· ·

Joy

You can rewrite stories in the moment. One phrase I use a lot is, "Did you have a bad day or a bad moment?"

For one week record any experience that reinforces your Sustaining Story.

To have joy, stop settling for a lesser, dishonest version of yourself.

Eagles on Posters Don't Fly

Make Values Actionable

*Daring leaders who live into their values
are never silent about hard things.*

—**Brené Brown, vulnerability expert, author, and speaker**

"A floating petri dish." That was my phrase about cruise ships whenever my husband would bring up the idea of a trip. Now, I'm in no way a germaphobe. The five-second rule is alive and well in our house, and I'll try a sip of your drink if you're offering. But a cruise ship? Everyone sharing the same water and air filtration system for days on end in the *middle of the sea*? My Enneagram Seven self could only imagine the terror of being trapped on a ship with a bunch of sick people and no escape.

Yet, for a big wedding anniversary, we embarked on a Disney cruise in the summer of 2023.

I have been a Disney fan since before I wrote my famous-Missourian biography on fellow Kansas City native Walt Disney in the fourth grade. But I hadn't "experienced" Disney in person until November 2022.* Let me tell you, the difference between knowing Disney is amazing, and experiencing it, is vast.

Two months later, I sat in Disney's Coronado Springs Resort on a retreat with business owners, enthralled by Terry Brinkoetter as he spoke about the organization. Brinkoetter, Director of PR for Disney Experiences, told wonderful stories as he fielded the myriad of questions from this group of thirty eager and intense leaders.

He shared how Disney uses its values to onboard cast members, steward its unique culture, and maintain its brand loyalty with billions of people. Disney's four core values—safety, courtesy, show, and efficiency—are more than words on the wall, nor are they in random order.[1] When faced with any situation, the first filter is always safety. (Or as my friend Erika likes to say as the car climbs the Mine Train, "Disney won't kill me.") Brinkoetter sat on a bar stool showing what these basics mean for Disney cast members each day, challenging me to consider how I lived by my values.

My five core values are connection, curiosity, joy, flourishing, and valor. And for decades, I had my arms crossed, fingers in my ears, deeply uncurious about Michael's desire to go on a cruise.

After Brinkoetter's session, I stood in the crowd that January night in the Magic Kingdom, tears streaming down my face from the joy of the fireworks. And I thought, *What if I were curious about a*

---

* The idea for this book began during my first Disney trip on the raft between the mainland and Tom Sawyer's island during School of Whimsy with Bob Goff at Disneyland.

cruise? What if I could show valor over my fears of the floating petri dish? Because I had experienced Disney's alignment of values and actions at that retreat, I reconsidered how I lived out my values. As for the cruise, I went from *hard pass* to *take all my dollars*, Disney.

I had identified my values before Brinkoetter's session. I'd named them, defined them, and even posted them on my office wall. But immersed in Disney's magic and knowing the business values behind it, I realized I wasn't living by them. And that was costing me connection with my husband. It compromised the integrity of my business. The misalignment removed me from purpose, and it was eroding my joy.

When Words Don't Walk the Talk

You've seen those framed posters with bold serif words and an eagle soaring over water. My eyes can't help but roll. Not because the words aren't true, but because in many organizations, those values aren't connected to the daily life of projects, meetings, and working together. Flimsy as that poster paper, performative versions of values can't hold up a Post-it note, let alone joy.

What's more, values slapped on the wall without follow-through past Friday aren't neutral—they're harmful. If actions and values don't match, the empty words sell false purpose and breed distrust. People spot hypocrisy fast. The posters become a constant reminder of the misalignment, eroding connection and leaving you unprotected and ill-equipped against difficulty.

In cultivating joy, values root you. They form the central taproot of the lavender image of joy. The taproot provides access to water stored deep underground, sustaining the plant even in drought conditions. Values must align with how you live every day, or you won't experience profound connection, especially when it gets hard.

Even when leaders and organizations do want to live by their values, they typically scramble the order of identifying values, purpose, vision, and mission.

The best definition of purpose I've ever heard comes from speaker and author Jade Simmons: "Purpose isn't what you do. It's what happens in other people when you do what you do."[2] Purpose grows from values. Your vision is what you want the future to be if you live out that purpose, based on values. Your mission is the action you take to achieve that vision. Without identifying values, you will misconstrue purpose, set unclear or even misguided visions, and go after unhelpful missions in your life.

Let's look at what values are, where they come from, and how aligning with your values fosters creativity, innovation, profit, connection, and joy.

Picking the Lens You Lead From

Clearly frustrated with the way a situation had gone down, a leader complained to his coach and mentor, Ken Black. The former Nike creative director calmly asked him, "How do you want to be seen in this moment?"

Pondering for a bit, the leader replied, "I want to be seen as someone who is steady, who is trustworthy, who is someone people can rely on."

"Are your actions showing that?"

"No," he sighed. "No. They are not."

"Well then, you have a chance right now to decide to act in alignment with the way you want to be seen."

When Ken teaches and trains on values, he says, "The eyes lead the body. Values are lenses."[3] This metaphor fits with the way we've been exploring self-awareness as you cultivate joy. Personality is the lens you're issued by design. Stories are the meanings you make from what you see through the lens. A value is a way of seeing the world through a lens *you* choose.

Back to Ken's story with his leader. The leader left the meeting with his lenses of *steady* and *trustworthy* in place. Within two weeks, everything shifted.

"It wasn't my direction," Ken told me on the *Joyosity* podcast. "It was because he made the decision about who he wanted to be." The leader named, owned, and acted on his values.

You already have values, and you will live by them some of the time. But if you don't name them, you have no idea which glasses to choose. That lack of clarity will always limit how well you can see, which will then limit your alignment, and ultimately, your joy.

The Art and Science of Alignment

Nick, a communications executive, landed a great new role. The company website promoted their purpose-driven culture and values of strategy, collaboration, integrity, and innovation. They hired him to create and oversee a digital transformation strategy—his sweet spot. He made his first presentation to the CEO, who said, "I love it. Let's bring it to the rest of the team."

The rest of the directors reviewed the strategy, made a few tweaks, and signed on. Six months later, the progress and initial results were strong. In the review meeting, one director sat back and said, "No one has ever done this before. This is how strategy should work." Nick left elated, ready for phase two.

Then, the wheels came off. Directors said yes but didn't follow through. People complained about Nick's team making changes and blamed them for dwindling results. Nick met with departments, asked questions, and tried to maintain the strategic course. Time after time, the CEO and directors pledged commitment to strategy and then bailed on actions. Frustration turned to infighting, and the outcomes got worse.

In a coaching session with me, Nick sighed, "I've realized they actually don't want strategy. They just want to say they're strategic on the website."

Over time, Nick got fed up with the broken promises and blame on his team. He left the "perfect job" that sold joy but ran on spin.

What you believe, say, and do need to match. Lip service harms people and breaks trust. Likely, you've experienced this too. And you've probably done it to yourself.

Owning who you are, fighting for authenticity, and living in alignment with your values feels exposed, vulnerable, and almost dangerous. That's why so many leaders take the lower-effort route—craft a word-salad vision and mission statement, toss posters on the wall, and move on.

It seems easier, but it's ineffective, exhausting, and infinitely harder.

You are most effective when you know who you are and what you value. And you are the most immature and incompetent when you live unaware.

Freedom begins with truth. Every time. To paraphrase Mark Groves, human-connection specialist, if you want to be free and have joy, stop settling for a lesser, dishonest version of yourself.[4]

Working in Sync, Not at Odds

To create joy, your goal is alignment in what you value and what you do. This means there should be a connection between your values, the organization's values, and the work that you do.

People whose values align with their company's purpose are 53 percent more satisfied with their job than those who are misaligned according to Strategy& and the *Harvard Business Review*.[5] When your work aligns with your values, that will always be purposeful work. According to the American Psychological Association, when you are out of alignment, you are 26 percent more likely to live most days at work tense or stressed.[6] Or, as Sustainable Brands reported, to leave the organization. Just over a third of employees in the United States resigned in 2023 because their company did not align with their values, and 51 percent would consider leaving for that reason.[7]

Consumers care too. In early March 2025, Target lost $12.4 billion in value because of organized boycotts after changes in its diversity, equity, and inclusion policies.[8] On February 28, 2025, an economic blackout of companies that rolled back DEI commitments drew international headlines. That day, the number of people in Target stores dropped nearly 11 percent, and Amazon web traffic dropped 4.6 percent. That same day Costco, who had gone all-in on its DEI efforts, saw an 8.3 percent increase in its web traffic.[9]

Connection to your rooted values not only creates joy for you as an individual, but it also matters to the economy.

Feeling the Click of Alignment

"What . . . in the world . . . is this move?" I shouted at Jonelle, the yoga trainer, even though she couldn't hear me, because she's on my iPad in an Apple Fitness workout.

After a year of regular yoga practice, I still could not maneuver my standing leg, arms, and balance. Determined, I came back to this workout about once a week for a month.

On the mat at the gym one day, I stood solid in a dancer pose—grounded right foot, holding my left foot behind me, bent forward with my right arm extended—for a full sixty seconds. I felt a powerful ease I could sustain. I was surprised when Jonelle's voice came through my AirPods: "OK, let's come out the way we came in."

Switching sides, my skin tingled with goosebumps as a warmth spread across my torso. I felt a lightness, and my breaths came easily. As I hinged forward, rooted and connected, I recognized this sensation as alignment.

Living in alignment isn't just a mental match-up game. When you are living in alignment with your values, you'll *feel* it. It's a practice you build over time. The alignment brings direction, peace to decisions (more on that in chapter nine), and a lightness in your leadership. But before you can experience this, you've got to do the work to identify the values you want to live by, and not just the ones you picked up or inherited.

What Shapes Your Values

Your world shapes your values. You absorb them from culture and family. Your Enneagram personality has plenty to say about what you value too. Often, you're acting on values you never consciously chose.

It's like wearing lenses that no longer fit who you are. And when those values go unexamined, you get uprooted. You lose alignment, and guilt and shame add more rocks to the soil. Joy withers.

When it's time to name your values, you want to choose what's true for *you*, not what someone else told you should matter. You want to see the world on purpose, through lenses that match who you are *and* who you want to be.

The Culture and Generation You Swim In

I knelt down on the industrial carpet, trying to get eye level with Kwame. He wiggled in place; eyes fixed on his shoelaces. He had gotten a little too excited with his body on the way out of my classroom, and knocked over a xylophone, scattering the wooden bars. We put the instrument in its rightful place, and there was no real damage. I asked Kwame what happened, but he wouldn't look at me.

"Hey, Kwame. Can you look at me, please?" I gently asked.

Eyes still on his shoes, he replied softly, "No, Mrs. Whitmer. That's rude. You're my teacher."

At twenty-four, still a fairly new teacher, I hadn't experienced this before. An earnest and sweet kid, I knew he was sincere. We wrapped up our quick conversation with his eyes on the ground, and I got curious. I asked my mentor teachers, who all confirmed what was new to me—maintaining eye contact is not a universal sign of respect.

Cultural values vary widely around the world. As we become a more global society, those differences surprise us. In a master's program in communication and culture, decades after this conversation with Kwame, I found one of the clearest frameworks for cultural differences: Hofstede Insights. Geert Hofstede, a Dutch social psychologist and pioneer in cross-cultural communities, identified six continuums he called dimensions. These measure countries on cultural values, and you can see how these values show up in you as an individual. The dimensions are low versus high power distance, collectivism versus individualism, high achievement versus quality of life, short-term versus long-term orientation, restraint versus indulgence, and high versus low uncertainty avoidance.

Kwame's grandparents emigrated from Ghana. Ghana ranks as a high power distance culture with a score of eighty on the power distance dimension.[10] People in a high power distance culture accept hierarchical order. Everybody's got their place in the hierarchy—no need to justify it. A sign of deference is to lower your eyes and not make direct eye contact. This deference of lowered eyes is common in many Black families, not specific to those from Ghana. Many African, Middle Eastern, and Asian cultures have the same practice. The United States has a comparatively low power distance ranking of forty, and eye contact is seen as a sign of confidence and respect.

As you think about what values you've picked up from culture, here are a few questions to ask:

- Who deserves respect and power? Who's important?
- Is it more important to take care of the group or make it on my own?
- Do you prefer doing what can be done quickly, or seeing what happens over long spans of time?
- Do you value the cutting edge, or do you want to stay with what feels more stable?

There are no wrong answers. The goal is to reveal how cultural dimensions impact your values, then decide if you want to keep it that way.

The Family Blueprint You Inherited

"Goffs aren't quitters."[11]

Bob Goff, *NYT* bestselling author, lawyer, and philanthropist, got this idea from his parents. I heard him share this idea in person at the House of Blues in Anaheim, California, during his School of Whimsy (proud graduate here). He also talks about it in numerous books and social media posts.

Turns out, that value kept him overextended and away from his family too much. The man commuted from San Diego to Seattle. Every day. So Bob flipped his script. He started quitting things on Thursdays. He encourages folks by saying, "It's Thursday. You can quit anything on a Thursday." But it's more than quitting a job or a hobby. He also encourages people to examine those old stories and change the values that aren't creating the life they want.[12]

The tricky thing about family values is they hide. You just think they're normal (remember the story about the flour in chapter three). Sometimes, they're overt: "Children are seen and not heard." "Work before play." "Finish what you start."

When my kids would leave for a friend's house or an overnight trip, I would say, "Be kind. Be polite. Be a Whitmer." Because I value connection, I was determined not to raise bullies and mean girls. I wanted them to show respect to other people and be helpful. I wanted them to remember they belong in our family, regardless of the situation.

As you examine your family values, you don't have to throw them all out. You will find parts that you want to keep and others that don't work for you anymore. Here are a few questions:

- What did my family teach me about privacy or secrets?
- What did my family teach me about emotions?
- How did my family handle conflict? What was considered a conflict?
- What were the rules?
- Who was in charge?

Your answers provide clues to what your family of origin values. As you reflect, you get to choose which ones you want to keep and which ones aren't creating the joy you want.

The Personality Patterns You Bring Along

Kristi, a technology director for a credit union, hopped on the Zoom kickoff meeting, excited. The project, a streamlined member app, brought together people she knew from other departments, but a few she hadn't worked with directly, including the team leader.

At the time, Kristi had been in my Joyosity Leadership Lab for a few months. She'd identified herself as an Enneagram Six and worked through my Navigate Values System. Like many Enneagram Sixes, she valued questions, but also belonging, structure, transparency, and preparedness. This project was the first opportunity to apply her expanded self-awareness in a new context.

The team leader opened the meeting with introductions and walked through the typical kickoff agenda: goals, objectives, budget, etc. Quickly, the meeting turned chaotic. The team leader presented two timelines with unclear deadlines. Decision-making roles remained ambiguous. People talked over one another. Kristi felt her anxiety rise.

As the meeting's end approached, she tapped the "raise hand" icon and waited. After several minutes, the team leader said, "Kristi, you have your hand up."

"Yes," Kristi began. "I have a few questions. I want to be prepared for our next meeting, and I'm not sure what to tell my team. So, first—"

"You'll have to ask your questions later," the leader interrupted. "I've got a hard stop, and I've got one more item."

Dismissed and frustrated, Kristi tapped "Leave Meeting" the moment the meeting wrapped. The encounter could have sent her into a spiral of scenario-building and overpreparing. However, Kristi had the self-awareness to pause and name what was happening.

First, the leader stepped on Kristi's values of questions, preparedness, and transparency. The leader didn't know she had done this, but that's what happened. Kristi also felt the team leader disregarded the credit union values of employee engagement and process improvement.

Then Kristi observed a deeper layer: the combination of her Enneagram Six personality and her values. Your personality lens will always impact how you see through the value lenses, as if you've clipped the values on top of your personality lens. Sometimes your values intensify the view, and that's what was happening for Kristi. Her Enneagram Six personality was shouting at her *"You're gonna get blamed!"* while the leader thwarted Kristi's values.

She called me to talk it through. After a bit of back and forth, I asked Kristi, "Do you want to align with your values?"

"For sure. I know I feel better when I do. Right now, I feel disjointed and unstable," she replied.

"So," I nudged, "Are you going to allow the team leader's behavior to determine how you behave?"

Kristi knew her answer. She chose the vulnerability of living by her values. She set time with the team leader to ask her questions so she could prepare a structure for her team's role in the new app.

Your values root you in joy, but only if you stay connected to them, understand how your personality interacts with your values, and choose to live by those values.

All of this means you must identify your unique values. You need to name them and define them for yourself. Not a vague sense of good ways to live, but specific, personal, and clear values that you write down. (You can head to the Lounge for a condensed process with the Values Identifier Guide. You'll find the full Navigate Values System in the *Playbook*.)

Once you've identified your values, life will test your character.

Choosing Your Character

Every Disney Pixar film includes a crisis, most of them shaped by legendary screenwriting expert Robert McKee. *Toy Story*'s Woody faces loyalty or popularity. Lightning McQueen from *Cars* faces ego or teamwork. In *Monsters, Inc.*, Sulley faces power or compassion. These crises are more than cartoon conundrums—they're a universal truth of life.

McKee writes in *Story*, "True character is revealed in the choices a human being makes under pressure—the greater the pressure, the deeper the revelation, the truer the choice to the character's essential nature."[13]

Remember, values are the lens you choose. You construct your character when you live by your values or leave them behind.

Our Disney cruise was a practice round for living aligned with my values. A few months later, my client Wendy complained about a payment issue. Our systems showed no extra charge; hers did. Weeks of my team wrangling chatbots, banks, payment systems, and emailing Wendy landed us in the same place.

If my values were just words on a wall, I could have pointed to our records and shrugged. Reasonable, but it would have cost me far more than one refunded payment. It would have damaged trust, lost me a long-term client, and communicated to my team that convenience matters more than connection.

Alignment with curiosity and connection required action. I called Wendy, listened to her hard feedback about feeling dismissed, and asked my team to dig one more time. Buried in a subsystem of a subsystem was the glitch. We made it right, both financially and relationally.

The legwork and the hard conversations were a struggle but aligned to my values. Living in alignment with your truest self is a choice of character that produces true joy.

You've explored your self and have been digging your foundation of self-awareness in this section. You understand your personality, you've identified your storylines, and you've named the values as the way you want to see and live in the world.

Joyosity

You're growing deep roots of joy by understanding what brings you profound connection, intense happiness, and true purpose. With clarity, alignment, and the ability to engage from a secure place, *aligned with your favorite self*, you are cultivating a character of joy.

The Gist

Values shape your daily reality. They're the lens you choose—guiding your priorities, decisions, and how you spend your energy. When your values are clear and aligned, you unlock the Joy Ratio: more joy, less toil, and a life that actually feels like yours.

> To have *joy*, stop settling for *a lesser*, dishonest version of yourself.
>
> —Jenn Whitmer

Connection

Finish the Values Identifier in the Lounge.

Is the work you're doing aligned with your values? Where do you feel alignment (or misalignment) with other people?

....

Curiosity

In what situations do you catch yourself saying one thing but doing another?

What cultural or family values still shape your decisions, at home and at work?

....

Joy

When you are living by your values (openly, consistently, and unapologetically), what is the impact on your coworkers, your family, or your organization? Write this down as a statement and put it where you can see it.

Part 2

I think the elephant in the room of the country today is humanity.

—**Howard Schultz, former CEO of Starbucks**

Engage

Complex People. Power Skills.

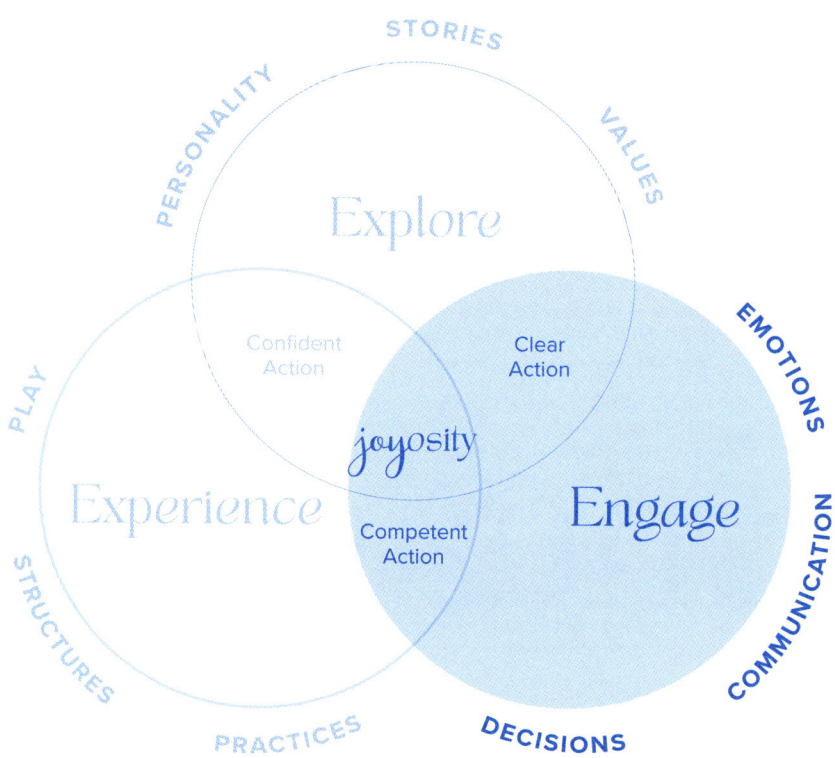

Slipping out of my bedroom, I silently padded to the alcove under the stairs. I lifted the receiver of the tattered beige phone and unfolded the scrap of paper filled with numbers.

It was 1996, and I was studying in Oxford. In a semidetached house on Windmill Road I shared with five other students, I perched on a tiny stool dialing what felt like 82,000 numbers to activate a special calling card that let me call Michael back in Missouri for 2 pence a minute.

Ring. Ring.

I yawned, somewhat annoyed with the six-hour time difference and our competing schedules that meant these 3 a.m. phone calls were the only window we could talk.

Ring. Ri— "Hello?"

A smile filled my face just hearing his voice.

But the conversation? Every week was a mixed bag. Because we were doing this on the super-cheap, the connection invariably scratched and wobbled. Also, trying not to wake the house, I whispered most of the time.

"What? Can you say that again?" became Michael's refrain.

We missed each other desperately, but these calls often brought more tension than connection. Frustration, miscommunication, or worse, an outright fight. And making decisions together? Challenging doesn't begin to capture it. Twenty-year-olds that we were, there was a lot of reactivity, and building trust on a timer in the middle of the night—well, at least we can laugh about it now.

Basically, we had to learn how to engage in a dynamic environment that frequently challenged our connection. This is where you are now.

In the Explore section, you've built a strong foundation, rooting yourself in the work of self-awareness. You're like, *This is great. I'm a solid seven outta ten. Let's go!*

But now, you've got to engage with other people: the ones who get under your skin, say things that make no sense to you, and have totally different goals—all while you're on a deadline. Welcome to the complexities of a scratchy phone line trying to connect to other people. It's easy-peasy to understand your personality, manage your stories, and live by your values until the *other* pesky, complex people show up.

The next three chapters will sharpen your people-power skills—the ones that actually help you get along with humans. Don't you *dare* call them soft skills. You'll learn to engage with your emotions, practice emotional regulation, and build trust. You'll also get practical tools for clear communication, conflict resolution, and decision-making with a repeatable process.

Roll up those sleeves! Welcome to the Messy Middle of the Joy Ratio, where cultivating gets real.

Feelings at the Table

Lead with Emotional Intelligence

As human beings, we can only experience life emotionally.
—Eduardo Bericat, professor of sociology

This is the tale of Rick Fisher, CEO of The Fisher Group (TFG), who built an empire on sharp thinking and relentless efficiency. Under his leadership, TFG became a global profit machine. But something was off.

Despite the record numbers, departments battled one another. Turnover spiked. Engagement plummeted. Innovation stalled. Profit declined. An air of quiet resentment permeated the company's sleek, glass-walled headquarters. And something inside Rick just felt . . . off.

He brushed it aside and grabbed his phone. "Work is about strategy and execution," he sneered as he swiped to his email. "Emotions are a distraction." But at night, he'd stare at the ceiling with a dull ache in his chest.

The board brought in a leadership consultant, Persephone Vull, but everyone called her Percy. Rick expected spreadsheets and slide decks. Percy showed up with a fountain pen and leather notebook.

After the initial pleasantries, she asked, "Rick, what hurts?"

He scoffed, "What kind of question is that? Profits are down. That's it."

"Not TFG. You," she persisted. "What hurts?"

That caught Rick off guard. While his mind tried to understand the relevance of the question, something inside him stirred. "Um, I'm not sure."

Over the weeks, Percy continued the perplexing questions: "What do you miss about your early days as a leader? When was the last time you felt inspired? What's something you used to care about that you no longer make time for?"

Slowly, Rick saw it. He wasn't just stressed about numbers. He'd exiled his feelings because he believed they had no place at work. But he'd cut off his emotional connection to everything and everyone. He'd created the same problem for his employees, and his company was beginning to fail because he had walled off emotions. With Percy's coaching, Rick worked on reconnecting to his feelings and increasing his emotional intelligence.

The transition was slow, but solid. Engagement ticked up. Innovation came back. There was even laughter in the office. TFG profits stabilized.

Rick didn't revive his business with the latest AI integration or market analysis. He realized emotions weren't a liability in leadership. Rather, his emotions (and the emotions of others) were an intelligence he needed. And for the first time in years, Rick closed his eyes at night, feeling whole.[1]

We've built artificial hearts, limbs, and voices. Artificial intelligence models can calculate, research, and even give solid advice. But no technology will ever replace human emotions. A machine might mimic tears or laughter, but it will never swell with wonder or tremble with grief. Emotions remain the sacred ground of our shared humanity, our most honest intelligence, and the very vehicle of profound connection.

You've invested in a book about how to create intense *happiness*. At some level, you believe feeling is the heart of what it means to be human. You cannot cultivate joy unless you're willing to wade into the turbulent, wild, and vulnerable waters of emotional intelligence.

Tin Man, Roller Coasters, or the Third Way

You may feel like emotions are totally inefficient and cumbersome—definitely not welcome in your 10 a.m. meeting. *Why do we need emotions when we've got logic to make work better?* It's easier to be the Tin Man, walking on the Yellow Brick Road, wishing for a heart.

You've come by this Tin Man perspective honestly. Western culture tells you emotions are weak (or, god forbid, feminine). Maybe someone wielding emotions as a weapon harmed you, and now emotions feel unsafe. Likely, no one ever modeled how to manage this domain of intelligence. I've forfeited far too much time there, attempting to outrun disappointment, fast-forward grief, and bypass fury so I wouldn't have to deal with my emotions.

Here's my question: Then what are you doing this all for? Because without emotions, you're walking through an existence devoid of meaning, not living a treasured and joyful life.

On the other end, you might be in the white-water rapids of emotions, feeling all the feels all the time and swimming for dear life. Checking your emotions at the door seems impossible, but the surging river isn't helping your relationships. The intensity of emotions steals your agency and imprisons you to the whims of your feelings, their feelings, and probably the feelings of your dog.

There's a third way: Whether you've been denying emotions or drowning in them, the solution to both extremes is developing the skill of emotional intelligence.

Why Emotional Intelligence Matters More Than You Think

Jewel's mom abandoned her at eight years old. After years of suffering under an increasingly abusive father, the not-yet singer-songwriter escaped as a teenager. She lived in her car and moved from one odd job to the next to survive, leaving her perpetually anxious, angry, and alone.

One day, utterly depressed with no clear way out, she hiked a bluff on the Pacific. She sat on the rocky ground, staring at the waves. "For about eight hours, I watched the tide go out and come back . . . so slowly, so imperceptibly," Jewel remembers. She started to connect the waters with her emotions. And she thought, "*Sometimes the tide is just out.*"

This idea transformed Jewel's life. "Because I felt so sad, like my sadness would be forever," she said. "But watching the ocean tide out and back in, I realized that change is a basic law of nature and physics. And I'm a part of nature and physics, so it would be impossible . . . it would be outside of the laws of nature and physics, for my bad mood not to change."

Since then, she has managed her emotions by seeing them as part of existing in the natural world.

"To this day," she said, "whenever I get sad, depressed, stressed, anxious, I say to myself, 'The tide is just out. I don't know how long it will take, but it will come back in . . . Nothing is permanent.'"[2]

Tsunami or Canal?

Even though emotions are part of the physics of life, workplaces tend to have two reactions to emotions: One, openly hostile toward emotions (oh, the irony), which sounds like, "Leave your emotions at the door" or "Don't get emotional about this," or two, unsure what to do with uncomfortable emotions, which sounds like, "Oh, don't cry," or "Let's look at the bright side."

I think we're afraid of the tsunami of feelings. We're afraid of losing control of our emotional responses, and of that tidal wave destroying our reasoning, reputation, and relationships. So we shove it all down and move on. We're so scared of emotional manipulation that we manipulate and gaslight ourselves by resisting and repressing emotions.

Multiple problems arise with the "no emotions" repression strategy, including a constant state of low-level irritation, unexplained physical symptoms, overreacting or underacting, and outright emotional numbness.

Instead, let's see emotions like Venetian canals. The canals absorb the tidal waters and change the flow of water into an intricate transportation system, connecting people across the Floating City. This is the image of emotional connection and emotional intelligence.

Our goal is to direct that water flow, not let it dry up or overwhelm the banks. **Emotional intelligence is directing the flow.** It's a skill set of awareness and actions: understanding your emotions, responding to situations, and connecting to other people.

This skill literally brings success to your life. A forty-year study from UC Berkeley found emotional intelligence was 400 percent more powerful than content knowledge in predicting achievement and success in leadership.[3] And *90 percent* of top performers have high levels of emotional intelligence.[4] AT&T found higher levels of emotional intelligence in any role were responsible for 20 percent more productivity than those with lower emotional intelligence.[5] Mountains of research show if you manage and regulate your emotions, you are generally more successful and happier.

Emotions, Feelings, and Moods: Not the Same

Before we go further, let's define a few terms. **Emotions** are energy in motion, the neurobiological signals of raw energy moving through your body that last six to ninety seconds.[6] **Feelings** are how we interpret those emotional chemicals moving through the nervous system. They are more "cognitively saturated" and last longer than the emotions. **Moods** are a more complex and general emotional state that last longer, from hours to days. A mood combines your environment, physical state, and mentality.[7] *

Syncing Your Three Centers

Houston had a problem: On June 14, 1989, the USS *Houston* dragged the tugboat *Barcona* a half mile into the ocean off the coast of Long Beach, California.

In the predawn darkness, the nuclear-powered submarine surfaced to periscope depth. As they ascended, sonar indicated the closest vessels were a safe four and half miles away. Suddenly, the watch officer saw a large black shape that filled the periscope. The commanding officer ordered an emergency dive, and the *Houston* plunged 300 feet without realizing the sub had snagged the cable connecting the *Barcona* to two barges, dragging the tug down with it. One man died, and two barely survived before being rescued by another tugboat.

On a submarine, three different types of data sensors keep the sub going in the right direction, staying in the right direction, and changing the direction if needed: sonar, radar, and radio. The sub needs all three of these centers working in congruence to travel safely. In the USS *Houston* incident, investigators determined one data center went into passive mode and catastrophe struck.[8]

You have three centers as well, three Centers of Intelligence: Doing, Feeling, and Thinking.** These Centers play an essential role in Enneagram work but appear in many traditions and psychological

---
* There's some debate about these definitions in the field. Alan Fridlund said, "The only thing certain in the emotion field is that no one agrees on how to define emotion."
** We'll come back to these three Centers again and again as a part of the Enneagram.

studies. Like the sub, these three work together to help you avoid obstacles, overcome challenges, and navigate your journey. Emotional intelligence requires all three.

Doing Center: Your Body Gets It Done

A newborn's cry is an example of the Doing Center. At birth, you haven't yet developed emotions or cognitive thought. But you *do* have reflexes and bodily sensations. (And sorry to break it to you, but that dreamy four-week-old smile? Probably just gas.) As you grow, the Doing Center of Intelligence becomes the way you get *anything* done. It's how you commute to work. It's how you write on the whiteboard, send the email, or create the design.

The Doing Center is where your five senses live, and gut instincts speak with an inner knowing before thoughts catch up. Researchers continue to discover how the body embeds trauma and memories as well as the mystery of how your internal storyteller connects with the rest of your nervous system.

Here's the key: Your Doing Center is a *way of knowing*. That's why we say *clarity is in the doing*. Your body is the vehicle of your work *and* part of your wisdom.

Feeling: Your Emotions Connect and Decide

As early as four months old, emotions develop alongside connections with a primary caregiver. Those smiles now? All genuine expressions of connection and trust.

Before this time, a cry was merely a physical response to a stimulus. But now, a cry not only *sounds* different, it *means* something different. A baby now feels fear and joy, disgust and sadness, and trust.

As your Feeling Center matures, it gathers data, stores memories, and makes decisions. (We'll talk more about decisions in chapter nine.)

With the Feeling Center, you relate to other people. You need this Center to lead effectively with empathy and authenticity. And, as we've been talking about throughout the entire book, you need your Feeling Center to *experience joy*.

Thinking: Your Strategy and More

Last to develop is the Thinking Center—what we typically associate with logic, language, and reason. You see this when a child can put all the blue things together, group the squares, and say, "Mama." As you develop, the Thinking Center becomes your ability to read, write, and do math. It's how you solve problems, strategize, manage time, and regulate your body—it's generally referred to as executive functioning skills.

Western society has elevated the Thinking Center, as if it's unerring and the highest form of correctness. (I'm looking at you, Enlightenment bros.) But I've got news: Your Thinking Center is just as imperfect as your Feeling Center and your Doing Center. You just happen to have more perceived control over it than the other two.

Each Center gives you different signals and information. To lead and live well, you need all three in balance. But in Western culture, we've spent centuries developing Thinking and Doing, while neglecting Feeling. And that neglect creates a dangerous imbalance. You're like the USS *Houston* operating with one of its data systems offline: You're navigating life without critical intel.

Western culture has historically derided the Feeling Center as weak and unimportant. It gets dismissed, intellectualized, or bypassed. Most people either shove feelings down like a genie in a bottle or indulge them like Grandma with a toddler. Here's why neither of those approaches cultivates joy.

You Can't Febreze Your Feelings

Feelings are like farts. They gotta get out, but in the right time and place.

Many people want to fix rather than feel. You move into your Thinking Center to "solve the problem." But like farts, emotions and feelings are not problems. They are a natural component of humanity. When you only think about your emotions or talk about them, you are "recycling" them. This sounds like a hamster wheel of thoughts and stories—reliving it in the shower or rehashing it with anyone who will listen:

- "I can't believe I said that. They must think I'm so stupid."
- "Why did I let that happen? I should have done something different."
- "What did they really mean?"
- "I should be over this by now. Why am I still thinking about it?"

All of this recycling shows up in the Monday status meeting. You'll get stuck in drama cycles where the same complaints loop without resolution—killing focus, blocking productivity, and stunting growth. Venting morphs into toxic gossip—sabotaging morale, disengaging your team, and driving people out the door.[9]

Remember, experiencing the emotion takes six to ninety seconds. We waste a lot more time recycling and causing unhealthy drama than we would by just feeling our emotions in the first place.

The other response most of us learn is emotional repression. Shove those feelings in a bedazzled box and lock them away. Likely, you had early experiences (either in childhood or your early career) that taught you that when you express emotions, bad things happen. Or possibly you learned some emotions and feelings are OK, and others are not. Shoving emotions into the recesses of your psyche only builds up, causing more pain and difficulty. And if you repress them for long enough, that energy gets trapped in your body, causing physical symptoms: acne, eczema, headaches, sleeplessness, joint pain, general fatigue, muscle tightness, and more.[10] It sounds like this:

- "If I just ignore it, I'll feel better."
- "Feeling this will just make it worse. I just need to push through."
- "Ah, TikTok. If I distract myself enough, it will just go away."
- "I don't have time for this. I'll figure it out later."
- "Crying is pointless. I should just toughen up."
- "Other people have it worse, so I shouldn't be upset."

Another clue you've been repressing emotions is what Brené Brown calls "chandeliering"—when the tiniest thing sends you over the edge (more on this in chapter ten). When you regularly repress feelings, they harden into more complicated moods. Anger solidifies into bitterness. Anxiety twists into hypervigilance. Sadness descends into depression.

The internal buildup doesn't stay inside. It spills out into the workplace. The glazed-over faces at the all-hands meeting, rising absenteeism, or the pervasive burnout you notice? Those are symptoms of emotional repression. And they're costly. Emotional repression erodes psychological safety. When repression is the expectation, creativity dries up, trust disappears, and health declines.[11]

You don't want a workplace full of unnecessary drama, but you also don't want one so sterile that it's joyless. Repressing and recycling feelings kill connection. So if those don't work, how do you actually feel the feels in the Venetian canal and get back to joy?

Name-Rate-Find: Three Steps to Master Emotional Moments

The first skill of emotional intelligence is recognizing and managing your emotions. This is how you, as a leader, regulate yourself when others fly off the handle. Self-regulation is also the beginning of practicing empathy. Put simply, empathy is feeling with people as they feel: not fixing or absorbing, but connecting.

Empathy elevates leadership from transactional to relational. Empathy fosters trust and psychological safety. You must have emotional connection for people to bring their full selves into innovation, creativity, and collaboration. Empathy is a connection brick in the pathway of joy, but that pathway is only walkable if you recognize and manage your emotions first.

In the Joy Ratio, emotional intelligence is how you navigate the Messy Middle, have resilience through toil, and experience the richness of joy.

Feelings at the Table

Decades of emotional intelligence research from Daniel Goleman and Marc Brackett to Susan David and Brené Brown reveal the same truth that we talked about with internal stories: Change begins with awareness. Enter Name-Rate-Find.

I've developed Name-Rate-Find from that research and from my experiences coaching hundreds of leaders. It's simple, repeatable, and effective in the messy moments of life. This is how you literally feel the feelings—how you apply emotional regulation when that inevitable meeting leaves you feeling some sorta way. Name-Rate-Find allows you to move from reactive and disconnected to resilient and joyful. Then you can lead yourself and others with empathy and clarity.

1. **Name** the emotions and feeling. Here's the sentence: "I feel [emotion]." Or "I'm experiencing [emotion]." Write it down or say it out loud. Say it to yourself or find a trusted person to talk to. This process, called "affect labeling," brings clarity and reduces the intensity of the emotional experience.[12] (Use this in the *Notice* part of SNAP from chapter four.)

2. **Rate** the intensity. Ask yourself: *On a scale of 1 to 10, how intensely am I feeling this emotion?* Don't overthink it. There is no right or wrong, and there's not consistent intensity. The higher the intensity, the harder self-control becomes. High intensity means take a break. Take a short stroll or find a place to feel the emotion and let it pass through.

3. **Find** the sensation in your body. Locate where in your body you are experiencing the feeling. The physical sensations of emotions exist in your body as energy, passing through as chemical reactions. When you locate the emotions in your

body, you get the Doing and Thinking Centers involved, helping you regulate your nervous system.[13]

You can find the quick version of Name-Rate-Find in the Lounge, complete with a list of more than 200 feeling words to help you *Name*, an intensity scale to help you *Rate*, and a guided body scan to help you *Find*.*

The complete system lives in the *Playbook*. In that deep dive, you'll find my proprietary Enneagram Feels Wheel, a fast track to emotional fluency that connects your personality to your emotional patterns. It's the tool that helps you recognize, regulate, and recover faster.

The real test of Name-Rate-Find? When the stakes feel high, and your emotions threaten to derail you.

Not long after I started my business, fellow Enneagram expert Sarajane Case invited me to speak at her Enneagram Summit along with Suzanne Stabile and other Enneagram greats. At the time, Sarajane ran one of the most popular Enneagram Instagram accounts, Enneagram and Coffee, with hundreds of thousands of followers—this felt BIG. This was my break! Since this was during COVID times, the sessions were prerecorded, and we engaged in the comments during the Summit. I wrote and rehearsed my talk so I could send in the recording on time. When I reviewed the materials before I recorded, I realized I'd missed an optional but amazing opportunity: being on the *Enneagram and Coffee* podcast, with millions of downloads.

The back of my jaw immediately tingled like I'd had a sour candy, and my chest collapsed. Tears pricked my eyes. All of these physical sensations instantly overwhelmed me, and I plopped my forehead on my desk. I'd missed my big break.

---

* This list of emotion words lives by my desk, and when our kids were younger, on our fridge. I pull it up in coaching sessions frequently.

When this happened, I'd been practicing Name-Rate-Find for years. I had already found the physical sensations in my chest and jaw, and I named the feeling as extreme disappointment. I rated this uncomfortable cocktail of shame, fear, anger, and sadness at a seven.

My Enneagram Seven self immediately wanted to reframe and repress to avoid this disappointment (that I was positive it would last for eternity). But I chose to breathe (still with my head on the desk) and just feel it. I felt a little embarrassed when I allowed myself to whimper. And to my surprise, after forty-five seconds or so, the emotional intensity dissipated.

I didn't lose more time spiraling; I could focus on the work at hand. I didn't have lingering emotional baggage; I could record my talk on Enneagram Types and Burnout with my fullest capability. Taking the time to process the emotions allowed me to do my favorite work well, the work that is the 35 percent, the Magic Third, in my Joy Ratio.

I imagine you've experienced a similar escapade. You missed a detail that had real consequences, and disappointment came rushing in. Name-Rate-Find is how you manage your emotions, and be fully human, no matter what comes your way.

Regulation isn't repressing or recycling. It's the clarity you need to process emotions in real time so you're leading yourself, rather than your emotions wreaking havoc like a tsunami or damming the flow of healthy connection. Use Name-Rate-Find to process, metabolize, and release emotions in a healthy, constructive way that opens the door to connection and better leadership. As Liz and Mollie write in *No Hard Feelings*, "It enables you to bring your *best* self."[14]

Who's Responsible for the Spread?

As a first-year teacher, I walked into the teachers' lounge curious and intimidated. At twenty-two, this was my first professional job, and I knew I had a lot to learn. I found out fast that the teachers' lounge was the place to pick up all the things you can't teach in an undergrad degree program.

There was a pair of fifth-grade teachers who had been teaching for decades. Both of them happened to be named Helen, so we naturally called them "The Helens." I loved listening to their stories and wisdom. They brought perspective to the initiative fatigue that can plague education and an even keel to the intense seasons of a school year. They brought delicious treats and shared the best recipes. Basically, I'd leave lunch feeling as good or better than when I walked into the lounge.

The next year, the schedule changed, and I had new folks in my lunch shift. After the first week, I quickly realized the gift (and the absence) of The Helens. This particular mix of educators was more volatile and pessimistic. Everything was "awful." They were a flurry of stressful activity. They loved to play the Olympic Games of Suffering, competing about whose class or workload was worse. I noticed how lunch changed from one of my favorite times of the day to connect with adults, to feeling like I was crawling from a cesspool in need of an emotional shower.

Have you been there when the emotional state of the room swings based on who's in the room? People describe that experience many ways, but I have a love/hate relationship with, "If Mama ain't happy, ain't nobody happy." But here's the nugget of truth in the old phrase that research demonstrates is true and that showed up in the teachers' lounge: Emotions are contagious.[15]

You Go First

If you want to be a leader with joy, you are responsible for practicing your own emotional regulation first. You set the tone, and others will reflect you. To be clear, this doesn't mean faking it, or toxic positivity, requiring you and everyone to have "positive vibes only." It does mean you model the emotional intelligence we've talked about in this chapter, and coach others in that direction.

You Are Responsible for You

Your second responsibility is owning your emotions. When you own your emotions, it sounds like this: "I feel frustrated by the team missing the deadline," rather than, "The missed deadline made me feel frustrated."

No one can *make* you feel something. You own your emotions and feelings because they are *your* response to stimuli. Projection or blame is a defense mechanism that releases you from being responsible for yourself.[16] Essentially, it's the "they made me do it" excuse and a sign of an immature Feeling Center.

You Can't Run Their Race

The corollary to this one is that you are also not responsible for the emotions of others. Sometimes, this one shocks leaders! *Aren't I supposed to keep my team happy?* You help your team develop their own emotional intelligence, not take on their emotional responsibility. Taking responsibility for other people's emotions is a passive-aggressive form of control that will leave you exhausted, resentful, and in a constant state of anxiety about how everyone's feeling.

Practice empathy. Acknowledge emotions. Have compassion for people. But you cannot not feel for them or fix their emotions. Just like you training for a 5K isn't going to increase the cardiovascular health of another person, you can't take on the responsibility of processing the emotions of someone else.

A Tale of Two Tearful CEOs

The Post Meme'd Round the World

His blue eyes, rimmed in red, stared straight into the camera as tears flowed down his cheeks. The caption with the close-up began, "This will be the most vulnerable thing I'll ever share." In August 2022, Braden Wallake, the CEO of HyperSocial, a marketing agency, began his LinkedIn post by sharing how much a recent business decision hurt him.

Like many companies, HyperSocial had to lay off employees. The difficult decision devastated Wallake. And in this now infamous LinkedIn post, Wallake (to his credit) said the layoffs were the result of his poor business management. But what happened next is what made Wallake internet-famous. The focus shifted to how bad *he* felt, how heartbroken *he* was, and he closed with, "I can't think of a lower moment than this."

The internet responded swiftly and furiously. The most common sentiments: "Read the room, dude," and "Too soon, bro." The laid-off employees weren't inspired by his vulnerability in that moment or by the medium. To many, the post felt self-focused on *his* pain, which came off as performative and out of touch—like the person who apologizes to you by telling you how bad they feel, rather than listening or making amends.

Some rallied to Wallake's defense, noting the moment of honesty in the polished, impersonal LinkedIn. And Wallake did use the viral moment to help people looking for work find a new jobs.[17]

This emotional fart landed all wrong. Wallake's mistake wasn't that he felt deeply. The post was misguided because he centered himself in a moment that required empathy for others. That's the difference between emotional expression and emotional intelligence.

The Tears of Connection

Fourteen years before Wallake's post, another CEO faced sleepless nights thinking about his first day back on the job and how to turn around a company. And what a first day it would be: Howard Schultz, returning to Starbucks as CEO, had to deliver bad news on a stage to 11,000 store managers. Everything hinged on this moment. He needed not only to reassure thousands of employees that the company could make it, but he also needed them to trust that he truly cared about their livelihoods.

Schultz grew up in public housing in Brooklyn. During Schultz's childhood, his father, a laborer, fell on the ice at work, fracturing his hip and ankle. Schultz knew firsthand the pain and vulnerability that the lack of health insurance and workman's compensation created for families. With Starbucks facing devastating forecasts, he felt like he was back on the wrong side of the tracks facing the same fears again.

On January 8, 2008, Schultz stood backstage in a navy-blue suit sharing his notes with other leaders. They were appalled! "You can't share that. You're going to scare the hell out of them." Schultz, connecting with his own emotional experience, disagreed. *How can I ask them to believe in the dream, in something larger than themselves, and trust me to lead them there, if they don't have the same information I do?*

Schultz said he walked on the stage "unencumbered and unvarnished" to deliver the truth. He talked about bureaucracy and lack of customer focus and took responsibility to solve those problems. What came next was the true surprise.

With tears, he said, "We're seven months away from insolvency, and if we continue on this track, you are going to be out of a job, and you and your families are going to be hurting. This is what we need to do individually and collectively to change course."

The weight of the responsibility, the connection to the people, and the hope he had for the future all came out in that emotional moment. But he didn't stop with his tears or dwell on his pain. He shared the comeback plan and asked for feedback from the frontline workers.

The managers in attendance witnessed far more than a CEO saying, "Chin up. We can do this." Schultz demonstrated a level of emotional intelligence that connected the people with him as a human, engendering their trust in him as a leader who genuinely cared about not just keeping the company sustainable financially, but the culture, the experience, and the people behind Starbucks. They responded with a standing ovation and thousands of emails thanking him for the transparency and humanity in a crisis.[18]

Schultz risked his reputation on his emotional intelligence. His genuine feeling humanized him and demonstrated empathy for his employees. His tears weren't for him; they were an expression of the reality of the situation and the damage that could come to everyone. His emotional intelligence built trust and made space for joy, even in hard times.

This messy, beautiful swirl of sensation and story that is emotional intelligence makes you human, not your productivity, spreadsheets, or perfectly crafted emails. It's your ability to feel—deeply, awkwardly, gloriously—even as a professional. Emotions are the very breath of life, the sacred signal that you're alive and connected. You don't have to run from them or drown in them. You can learn to guide their flow, like water through a Venetian canal, toward joy.

Joyosity

> ### The Gist
>
> Unchecked emotions will wreck trust and tank performance. Emotional regulation is how leaders stay clearheaded, connected, and calm under pressure. Without risking the wild and beautiful waters of emotional intelligence, the Joy Ratio is just a meaningless math problem.

Emotions *are the* very breath of life, the sacred signal that you're alive and connected.

—Jenn Whitmer

Connection

Rate your emotional intelligence abilities on a scale of 1 to 10. What does connecting with other people look at that level?

What is one step you can take to increase your emotional intelligence skill by half a point?

. . . .

Curiosity

Do you live as the Tin Man or on a roller coaster? What impact does that extreme have in your life? What scares you about the Third Way?

How often do you say, "They made me feel" or "It made me feel"? Practice saying "I felt _____ when . . . "

. . . .

Joy

Download Name-Rate-Find from the Lounge and put it where you can see it. Practice it once a day for a week.

Note what is happening around you when you feel connected, playful, peaceful, happy, excited, or joyful. Note those experiences or situations in your Joyosity Explorer Map.

The goal of communication is shared meaning.

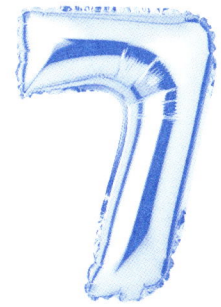

Clean It Up
Better Communication Now

> Every act of communication is a miracle of translation.
> —**Ken Liu, *The Paper Menagerie and Other Stories***

A vacation to Chicago with our four kids ranks as one of my favorite experiences as a family. Our children were nine, eight, six, and almost three. We rented a high-rise condo overlooking the Museum of Natural History and Lake Michigan, just a mile from the Bean and the Art Institute.

We parked the van for a week, walking or riding the El everywhere. We had the best pizza (because really, is there anything better than Chicago deep-dish?), took in the views from Sears (yes, I know, Willis) Tower, ran around the Museum of Science and Technology, and walked through exhibits at the Art Institute. We did all the things.

When the youngest grew weary of sightseeing, she would say, "Are we go back to our Chee-cagoh howme, now?" and we would swim in the rooftop pool. This vacation plays in my highlight reel of great family vacations.

Five years later, I wanted to recreate the magic. I would drive up with our oldest to see *Hamilton* in Chicago, and the rest of the family could take the train to join us when their spring break started. Michael? Not a fan of the plan.

"Why? Our last trip was amazing. And they're all older now! It will be even better!" My relentless optimism was set on convincing mode.

"Jennifer," Michael stared at me. "That trip was a disaster."

My head did one of those spirals. "What?! I don't understand."

He began to count off on his fingers, "Don't you remember our eight-year-old fighting with me in front of the lions at the Art Institute? I was so angry, I wanted to leave him right there. And the six-year-old wailing the entire two blocks from Sears Tower to Giordano's Pizza?"

I remembered none of that. *Not. One. Bit.*

I was shocked! How could two people be in the same place, together the entire time, and walk away with completely different experiences?

Because everyone sees the world differently. And we all bring different perspectives into every communication.

You cannot assume that anyone sees, thinks, feels, believes, or—here's the kicker—interprets information the way you do. And that's what makes communication complex and dynamic.

The Goal of Communication Is . . .

We are constantly communicating and making meaning (as we talked about in chapter four).

Let's do a little thought experiment: Imagine a high-heeled shoe. Got your picture? Did you just picture a black patent-leather Louboutin stiletto, or a men's buckled shoe with a red heel from the seventeenth century?

I would put some Vegas odds that the modern red sole (or something similar) filled your imagination. It's unlikely that Louis XIV's *les talons rouges* (the red heels that screamed royalty) popped into your head.[1]

When I asked you to imagine a high-heeled shoe, you took those letters in that order and found the pattern "high-heeled shoe" familiar to you. Then you made meaning from that. Even if you didn't go for the red-soled luxury brand, you probably didn't think of a men's shoe, unless you are a historian particularly versed in the Sun King's fashion choices.[*]

The goal of communication isn't to tell people the next steps. The goal isn't even to listen to other people. **The goal of communication is shared meaning.** When I speak on communication, I have the audience repeat this phrase over and over during the talk, like a call and response. You can practice, too: "The goal of communication is . . ." (and then you say to yourself) *"shared meaning."*

In this chapter, I'll remind you of communication foundations and best practices with my CLEAN communication framework. Then

---

[*] It's really fascinating if you want to read more about shoes, status, and gender from the Getty Museum.

we'll walk through what you do when you're facing hard conversations and genuine conflict in the next chapter.

The Players in the Communication Game

"What do you mean you're in Illinois?" I blurted out.

Michael's voice came through the speaker, "Because the car was in O'Fallon."

A couple of years ago, my husband and our son Stuart were out shopping for a used car. We had five drivers and one reliable car. So on a cold January Saturday, they hopped in the van to see a car in O'Fallon.

When that car didn't work out, I texted Michael links to others near O'Fallon. From the passenger seat, Stuart texted back that all of them were too far away. We were all confused, so they pulled over, and Michael called me.

"We're in Illinois. All those cars are an hour away." This is when I blurted out my shock. Then, slowly, I huffed a laugh and slapped my forehead.

We live on the Missouri side of St. Louis, just across the Mississippi River from Illinois. For reasons unknown, both states have an O'Fallon—about an hour apart, each thirty minutes from us. You can guess where I thought they were looking at cars.

I'm sure you've had an experience like this. One word, one phrase, very different meanings.

Let's look at the basic model of communication to help visualize how communication happens and how you get to shared meaning.

The Model: Show 'Em How It's Done

You will communicate more effectively if you envision communication as a cycle, a two-way path that has many players, parts, and obstacles.

The basic communication model looks like this:[2]

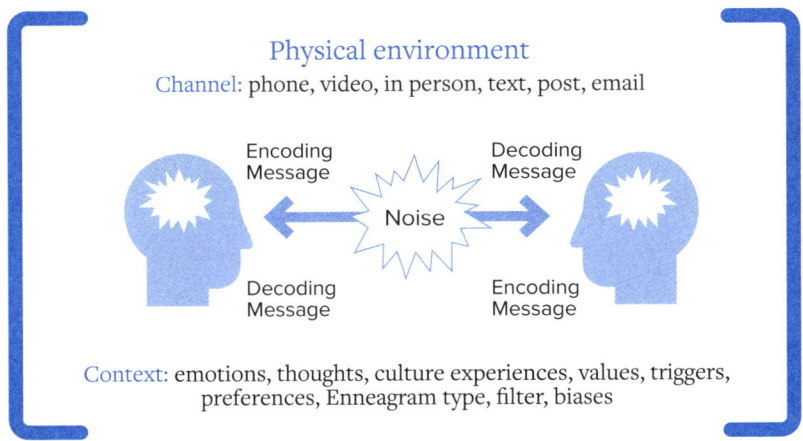

Message: the information

Encoding: how the sender creates the message

Decoding: how the receiver interprets the message

Channel: the communication method

Noise: internal and external disruptions to the message

Context: physical and psychological factors surrounding the communication

When you communicate as the Sender, you have a message inside your brain that you encode into words in the English language (if you're an English speaker). Your brain then tells your mouth to form shapes that create soundwaves that move through space and vibrate the ear drum of the Receiver. The Receiver then decodes those soundwaves into words that have meaning inside their brain.

Straightforward and simple, right? As if that isn't complicated enough, the noisy neighbors show up.

The Noisy Neighbors: Bless Their Hearts

Nothing will zap joy faster than communication barriers—technically, and aptly, called *Noise*. The Noise includes internal and external factors that disrupt the message:

- Literal noise, hearing abilities, rate of speech
- Physical environment that blocks eye contact or gestures
- Medium mismatch, between handwritten notes, text message, email, phone call, Zoom, or in person
- Personal factors including the way you see the world, your emotional regulation, thought patterns, culture, past experiences, personal values, generation, psychological triggers, preferences, Enneagram type, physical condition, filter, or unconscious biases

We use everything at our disposal—vocal tone, body language, facial expression, gestures, gifs, punctuation, word choice, fonts—to develop shared meaning.

And yet the same word, gesture, image, tone, etc., can hold different meanings. Just like the two O'Fallons.

The Noise flies in from every direction. Trying to have a conversation in the Phoenix airport? Good luck. Loudest PA system on the planet. Want to clearly communicate your intention over Teams messaging with your boss? Godspeed, my friend. Want to have a productive conversation at 3 p.m. with your colleague who's not eaten all day? Hard pass.

Some of the Noise is 100 percent your responsibility and within your control. Some of the Noise will never be in your control, and you will have to manage through it. Engaging with other people in healthy communication is dealing with the Noise so you can co-create shared meaning.

When you can't manage all that Noise, the Messy Middle turns into toil. In the United States, 80 percent of employees experience stress because of ineffective communication. And failures? Well, 86 percent of the workforce cites poor communication as the number-one cause of corporate failures.[3] I could cite statistics for pages, but pause for a moment.

Think about all the time wasted, emotions whipped up, and work lost when unclear communication leads to assumptions that turn into conflict. No, really, pause to think about the actual hours. Consider the emotional angst and division from gridlock in the conference room. Ponder the great ideas never implemented. The creative solutions never developed.

Does that feel at all like joy's profound connection? Far from it.

Now imagine communicating effectively. What could you create? How much more effective could you be? How would your relationships feel?

Improving your communication skills decreases conflict, improves creativity, increases productivity, enhances confidence, and just generally makes life more peaceful and, of course, joyful.

AI or the new company communication tool isn't going to fix this for you. Because they are only as good as what you put in. So if messy communication is this costly, work at cleaning it up. John Powell, who composes scores for movies, reminds us, "Communication works for those who work at it."4

CLEAN Communication

The CLEAN framework will help you create shared meaning, stopping miscommunication before it starts. It looks like this: **C**lear, **L**isten with Curiosity, **E**motional Regulation, **A**bsorbing Stories, and **N**onverbal Awareness.

I developed this framework as an easy way to remember how to manage the Noise that happens in the Messy Middle. Below is a condensed version with the basics. For the full framework with examples and scripts, head to the *Playbook*.

Clear: Setting Expectations

When Jen's small engineering firm promoted her to manager, she was thrilled to hire her first team member. Brian had the right training, notable experience, and was a great culture addition. She felt confident he could replace her in the day-to-day work, including updating the team dashboard every Friday. Finally, she could focus on strategy and team development.

During Brian's onboarding, Jen gave him access to the dashboard, walked him through the process, and moved on.

Friday afternoon came, and the dashboard wasn't updated. The next week, the dashboard was updated, but the format was off. The next week, he'd left out a section.

Clean It Up

Staring at a dashboard that wasn't meeting her expectations three weeks in a row, she started grumbling. *Why can't he figure this out? Can't people just follow simple directions? I should just do it myself.*

But she paused and took a breath. *Brian was reliable in his other work. Something about this dashboard is unclear.* And that's her job as the leader to clarify.

Surely "complete the dashboard on Friday afternoon" is clear. But it's not enough. Effective leaders consistently clarify their expectations. Brené Brown gets straight to the point: "Clear is kind."[5]

In communication, you can point and paint—some people naturally bullet the highlights and others paint the picture. While there is absolutely a place for bullets, you will communicate with more clarity if you, as Brown calls it, "paint what done looks like," and share your expectations fully and specifically.[6]

So, if you find yourself thinking, *Ugh. They should know this!*, it's probably time to clarify expectations. If you always revert to doing it yourself, you are the bottleneck. You're not communicating, and you will never grow past your own limitations.

When communicating clear **expectations**, they must be:

1. **Spoken.** You must say them with your out-loud voice.
2. **Agreed upon.** Edicts rarely work. You need people to agree, again, with their out-loud voice.
3. **Reasonable and resourced.** What you expect must be grounded in reality (much like self-efficacy) and within the scope of available resources.

Clear communication is the first step to creating shared meaning and keeps the avalanche of miscommunication from falling on you.

Listen with Curiosity, Not Judgment

Ted stood on the precipice, about to win or lose it all, with the throw of a dart.

If you've missed *Ted Lasso*: Ted, a relentlessly positive Kansas City native and college football coach, finds himself the head coach of a Premier League soccer club in England. He's coaching a sport he knows nothing about at a level he's never experienced.

A jilted wife has taken ownership of the club from her ex-husband. Ted wins over the team and the owner by leading with curiosity and questions. But the ex keeps trying to weasel his way back into the owners' box, literally and figuratively.

One day at the pub, the smug ex challenges Ted to a game of darts. The wager: £10,000. Ted raises the bet: If the ex wins, he picks the starting lineups. If Ted wins, the ex is banned from the owners' box. They shake on it. The ex pulls out his silver dart kit. Ted, dart in hand, grins, switches hands, and chuckles, "Oh, I forgot I'm left-handed." This might not be so simple for the ex.

And yet, by end of the game Ted must pull off a near-impossible set of three throws to win—two triple 20s and a bullseye. Ted begins to wonder aloud about curiosity.

"Be curious, not judgmental," he quotes Walt Whitman, landing a triple 20. The pub crowd gasps.

He continues, "All those people who belittled me? They were never curious. If they were curious, they would have asked questions. Questions like: 'Have you played a lot of darts, Ted?'" landing a second triple 20. The crowd roars.

"Why, yes, sir. Every Sunday afternoon at a sports bar with my father, from age ten 'til sixteen, when he passed away."

Clean It Up

Ted twirls the final dart through his fingers. Breathes. He says to himself, "*Barbeque sauce.*"

Bullseye.

Curiosity brought success to Ted far beyond that pub showdown. And a lack of curiosity cost the ex dearly.

Curiosity is an interest in the gap of knowledge, understanding, or experience, and becoming emotionally and intellectually invested in closing that gap through exploration.

Curiosity changes how you listen because you're actively invested in exploring the way to shared meaning. You're not just waiting for your turn to talk. You're leaning in and asking better questions.

To listen with curiosity:

1. *Notice your thoughts and bring them back to the conversation.* Are they wandering away to what you want to say or prove? Have they meandered to *When is this meeting over?* or *What's for lunch?* Bring your thoughts back.
2. *Avoid assumptions and turn them into theories or stories.* You can say, "My theory is . . . " or "The story I'm telling myself is . . . "
3. *Use the word curious.* Words have power. So in your questions, say, "I'm curious about . . ." or "What I'm curious about is . . . "

Also, communication isn't a DoorDash, no-contact delivery. Expect questions and ask questions again, as you create shared meaning.

Also (*climbs up on soap box*), **when you ask a question,** *wait for the answer*. Have you ever been in a meeting or a conversation and the person in charge says, "Any questions?" and then without another breath says, "Great," and moves on? You receive the message: Questions aren't welcome.

People need time to first decode what you've said, comprehend it, and then analyze their own thoughts before synthesizing a question. (Let alone get over the fear of looking stupid for asking a question.) That process takes *time*. After you ask a question, **silently count at least to eight, if not twelve, in your head**. It will feel like an eternity at first, but it communicates you actually welcome questions. (*Steps down.*)

Curiosity engages you in the collaboration of creating shared meaning, so you hit the bullseye.

Emotional Regulation: What's OK and What's Not

In the Hatch, Chick-fil-A's innovation center, a team leader asked me, "Well, but what do you do with wrong emotions? Because—"

I interrupted him: "I'm going to pause you, because there are no wrong emotions. There are no good or bad emotions." There was a collective intake of breath from the team. This wasn't someone they often saw interrupted or challenged.

To his credit, the team leader paused, leaned back, and asked, "Can you tell me more?" (He'd been listening in our training.)

"Yes!" I love this question. "Emotions are signals. They can be uncomfortable, but they are not wrong. There are, however, helpful and unhelpful, appropriate and inappropriate behaviors."

"OK. Soo . . . " his eyes drifted to the left as he processed and formulated his question. "What do we do when emotions turn into behaviors that stop communication?"

Now that's a good question!

Clean It Up

When you ignore emotions, you will miscommunicate and make poor decisions. (Go back to chapter six if you need to.) Remember, you don't want a tsunami or dry bed of emotions—you want a Venetian canal.

If you buy into the thinking that emotions take too much time, you're going to cost yourself more than just miscommunication. Brown says, "Leaders must either invest a reasonable amount of time attending to fears and feelings or squander an unreasonable amount of time trying to manage ineffective and unproductive behavior."[7]

A few guidelines about emotions in communication:

1. *Tears are OK.* When tears come, folks often get nervous. Tears activate the mirror neurons in other people, so you may feel the intensity as well. That could be what makes you uncomfortable.[8] But tears mean something matters, and it's time to lean in with empathy and curiosity. This isn't a time to dismiss their argument or do whatever they want so the tears stop. It's especially not a time to say, "Don't cry."

2. *Yelling is not OK.* Yelling activates fight-or-flight responses and erodes empathy. Most people yell because they feel afraid, unheard, or it's worked for them before. Instead of yelling back with your own, "Oh, you wanna go?" or shrink away, use Name-Rate-Find to regulate yourself first.* Then reflect back to that person what you're observing and stay curious by asking questions. Later, when calmer tempers prevail, express empathy and reestablish expectations.

3. *Breaks are OK.* If emotions become too intense, take a break. Emotions work through the body in ninety seconds, and ten

---

* If you feel like you are unsafe and someone is threatening you, you do not need to stay. Leave the situation.

minutes is typically enough time for you to practice SNAP or Name-Rate-Find, regulating yourself.[9] Ask for a break or offer one to the group. But don't leave the conversation just hanging out there; make sure to set a specific time to return to the discussion.

Emotions will always be around in communication, and you need them. They're not wrong or bad. We just need to keep them from overflowing the canal and flooding your conversation.

Absorbing Stories to Hook, Connect, and Persuade

It glistened in her hands. Bright pink with aqua seats. Michelle stood in front of our fourth-grade class holding the latest and greatest Barbie and the Rockers Tour Bus. She proudly placed the treasure on Mrs. Ott's teacher table so she could take out the deck chairs and table for show-and-tell.

But then, she brought out the pièce de résistance, the cassette player and microphone. She popped in a clear cassette and pressed play. The brush and triangle percussion sounds came out of the tiny speakers, and Michelle started singing into the microphone, "Shout, shout . . . " along with Curt and Roland of Tears for Fears.

The entire class, even the boys—who were very '80s nine- and ten-year-olds, unsure about this whole Barbie thing—joined in, "let it all out."

Let's pause the story for a moment: What memories did this bring to your mind? What emotions? What connections are you making?

You may have noticed I've loaded this book with more stories than your typical leadership book. While hopefully entertaining, their purpose is strategic: Stories create shared meaning.

Here's what's happening in your brain when you hear a story and how stories improve communication:

1. *Oxytocin floods your system.* Hearing a story releases the trust hormone that builds connections and changes behavior. Paul J. Zak, a neuroeconomist, found "emotionally engaging narratives inspire post-narrative actions," because your trust in the storyteller increases.[10]

2. *Mirror neurons fire.* Much like empathy from tears, mirror neurons create the sense you're in the story. Trust, empathy, and shared meaning increase.[11]

3. *Dopamine gives you a "pay attention" kick.* Retention requires attention. A story directs attention and pleasure because of the novelty. But the magic of dopamine and the HOME (human oxytocin-mediated empathy) means you will remember a story—and its point—far longer than simple facts.[12]

4. *The crossed-arms skeptic in your brain goes to sleep.* When you are engaged in a story, that critical part of your brain relaxes, regardless if the story is true or not. Sally Zimney ("Sally Z."), speaker and expert storyteller, says simply, "[Stories] are one of the only things that can get past the walls that divide us and sneak past people's defenses."[13]

5. *The prefrontal cortex lights up, and the parasympathetic nervous system relaxes.* Effective stories engage the wonder part of your brain: the C-suite, prefrontal cortex that integrates new learning and the vagus nerve that tells your body it's safe. In *The Wonder Switch*, Harris III describes wonder as the state where we are "awake to possibility."[14]

Joyosity

As digital, disrupted, and asynchronous communication increases, activating mirror neurons becomes more challenging, meaning you need *more* stories and fewer AI summaries.[15] I didn't give you an executive summary of what happened in fourth grade: For show-and-tell, Michelle brought her Barbie and the Rockers Tour Bus and sang in front of the class. The story had characters, emotions, a setting, colors, sounds, and more.

When you need to "paint done," contextualize data, pitch a client, or train on a process, start with a story. You can use your stories from work, home, even elementary school, or borrow them from a friend or client. Use part of a book, movie, or fable. Stories don't have to be elaborate, they just need to be rooted in *one* tangible moment, with visual details, emotions, and a point.

Stories build trust, create understanding, and enable possibilities.

Nonverbal Awareness: The 93 Percent You're Not Saying

Imagine you walk up to your coworker's desk for a coffee and a chat. All three monitors are full of windows and text. They glance over to you, shoulders tense, eyes narrowed, and they mutter with tight lips, "Yes?"

Are you pulling up a chair for that chat? Probably not.

Because we believe the body over words. Every time.

Nonverbal communication makes up 80 to 93 percent of communication, including facial expressions, gestures, silence, scent, digital haptics, personal space, and even your relationship with time.[16]

You need to be aware of what that 93 percent of you is communicating. When you match your words with your body language and tone, you build greater levels of trust with people, and your communication is clearer.

Here are a few simple nonverbal cues to communicate safety and improve shared meaning that are generally universal:

1. *Relax your shoulders, open your palms, and face the person you're talking to*. When your shoulders are up, people interpret that as defensive or insecure. An open palm, especially with fingers pointed down communicates "I've got nothing to hide." Facing the person not only improves your focus and listening but communicates their importance.[17]

2. *Remove physical barriers*. You know that if the phone is out, you're distracted. Put away phones and remove laptops between you. If that's not possible, position your body so there is open space between you and your conversational partner.

3. *Manage your vocal tone and volume*. A lighter tone generally works better than an intense tone. A volume that matches the room is also important. As someone with a naturally louder voice, I have to work on modulating my volume.

4. *Find the mute/unmute button for your face*. If every emotion passes through your face before you open your mouth, you might need to work on dialing down your facial expressions. If you have been told you're hard to read, you might need to intensify your facial expressions to communicate clearly.

During the O'Fallon fiasco, I just assumed where Michael and Stuart were. So in that face-palm moment, I changed my approach. I listened with curiosity and asked questions. Michael pulled off on an exit so he could focus on the call, showing his nonverbal awareness. We both got clear on the goal: Find this black Hyundai at the dealership on Olive Blvd. If it checks out, buy it. Michael had already told me the absorbing story of their misadventure at the first car lot. I shared I felt anxious that the car we wanted wouldn't be at the second dealer, practicing emotional regulation.

CLEAN communication got us to the goal with less wasted time and far more ease and joy. It also got us Jack Kelly, our Hyundai Santa Fe. If you use CLEAN, you will clear up most miscommunication.

From Misfires to Meaningful Connection

As a leader, you need to work with and through people to accomplish a common goal. You're not a solo act. Communication is the main engagement tool you use to get anything done with others. For an activity we do all day every day, many of us are surprisingly ineffective communicators. Mismanaging the noise that creates miscommunication costs you actual dollars—approximately $11,000 per employee for large companies, and up to $420,000 a year for smaller businesses, according to Zippia.[18] And nearly half of businesses have lost clients as well. All because of miscommunication.

Communication is the external vehicle of connection in every relationship—from your closest family to your newest team members. Of course CLEAN communication improves productivity and reduces stress. But it also saves jobs, restores relationships, and inspires movements.

After Michael and I realized we had wildly different versions of that first trip to Chicago, we could have disconnected or denied the other person's experience. Instead, we clarified our goals, expressed our fears, and worked through what we should do for that potential spring break trip. What could have been an ugly tug-of-war or a quiet wedge in our relationship turned into a shared laugh and collaborative decision to venture again to the Windy City.

Those noisy neighbors aren't moving. CLEAN won't eradicate miscommunication from your life. But the more skilled you are at clear, effective communication, the more connection and joy are possible in every area of your life.

The Gist

The CLEAN method gives you a clear, kind, repeatable way to face the mess of miscommunication, speak the truth, and actually get somewhere in the conversation. When you choose to work for communication, you are cultivating joy.

The goal of communication is shared meaning.

—Jenn Whitmer

Connection

Whom do you miscommunicate with the most?

Which one of the noisy neighbors is getting in the way?

How can you use CLEAN to build better connection?

· ·

Curiosity

What section of CLEAN is your strongest?

What section of CLEAN is your weakest? Choose one tool from CLEAN to practice for a month. For example, to work on Nonverbal Awareness, practice removing physical barriers, like putting your phone down, when you're communicating.

· ·

Joy

What methods of communication consistently steal your joy and feel like toil? Email, phone calls, DMs?

What's the communication channel that makes you feel the most connected? FaceTime, voice notes?

Switch communication media when you want, so that 35 percent (the Magic Third) of your communication time makes you feel connected, and only 10 percent of the time is toil.

If you avoid conflict, you manufacture fake peace.

Conflict Is Opportunity

Lead with Curiosity

> Peace, however, is not merely a gift to be received: It is also a task to be undertaken.
>
> —**Pope Benedict XVI**

My friends Chandler and Monica started dating, but secretly. (Yes, those *Friends*. Work with me.)

They go on a romantic weekend away and have had their first real argument over Monica's insistence on several room changes and Chandler's preoccupation with a high-speed car chase. After the row, Monica storms out.

Once back home, Chandler says to Monica: "Yeah, so I guess this is over."

Monica: "Why, exactly?"

Chandler: "Well, because of the weekend. We had a fight."

Monica: "Chandler, that's crazy. If you give up every time you have a fight with someone, then you'd never be with anyone longer than . . ."

You can see the wheels turning for both of them in the giant pause, then, "Oooohhhh . . ."

Chandler's unsuccessful relationships weren't just because he was insecure, had issues with his dad, or hadn't found the right person: Chandler thought a fight was the end.

Don't we often think that? That conflict means disconnection and trouble and the end. Luckily, research shows us something different.

In the *Journal of Social and Personal Relationships*, communication researchers report, "Conflict is a natural and even inevitable aspect of ongoing close relationships."[1]

But Jenn! You just said I could use CLEAN communication and create shared meaning. We sing kumbaya and it's all OK! CLEAN goes a long way, but you'll still face conflict.

Let's shift this Chandler conflict paradigm and completely disrupt the narrative that conflict means disconnection, trouble, and the end.

Conflict is an opportunity to build the very thing it feels like it isn't—connection and joy.

I know how that sounds. I'm a card-carrying recovering conflict-avoider. Here's the thing: That's the norm. In general, we don't have enough conflict, especially at work. Dr. Ramani Durvasula, narcissism expert and licensed clinical psychologist, writes, "When fighting goes away completely . . . people have checked out."[2]

The problem is, we're getting worse at healthy conflict. You feel it every day when your phone dings news alert after news alert of conflicts playing out in the public arena. Or you glance at the comment section of a post, where faceless users and even your friends descend into name-calling and eyerolls. Or you have the meeting before the meeting so there "isn't any conflict."[3]

All across the spectrum, people are hurting and broken because we don't know what to do with conflict. And it's costing us joy.

When Ducking Conflict Costs You More

Headset mic around my ear and presentation clicker in hand, I ask, "What would you do if I gave you three more hours a week?"

I've stood in front of thousands of people and asked that question. The most common answer? Sleep.* This is typically followed by some kind of self-care like exercise or reading, and then social activities like time with family and friends.

Why three hours? CPP (now The Myers-Briggs Company) found you spend, on average, nearly three hours a week managing the effects of unresolved conflict at work. That's nearly four weeks of workdays per year. If you put that into dollars, based on the median salary of a team leader with ten to fifteen years of experience in the United States, that's $9,855 a year wasted in ignoring someone's messages, turning off your camera because you can't control your face, or rewriting and rewriting and rewriting that email so it "doesn't make anyone mad."[4]

Besides all that angst, you lose people and talent and friends when you avoid conflict. Without facing conflict, relationships end. That's what Chandler did (or, rather, didn't do) time and time again. As

---
* More on sleep in chapter eleven.

much as you desperately want to solve conflict by sidestepping it . . . You can't go over it. You can't go under it. You gotta go through it.

If you avoid conflict, you manufacture a fake peace.

And fake peace will destroy profound connection and dissolve purpose. Conflict is inevitable, so engaging with it is a necessary part of cultivating joy.

The Real Definition of Conflict

Conflict isn't miscommunication. It isn't a fight. It isn't failure. From superpowers to small teams, **conflict is the struggle between limited resources and differing goals.**

Framing conflict as a struggle between limited resources and differing goals changes it from a clash of wills with a winner and loser. Conflict instead becomes a problem to be solved, and that's just a negotiation.

When you stop viewing conflict as a failure and see it as a problem to solve, everything shifts. You stop the power struggle and the pulling away. Instead, you move closer to other people, connecting and collaborating. Can you feel the difference? When you stop fighting against people, you can work for the hidden joy in conflict—deeper trust, stronger connection, and real change.

Let's define the parts of the problem:

- **Limited resources** fall into one of these four categories: time, money, space, and people.
- **Differing goals** aren't just how you want to spend the social committee funds, what should go into the strategic vision, or where to go on spring break. They go all the way down to the core: love, safety, and belonging.

Recognize those motivations? Way down deep, those Enneagram motivations aren't just trying to drive the bus again: This time they're trying to set the engine on fire with a flame thrower and gasoline.

Enneagram Conflict Styles: Your Default in the Heat

Joy has a nemesis. It's sloppy or sidestepped conflict.

I spent years trapped in toxic positivity, avoiding conflict and manufacturing fake peace like my life depended on it. The fallout of my work environment, embroiled in conflict, wrecked me. Yet, I still pretended it was all fine. Then the Enneagram threw me a lifeline. It helped me name what was in the Unknown of the Johari Window (what I and others couldn't see). The Enneagram led me out of denial and into healing.

Learning the Enneagram through the lens of conflict was my first real understanding of how self-awareness could change me, not just as a human but in how I lead others. It transformed me from conflict-avoider to conflict expert. It's the tool I start with to help myself and my clients work through conflicts every day.

The Enneagram shows you, with achingly accurate detail, how you show up in conflict and hard conversations. And without that knowledge, conflict will continue to baffle and destroy you because you don't understand what motivates you, or respect what motivates other people.

All those Enneagram motivations roar during conflict. When you understand your Enneagram conflict style, you have the tool to move from reaction to response, from avoidance to negotiation, and from fake peace to joy.

Joyosity

I call the three Enneagram conflict coping styles **Dynamite**, **Cool Cucumber**, and **Silver Lining**.* Each group of three shares a common response to disappointment, adversity, loss, and of course, conflict. As you read, you might think, *I don't do that!* No, not all the time, but be honest about your initial reaction that comes before all the polished coping strategies kick in.

Each group has a joy strength that is the good thing they bring to conflict and a joy snag that will trip them up. Here you'll see one joy shift that will help you pivot toward joy. For more, see the *Playbook*.

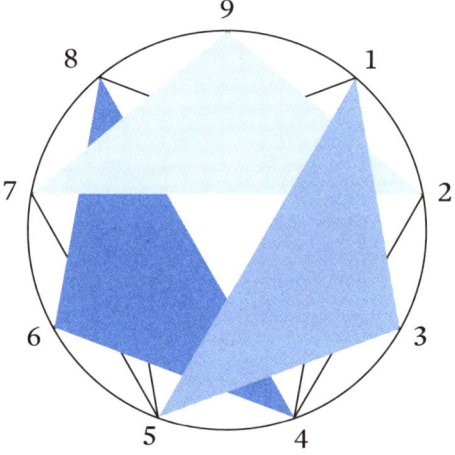

Dynamite

Enneagram Fours, Sixes, and Eights

Outside: "Aren't you upset about this?!"

Inside: *Can I trust you?*

Dynamites react fast and furious when facing disappointment—both your own and others'. You can Hulk out and express your frustration before others even know there's a problem. Some Dynamites

---

* Many Enneagram teachers call them the Harmonic Approaches.

explode; others implode. Either way, you connect to the problem emotionally. And you want others to react similarly. If other people dismiss or reframe, you may become more aggravated and expressive. Dynamites don't trust others easily. And when others' reactivity matches yours, you feel as if you can trust them more because you see where they stand.

While Fours, Sixes, and Eights share this approach, they ask slightly different questions when they sense a conflict.

- Fours: See how hurt I am? No one feels like I do.
- Sixes: Can I trust you to handle this? Can I even handle this?
- Eights: Will this leave me exposed? I'm not shouting. I want you to hear how mad I am.

Dynamite joy strength: You bring out the feelings in the room, and we need that. As we've said repeatedly, the emotions are already in the room, so we need to deal with them.

Dynamite joy snag: You can overwhelm other people with your emotional intensity. The intensity escalates quickly or shuts others down, solving nothing.

Dynamite joy shift: Learn to lower your intensity. When you stop using emotions as a shield to protect yourself against others and disappointment, you find solutions. You don't need to be completely calm and serene. But imagine a dial all the way up at 100. Breathe in and exhale as you visualize that dial coming down to 65 or so. That's still elevated, but not so much that it blocks solutions and connections.

Cool Cucumber

Enneagram Ones, Threes, and Fives

Outside: "Let's just stay objective, OK?"

Inside: *I have failed.*

Cool Cucumbers want to be competent. In conflict, you look for objective frameworks and structures that prove you've got it handled. You want facts, data, and solutions—skip the messy feelings, please. You typically cram your emotions into a bedazzled box and overlook others', excusing it as "objectivity." Conflict feels like failure, so you rush to close it, name some action steps, and call that "efficiency." In speed, you bypass effective. You can easily skip over the root issue, practically guaranteeing the conflict will boomerang back and increase your sense of failure.

Like the first group, Ones, Threes, and Fives have unique internal soundtracks when conflict starts.

- Ones: Let's be adults here. I'm holding it together—why can't you?
- Threes: I've got this handled. Just follow me, and I'll win.
- Fives: I need time to go into my mind castle. Too many feelings. Not enough data.

Cool Cucumber joy strength: You spotlight solutions. With facts and shared data, you help shift messy conflict into focused problem-solving.

Cool Cucumber joy snag: "Just the facts" ignores the humans in the room. Dismissing emotion may feel efficient, but it backfires because people feel dismissed. And the solutions will fall flat. (See chapter six.)

Cool Cucumber joy shift: Slow down. Incorporate feelings into the conversation and understand the emotional impact of the problem. Look for the big picture (stop majoring in the minors). Focus on the broader purpose and implications, not just what the rules say.

Silver Lining

Enneagram Twos, Sevens, and Nines
Outside: "Well, at least . . . "
Inside: *If I can find the good, I don't have to deal with the bad.*

Like your name implies, Silver Linings reframe difficulty into something positive—and sometimes moonwalk out of the conflict altogether. You want to feel good and help others feel good too, so positivity feels like the obvious choice. Conflict causes discomfort, so you avoid, distract, or downplay. It sounds like, "It'll all work itself out." Your positivity is a gift, but lean too far in? You become toxic by denying reality. You may ignore deeper issues, especially your own. When you only focus on the bright side, you miss the growing darkness of unresolved conflict. Left unexamined, conflict festers, spoils, and eventually explodes. Because you said "no drama here," you invited danger and damage.

Again, each type in this group has a specific story it tells when they get a whiff of conflict.

- Twos: Let me help you with your problem. Because I am not the drama. Right?
- Sevens: Not my circus. I'm on tour with merrier monkeys.
- Nines: Nope. No conflict here. (Dear Reader, conflict is everywhere.)

Silver Lining joy strength: You can see what happens if it all works out. So you bring solutions that connect to purpose and provide a hopeful vision of what could be.

Silver Lining joy snag: Avoiding conflict, brushing it all under the rug, means you end up with a Dr. Seuss–style *vug* under that rug. Complex problems mean complicated (and expensive) solutions.

Silver Lining joy shift: Actively address conflicts before it feels necessary to you. In general, small problems have simple answers and cheaper solutions.

When you manufacture fake peace instead fighting for connection, the cost is steep: lost productivity, constant tension, broken relationships, and an entire trail of damage that leads far from joy.

Conflict isn't the enemy, but a problem of limited resources and differing goals. When you see conflict this way, you have access to better tools, like your Enneagram conflict style. You can see how your Enneagram conflict style fuels the flame of conflict or is the fire extinguisher of repair. Let's look at how to resolve conflict with curiosity, so you walk away with connection *and* joy.

The Curiosity Conflict Fix

So with all this self-awareness and all these definitions, how do you walk toward connection through solving conflict? You need the right posture, kind confrontation, and good questions.

Shifting Sides: Standing Together in Conflict

Imagine for a moment that I ask you to replace a faceplate on a light switch. You've got all the right materials and tools: Faceplate? Check. Screws? Check. Screwdriver? Check.

Now imagine turning away from the wall where the light switch lives. Grab that faceplate and screw, and bend backward, tilting your head back so you can see to screw the faceplate in place. Now grab that screwdriver.

At this point you're like, What is happening? Even with all the right tools, you'll struggle mightily to get the faceplate on the wall because you're in the wrong position. Conflict is the same.

Conflict resolution is first a posture, then a set of skills.

You read the book, memorize the frameworks, and collect Enneagram insights all day long, but if you're in the wrong posture, they're virtually useless. You'll stay stuck and frustrated, wondering why the tools aren't working.

Most people picture conflict like a face-off: fists up, ready to strike. That posture will always fail to bring you joy.

Instead, think of the game red rover. In this version, everyone in the conflict is on the same team. It's the two of us, or the team of us, side by side, elbows hooked, facing the same direction, and looking at the problem out there.

This is the posture of healthy conflict resolution: It's *us together* against the problem out there. *Red rover, red rover, send the problem right over*. We're ready to face it together. No one's getting through us.

You'll move through conflict to connection when you shift your posture from "me versus you" to "us versus the problem." Now you can use curiosity and creativity instead of attack and counteroffensive. You're in a posture that allows you to use all your tools and skills to solve the limited resources and differing goals struggle of the Messy Middle, while staying connected to other people.

Time to Speak Up

"Angela, come over here a sec," Julie beckons in the lobby of the conference. She ducks behind a post, and Angela follows.

"You've got a black speck on your tooth," Julie whispers, pointing at Angela's mouth.

"Ugh!" Angela scrapes her tongue over her teeth. "Did I get it?"

Julie squints, "Not yet."

After a few failed attempts and frantic fishing for a mirror or toothpick, Angela stress-laughs, "Ahh. Just get it for me!" and flashes all her front teeth—top and bottom.

Julie hesitates, then extends one magenta-manicured finger and swipes away the offending stowaway from lunch.

"Oh my word! You are a true friend!" Angela giggles. "Thank you!"

When Angela told me this (yes, real) story, I immediately thought: *This is what kind confrontation looks like.* Awkward? For sure. But it's also kind, vulnerable, and courageous.

Every offense, slight, or issue doesn't need a confrontation. Talk about exhausting. So if you're going to go through all the discomfort of having a conversation that makes your hands clammy, you need a way to discern when it's worth it.

Here's the decision tree for when to have a kind confrontation. If one of these is happening, it's time.

1. *Harm:* Harm includes damage and lasting negative impact. Harm isn't the same as accountability, discomfort, or even

hurt. Harm is breaking agreements, commitments, laws, and codes of conduct in ways that negatively impact you, someone else, or a group. Harm needs a kind confrontation.

2. *Break:* Actions that break trust, cause friction in a relationship, or divide people unnecessarily need a kind confrontation. And in general, the closer the relationship, a smaller break qualifies for a confrontation.

3. *Pattern:* If you see a pattern of behavior that causes friction, it's time to have a kind confrontation. We're all imperfect and make mistakes, but patterned behavior will eventually harm someone or break trust. How many times is a pattern? Fewer than you think. In general people give others more chances because they don't want to be "the fussy one" or the "bad guy." But the sooner you address a pattern, the better your chances of success. My rule? Three times, then have a kind confrontation.

Kind confrontation shines a light on the problem and stays present until the flake on the teeth is gone. It's rooted in curiosity, connection, and care. Avoiding the discomfort might protect everyone from a moment of tension, but it ultimately robs you of trust and manufactures that fake peace. When you lean in with courage and name the problem—even if your voice shakes—you cultivate real relationships and joy that don't float away when things get hard.

Listening Three Ways

On the *Joyosity* podcast, Kwame Christian, negotiation expert, reminded me, "The person asking the questions is the person in charge."[5] So if you're going to lead into joy through conflict, you need great questions. You need to rely heavily on the L and N in CLEAN here: Listen with Curiosity and Nonverbal Awareness. You're exploring with questions and your tone matters!

I can't give you every possible question that will help you wade through the Messy Middle of hard conversations. Use this Three Question Model for categories of questions to lead through a conflict or prepare yourself for one.

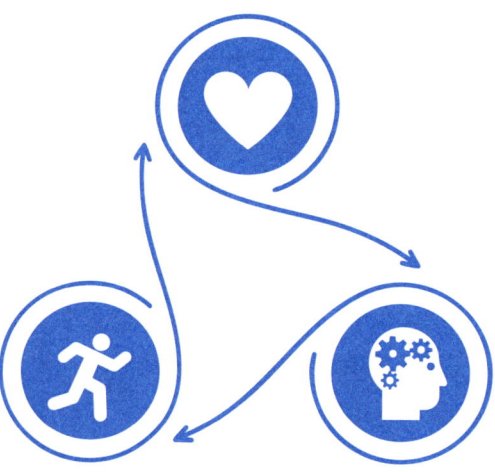

How do you feel?

We start with *How do you feel?* because all decisions and problem-solving must go through the limbic system where your emotions are. As we talked about in chapter six, naming emotions reduces their intensity. There are only a couple of ways to ask this type of question:

- How do you feel about this?
- What are your emotions about this?

Next is my all-time favorite question in any conversation ever. (Did I hype it up too much? Probably not. It's amazing.)

- Can you tell me more?

And then zip those lips and let the question and silence do their work.

What do you think?
What do you think? gets at someone's logic. It's the chance to understand their data sources, thought process, and interpretation.

There are many ways to ask this question:

- What do you think about this?
- What are your reasons?
- Is there information I'm missing?
- What assumptions are we making?
- Where are you looking for information?
- What conclusions have you made?
- What context would you add?

Quick note: It's tempting to ask *why* when asking about thinking. But asking *why* in conflict puts people on the defensive. Swap *why* for *what*, and you'll get more detail and less defense.

What do you want to do?
This is the action question that's tied to emotion. When you ask about want, you're asking for emotions. And that's OK. What people want matters, but we're looking for action steps.

- What do you want to do?
- What actions will you take?

- What solutions do you suggest?
- How do you want to make this right?
- What feels like a win to you?
- What outcomes do you want?
- What do you want me to do?

See the Lounge for "Twenty Helpful Questions in Difficult Conversations." The *Playbook* has so much more for you too.

This Three Question Model—How do you feel? What do you think? What do you want to do?—unlocks the answers you need to move *through* conflict and actually resolve it, so once you're through it, you walk away with connections and joy intact.

The Right Help at the Right Time

Sometimes the path to joy means expanding the team.

When you're in a conflict and it's just not getting solved, it's time to call in help. The rule of three works well here: If you've had three conversations and nothing is changing, it's time to ask for help from a third person.

The appropriate person is always someone who has the responsibility and authority to help solve the problem. That could be your mutual manager, higher boss, a counselor, or human resources. It is *never* a subordinate.

The Day I Stopped Buying Fake Peace

Part of my story includes a war zone of conflict. Though it was a school library, not a French battlefield.

"I'm sorry. Can you repeat your answer?" a member of the committee asked the external candidate.

"Um, sure," the candidate replied, confused.

She repeated her answer while glancing nervously at the four of us on the interview committee. Tension filled the room. One committee member had a splotchy face and red-rimmed eyes from crying. Another seemed to be taking inventory of the books. The committee head hyper-focused on the candidate, emotions pushed aside. I had plastered on a stiff smile and raised my eyebrows, but my eyes looked blank.

After a few more questions, the committee head thanked the external candidate and walked her out. As the door closed behind them, the other two committee members packed their totes and left without a word.

After years of toxicity brewing, everything had come to a horrific climax in this one week. I slumped on the library couch, drained by grief and loss. Gossip. Gaslighting. Manipulation. Career sabotage. All of it exhausted me.

Before this interview, we were reviewing the qualifications of the external candidate together. The committee head and I were eager to interview her because her certifications and experience seemed exactly what the role needed. The other two members of the committee wanted to hire an internal candidate, but that teacher lacked the necessary training and certifications.

Five minutes before the external candidate's interview, that internal candidate burst into the library with all the emotional baggage that came with her (including that she was married to our leader and had lobbied the board for an exemption so she could have the position).

It's hard to remember how everything unraveled in those five minutes before the interview. I only remember raised voices, sobbing, and damage everywhere.

Alone on the couch, thinking back over the destruction that hour had brought, I felt burned by the crucible of leadership—not just in that moment, but in the months and years that created the powder keg which fueled that explosion.

I had enabled. I allowed. I was quiet.

I ignored best practices. I didn't get help. I didn't set boundaries.

I avoided kind confrontations and hard conversations.

And now, a wonderful candidate had gone through an interview nightmare and—a surprise to no one—said "No thank you" to the offer.

The fallout continued. Within three weeks, one admin had quit, my position was eliminated, and the organization began to come apart at the seams.

Situations are impossible. People will fail. And sometimes, the outcome is rocks and acid in the soil rather than sunshine and rainbows.

When I think about the pain of the interview explosion, I see how disengagement fueled miscommunication that transformed into the destruction of mishandled conflict. Talk about the Joy Ratio being out of whack.

Although that experience reminds me of the cost of sloppy or sidestepped conflict, there are so many other stories of the joy of working *through* hard conversations:

The times I used CLEAN to clear up miscommunication before it snowballed. When I noticed my Silver Lining impulse to reframe and chose kind confrontation instead. When I firmly hooked elbows in the red rover posture and spoke up to say, *I'm working for us*. When we cultivated something profound and mighty. And goodness, all the clients I've helped do the same.

Like Monica and Chandler choosing to stay with each other instead of choosing an ending, these moments tell a different story. In those stories, we came through to the other side of conflict, becoming more connected. And those experiences are the ones in the Joy Ratio.

Conflict is inevitable. Your joy as a leader will rise and fall on your ability to solve it. So you can work to avoid conflict, fueling it, or you can get in the right red rover posture, pick up the tools, and work for joy.

What will you choose?

The Gist

Conflict isn't the problem; avoiding it is. In general, you probably don't have enough conflict, but that will upset your Joy Ratio. Working through conflict is the work. Choose to work for joy.

> *If you avoid conflict, you manufacture fake peace.*
>
> —Jenn Whitmer

Conflict Is Opportunity

Connection

Write down the names of the people that came to mind with whom you have unresolved conflicts.

What could be one next step to connect with one of them? Do you need to apologize? Or forgive them even if they don't apologize? Do you need to pick up the phone or write a letter?

....

Curiosity

How does your Enneagram conflict style show up at work?

How does your Enneagram conflict style show up with your family?

How does your Enneagram conflict style show up online?

....

Joy

Where is avoiding conflict stealing your joy right now? Do you need to have a kind confrontation?

Are you in any conflict right now that you've tried to resolve? Do you need to get the right help?

Don't chase the fleeting. Choose the freeing.

The Wisdom of Tomatoes

Decision-Making Under Pressure

> The need for certainty is the greatest disease the mind faces.
>
> —Robert Greene, *Mastery*

"And we've come to the final award of the night. Seconds from now, this stage will be filled with producers," Whoopi Goldberg quips, earning a ripple of chuckles from the audience.

It's 2008 at Radio City Music Hall for the 62nd Tony Awards Ceremony, and *In the Heights* has eleven nominations and three wins at this point in the night. Goldberg announces Best Musical: *In the*

Heights. Lin-Manuel Miranda, the idea-generator, composer, lyricist, and lead actor, dances with Goldberg as he receives his medallion. Director Tommy Kail, the producers, and about fifty other people in formal wear stream up the stage-left stairs to celebrate the award.

After the producer Jill Furman delivers the thank-you speech, the company lifts Miranda up on their shoulders. "We love Broadway!" they erupt to waving, fist-pumping, and huge smiles all around.

Goldberg closes the show, and forty-four seconds after winning the crowning achievement of theater awards—and eight years after seeing the script for the first time—Kail stands alone on the stage. The house lights come up, and the audience spills out of the red velvet seats. Alone in the rustle of dresses and the buzz of voices, Kail has a revelation.

At thirty years old, Kail had spent most of his adult life developing and working on *In the Heights*. Now, left under the fading heat of the lights and the audience moving on, he remembers noticing the win was over in a flash. On the podcast *Little Known Facts*, he recalls thinking it can't just be about the result. He said, "It has to be about something more."[1]

If you do the math, the forty-four seconds the company of *In the Heights* stood on the stage of Radio City were about 0.00001743 percent of the eight years that Kail had invested in bringing the show from words on a page to the stage. What if the show hadn't won the Tony? Did he waste eight years? Kail's revelation was this: The outcome cannot be the only measure of the success of a decision.

People tend to assume a good outcome equals a good decision and a bad outcome means a bad choice. Annie Duke and other professional poker players, who deal with luck every day, call that *resulting*.[2]

We do this *All. The. Time.* As a culture in general, but *especially* in the corporate world. We shackle ourselves to results. (Remember our obsession with measurement from chapter two?) If you don't lose four pounds at the end of a month of workouts? Wasted all that time. Didn't land the big client? Shouldn't have pitched them. Didn't make your sales numbers? Worthless quarter.

Resulting is essentially saying if you don't win the Tony, you made a bad decision.

The Trouble with Resulting

Resulting steals our joy in two ways.

One, you Monday-morning-quarterback your own decisions. You *shoulda coulda woulda* yourself. But in the Messy Middle moments, you can only make decisions from where you are with the information and resources you have. Shame doesn't grow joy.

Two, you believe you control the outcomes far more than you actually do. There are more factors that shape the outcome of events that you don't control. The idea pervades American popular culture so much that we have a name for it—the Bootstrap Myth.[*] The myth preaches the fantasy that you can achieve the outcomes you want all by yourself through hard work, effort, and wits alone. You're not a victim of circumstances; you rise above them without support or resources.

The shadow side of resulting is the shame you experience when your decision didn't create the outcome you wanted. If you're armed with hindsight and the fallacy that you had all the control, then the outcome is also all your fault. And we don't like that so much. Duke

---
[*] For more, see "The Bootstrap Myth" in "Stories That Didn't Fit" in Stories, Study Stacks, and Citations.

reminds us that "outcomes don't tell us what's our fault and what isn't," just as much as outcomes are "never 100 percent due to luck or skill."[3]

Resulting increases anxiety, cynicism, and delays, robbing you of joy.

Multiply that by the sheer number of decisions you make every day. In the early 2000s, researchers found that the average adult makes 35,000 conscious decisions each day.[4] And those are just the ones you're actively thinking about. Harvard Business School professor Gerald Zaltman found 95 percent of decisions are subconscious.[5] So if we play with math again, that's 700,000 decisions a day. Some experts estimate that leaders make twice as many decisions as their employees.[6] (Which, in case you didn't want to do that math in your head, is 1.4 *million* decisions a day.)*

And if you feel like you have to make more decisions now than you used to, you're not alone. Business leaders reported that from 2020 to 2023, the number of decisions they made each day increased tenfold.[7]

No wonder you're exhausted.**

What if the exhaustion and lack of joy originate in *how* you make decisions, not in the outcomes? What if the way you're evaluating decisions steals joy? If you measured success differently, would you learn to make wiser decisions with less stress? If you haven't guessed, the answer is yes.

---

* That's 70,000 conscious decisions and 1.4 million total decisions in a day. Thanks here to my oldest son, Chase, who helped me with the algebra because I forgot how to do math. (But if it had been a sale discount, I'd have had it in a heartbeat.)
** More on reducing the number of decisions, and decision fatigue, in chapter twelve.

The process of making decisions is more important than the decision itself. With a wise process you make *informed choices*, independent of results, growing resilient joy—regardless of the outcomes.

What's a Tomato Got to Do with It?

New tariffs meant a new tax, and John Nix of New York raged. For nearly fifty years, John Nix & Co. had imported its products into the state, but the new tariff act cost Nix 10 percent more than before.[8] Fed up, Nix filed a suit against Edward Hedden, the collector of the Port Authority of New York, to "recover back duties paid under protest" that went all the way to the Supreme Court.[9]

The contested issue? Whether or not tomatoes are a fruit or a vegetable according to "'Schedule G.—Provisions' of the Tariff Act of March 3, 1883." Chester A. Arthur, the twenty-first president of the United States, signed the Tariff Act of 1883, which included a 10 percent tax on the value of imported vegetables, but not fruits. Nix claimed that because they grew from the plant's flowers, the tomatoes his company imported from Bermuda were fruits, and thus exempt from the tariff.

The nine justices of the Supreme Court listened to witnesses for the plaintiff respond to definitions from three separate dictionaries. The defense then read into evidence definitions for pea, eggplant, cucumber, squash, pepper, and finally, tomato.[10] In their stirring rebuttal, the plaintiff read definitions for potato, turnip, parsnip, cauliflower, cabbage, carrot, and bean.[11] What a day to argue before the Supreme Court.

After a rousing look at the judicial precedent of classifying beans as seeds and where vegetables go on a dinner plate, the justices rendered their unanimous verdict. Tomatoes, for the purposes of the tariff, are a vegetable. Case closed.

The entire case was a legal spin on the old joke: Knowledge is knowing a tomato is a fruit, but wisdom is knowing not to put it in a fruit salad.

Albeit humorous, *Nix v. Hedden* illustrates a lot about decision-making. Agree or disagree with the verdict, the decision-making process included personal perspectives, values, data, emotions, parties responsible, and outcomes few expected.[12]

Not every decision in your life as a leader rises to the level of the highest court in the land. The decisions you make every day range from simple binary choices—whether to call or text—all the way to complex arrangements that impact groups of people in your care—the conflicting schedules of summer camp transportation and the town hall meeting.

Knowledge is rote recall and basic facts: A tomato comes from the flower of a plant and has seeds. Wisdom is pulling apart context, evaluating options, and synthesizing a way forward: How do you use a tomato in real life?

Wisdom includes increasing your awareness of what *influences* your decisions—time, people, preferences, values, and desires. Then you can integrate those influences to make a decision. Because you make an informed choice, you can release the results (well, at least a little bit easier). Your joy doesn't hang on the forty-four seconds of standing on the stage of the Tony Awards.

Wisdom plays a stronger game of joy than knowledge ever could.

The Wisdom of Tomatoes

Before You Decide, Know Who's Deciding

I totaled my dad's car when I was sixteen—in my own driveway.

I backed the '82 Cutlass Supreme into a random F-250 black truck with an enormous tow hitch that had chosen that moment to turn around in our *h*-shaped driveway.

What didn't I use that morning? My mirrors.

It cost me a lot of time scooping ice cream at Baskin-Robbins to pay for the damage!

If you want to cultivate joy in decisions, you need to know your internal influences. Or, like me forgetting my mirrors, it will cost you too. Do you remember the way out of the Blind Spot in the Johari Window? Feedback. A mirror gives feedback, showing you what's hiding in your Blind Spot, both the best parts of you and the worst parts of you. Because when you misuse or overuse your strength, it becomes your weakness. The mirror also shows you how your Enneagram motivations influence your leadership.

To understand the Enneagram leadership styles, we need to expand on the Centers of Intelligence (remember those from chapter six?) because the Centers and how you use them absolutely influence your decisions.[*]

One Down, Two Overworking

At Baskin-Robbins, I scooped ice cream and an absurd amount of Daiquiri Ice. If you like Daiquiri Ice, we can still be friends, but I never want to scoop it for you. It's in the name—*ice*.

---

[*] Enneagram teachers often call these stances, or "the Hornevian groups," based on Karen Horney's theory of self.

From those months of scooping, I developed a Popeye forearm on my right side. I didn't notice it until the spring, when Coach Holder started fussing at me at swim practice.

"What's wrong with your stroke?" he shouted.

"What do you mean?"

"You're not stroking evenly," he said. "You're going to get disqualified!"

My Popeye forearm sliced through the water faster than my left. An uneven stroke disqualifies you in the butterfly. I know this sounds ridiculous, but that Popeye arm was about to cost me my first season on varsity. And there was *no way* I was getting disqualified in a stroke I'd been swimming since I was six.

Now, was I going to weaken my right arm? No, of course not. I had to *strengthen* my left.

So I had to use that strange triangle-shaped coiled squeezy thing, trying to develop strength in my left arm. It felt all kinds of awkward and ridiculous, but if I wanted to compete, I had to balance my strength.

Your Centers of Intelligence work like this as well. Back in chapter six, you met the Doing Center, the Feeling Center, and Thinking Center:

- *Doing Center*: Instincts, reflexes, physical senses
- *Feeling Center*: Emotional connection, decision-making, meaning-making
- *Thinking Center*: Strategy, logic, language, regulation

The Wisdom of Tomatoes

What we *didn't* talk about in chapter six is what happens to those Centers in your developmental years. After Thinking, Feeling, and Doing make their appearance, they're not fully developed. (If you've spent any time with a four-year-old, you know this.)

Along the way to adulthood, something happens that hurts a Center. Maybe someone said, "Why are you always moving around? Can't you just sit still?" And your Doing Center goes into hibernation. Or, "Stop being so emotional. Why are you crying all the time?" And your Feeling Center locks the vault. Or, "Why are you thinking so much? Can't you just get it right the first time?" And your Thinking Center retreats.

As you mature, that Center doesn't get as much practice, so it's inexperienced and weaker. Another Center of Intelligence steps up and shouts, "Don't you worry! I will overfunction for the rest of you!" So you become out of balance—just like my Popeye arm and my wimpy arm.

The grip trainer made my wimpy arm stronger. You need to do the same with your unpracticed Center: This deeply affects how you make decisions. It also explains your leadership style, which developed out of your underdeveloped Center. (More on this below.)

Without strengthening that unpracticed Center, you live out of balance and ignore a key piece of wisdom in decision-making. And to make it even more challenging, most workplace cultures push you further out of balance, overvaluing Thinking and Doing while undervaluing Feeling.

Because of the imbalance, you've heard or even said "I don't want to make an emotional decision." **The truth is, all decisions are emotional decisions.**[13]

Undervaluing emotions works against the reality of your neurobiology. We touched on this in previous chapters, but all decisions move through the limbic system that holds your emotions before moving to the prefrontal cortex.[14] Daniel Kahneman, Nobel-winning psychologist who studied judgment and decisions, also saw balance as a key part of decision-making: "Any decision had to account not just for the financial [logical] consequences but for the emotional ones, too."[15]

Remember the USS *Houston*? All the data systems online and in balance would have avoided the disaster of the tugboat. You have to know which of your Centers is offline, and that starts with knowing your Enneagram leadership style.

The Wisdom of Tomatoes

Enneagram Leadership Styles: How You Lead in the Moment

Like the conflict styles, there are three Enneagram leadership styles. I call them the **Trailblazer**, the **Connector**, and the **Professor**. The three types in each group share the same unproductive Center of Intelligence, orientation to time, and approach to people. Each group shares similar joy powers and joy pressures. Joy powers are leadership strengths that lift joy and multiply it. Joy pressures are tendencies that squeeze joy and diminish it. Here I'm giving you a quick joy pump to boost your joy, and of course there's more in the *Playbook*.

Joyosity

Your style gives you unique powers and pressures that influence your decision-making.

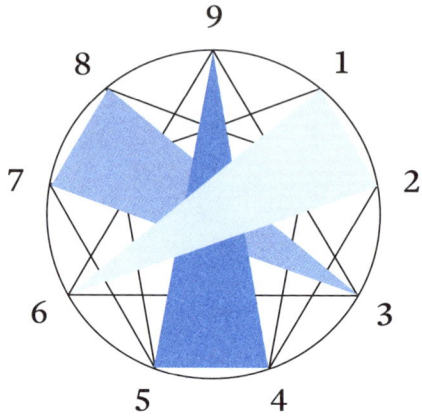

Trailblazer

Enneagram Threes, Sevens, and Eights

Time: Future

People: Independent, out front

Unproductive Center: Feeling

People perceive Trailblazers as quick thinkers and problem-solvers, often labeling them "natural leaders." You're the one who sees the vision and starts solving problems quickly because you're already living as if you *are* in the future.

Your independence means you forge ahead on your own track. You'll invite others along, but you rarely wait for permission. At times, other people find that assertive or even aggressive—you pushing against them. But from your perspective, you're just taking care of yourself and solving the problems you see.

Now, when it comes to the *unproductive feeling*, Threes, Sevens, and Eights manage that differently.

Enneagram Three: You take in emotional information but don't use it to make sense of what's happening, particularly ignoring your own emotions. Instead, you tune into the emotional energy of the room to choose your persona. That disconnection makes it hard to stay authentic, and you chase the goal of approval instead of joy.

In decision-making, emotions feel incredibly inefficient. You might rush past them or do what makes you look successful. That can lead to decisions that skirt the rules, or are even unethical, when looking good outweighs values.

Enneagram Seven: You use the Feeling Center to chase "good" emotions—the ones that feel exciting, positive, and full of possibility. You have *absolutely zero* interest in the emotions that are uncomfortable or "bad." That discomfort feels like pain and fuels your Fundamental Fear.

When you make decisions, your emotional focus on "good vibes only" leads you to delay, distract, or dream up more options—anything to avoid the pain. When you bypass difficult emotions, you'll hop to every shiny object that hints at happiness. But real joy roots in connection, even when decisions bring discomfort.

Enneagram Eight: You tend to be *very* comfortable with anger, and the rest of us could learn a lot from you. Your other go-to emotion is passion. Everything else feels vulnerable, striking at the heart of your Fundamental Fear.

When you avoid vulnerability, you limit access to the full emotional data you need for wise decisions. You start making decisions that protect power instead of build trust, blocking real joy.

Trailblazer joy power: See and solve.

You're an incredible brainstormer, goal-setter, planner, and systems thinker. So when it comes to making decisions, you've probably already identified the problem and come up with creative solutions. You're thinking, doing, and getting to the action items quickly.

Trailblazer joy pressure: Go solo and burn out.

Your high level of independence makes delegation feel inefficient, or even raises the "nobody else can see it the way I see it" issue. You can run yourself into the ground or run other people off the team. With your decision-making pace, others can feel shut out, and they don't buy into the decision.

Trailblazer joy pump: Feel fluently.

Use Name-Rate-Find to practice slowing down and feeling your emotions. This is how you strengthen the Feeling Center.

Connector

Enneagram Ones, Twos, and Sixes

Time: Present

People: Compliant, dutiful, dependent, moves toward others

Unproductive Center: Thinking

Connectors are the glue of society. You naturally build relationships, develop people, and link others to ideas and resources. You orient yourself to here and now—What task happens now? What does the person in front of you need? How do you prepare right now? Of course you think about the past and future, it's just that your primary attention is on the present.

You move *toward* other people. If the Trailblazers face forward, independent, you face the person in the room and lean in. When you're in a room with others, you naturally attune to them.

You have an underproductive Thinking Center—specifically, overthinking that doesn't always lead to a clear decision. And Ones, Twos, and Sixes each overthink in their own way.

Enneagram One: Arguing with your inner critic traps you in unproductive mental loops. Because the critic demands absolute perfection, every decision feels like a high-stakes test of belonging. One wrong move and you're out. You spin and tweak and perfect, paralyzed in indecision pursuing the fantasy of perfection. You allow your inner critic to grade every decision—before, during, and after—on a sliding scale that is never in your favor. Joy will never flourish there.

Enneagram Two: You're overthinking about relationships—Am I okay with this person? Is this person okay with me? Is this person okay with *that* person? Although it connects you to people in your mind, it becomes unproductive when it takes over your thoughts. You start making decisions that keep everyone comfortable and feeling good about you. I'm sure you've heard this before: You can't please everyone. Sometimes the decisions that bring the most joy don't feel good at the time.

Enneagram Six: You and your internal writers' room can spin out full one-act plays for every scenario that might possibly, tentatively, hypothetically happen. That kind of overthinking keeps you tense, stuck in indecision, and doubting yourself. You're working so hard to show your loyalty, and avoid blame, that of course others trust you. But the problem becomes that you don't trust yourself to make good decisions, so you block your own path to joy.

Connector joy power: Develop and connect.

You have an ability to develop individuals and draw a team together—not just to work well, but to *function* well.

Connector joy pressure: Overthink and overfunction.

You easily overextend yourself under the assumption that *everything* is your job. You *should* all over yourself. That obscures your *actual* capacity in decision-making. You often measure what's possible based on *your* ability to get it done, rather than the capacity of the entire team.

Connector joy pump: Get a trusted thinking partner.

Strengthen your Thinking Center by using SNAP to rewrite stories on your own and get a trusted thinking partner to get the thoughts out of your head. Tell them what you need: Either "I need you to listen while I work this out," or "I need you to help me think differently and decide."

Professor

Enneagram Fours, Fives, and Nines

Time: Past

People: Away from people, withdrawing

Unproductive Center: Doing

Professors lead people deeper and remind us that not everything has to happen right now. You reach for previous experiences to guide you. Your strong tether to the past helps you hold incredible institutional knowledge. You help others pause and connect this moment or the future to what *has* happened before.

You *withdraw* from other people. If Trailblazers independently jump out front with "I'm going here. You coming?" and Connectors lean toward people with "How can I help you?" you're the one quietly stepping away to the corner of the room, happily sipping your club soda, observing. You might assume you're not needed—or even wanted.

You have an underproductive Doing Center. You feel like you're doing, but your actions don't always take you where you want to go. And it looks different for Fours, Fives, and Nines.

Enneagram Four: You have multiple decisions loops open while you cycle through having feelings, then thoughts about those feelings, then feelings about thoughts about your feelings . . . Making a decision that isn't *perfectly* authentic or aligned feels impossible. So you might start creating or doing *something*, but it's not actually moving you toward deciding. You get caught in making the most unique and meaningful solution that you don't make simple decisions. Joy doesn't require transcendence, but it does require action.

Enneagram Five: You do. You gather knowledge, collect data, build decision trees, and construct layered plans. But you often confuse *planning* with *acting*. You want more time to find more information before you decide. The struggle comes when you don't know when to stop researching and start *doing*. You will never have enough information to feel comfortable. Joy asks you to trust in the mystery of discovery that happens in the doing.

Enneagram Nine: You look busy, bustling even, but not necessarily on the tasks that matter most. Everything feels equally important, and prioritizing seems insurmountable. Underneath is the fear that choosing will bring conflict or disconnection. So "whatever you want" feels easier when you're faced with a decision. But when you just do what others want, you abdicate leadership and trade your voice for comfort. You disconnect from yourself, and joy moves out of reach.

An important note on Professors: It's easier to hide unproductive feeling and thinking than unproductive doing. "Leave your emotions" at the door is so pervasive that I've talked about feelings for the last four chapters. Overthinking gets a pass as long as you're checking boxes and meeting numbers. Corporate culture *overprioritizes* efficiency and productivity, making unproductive doing a betrayal that the hustle-happy cult won't forgive.

Here's the truth: Overthinking and emotional avoidance damage your decision-making just as much as inaction. I want you to recognize that, especially if you are a Professor (or you're working with one). Professors aren't slow thinkers or too cautious. We just live in a system that idolizes high-speed output and confuses speed with wisdom.

Professor joy power: Observe and strategize.

Because you see from a different vantage point, you bring a new perspective. You connect the dots others miss. And your strategies and wisdom come out in ways that slow the rest of us down in a beautiful way.

Professor joy pressure: Withdraw and delay.

Because you want to wait to decide until something feels *authentic enough*, or you have *enough* information, or until you're *sure* everyone will agree, you unnecessarily delay decision-making.

Professor joy pump: Use rhythms and rituals.

The Experience section is full of rhythms and rituals that help you practice productive doing (and reduce your decision fatigue.) In the meantime, here's a quick trick when you're stuck in inaction: 5-4-3-2-1 *Do it anyway*. Something about the countdown is magic. 5-4-3-2-1 Get up. 5-4-3-2-1 Send the email. 5-4-3-2-1 Pick the restaurant. It's a jump-start to strengthening your Doing Center.

Each of these leadership styles brings a powerful set of skills to the workplace. Grab the *Playbook* for ways each type can grow and work better together.

When one Center takes over and another sits in a corner, your decision-making process falls short. Recognizing your leadership style enhances your decision-making by bringing to the light what's hiding in your Blind Spot. Your style is the mirror that moves you into Open—the space where others can help and change happens. Strengthening your unpracticed wimpy arm gives you more balance and stability, and you can lean into the joy power of those around you to alleviate some of your joy pressures.

Let's bring this awareness to your chosen lens. It's time to connect decisions to your values.

Values: Your True North for Every Decision

Did you do your work through identifying your values?* Gold star. Now it's time to integrate those words on the wall into your decision-making.

When faced with a decision, you must know your values. Use those values as a filter when faced with a decision. Just as Disney's first filter is safety, your values filter out fleeting impulses and distracting influences, so you stay rooted and connected. And they guide you in evaluating the next thing you need to understand: your desires.

---

* The *Playbook* has a more extensive process of using values in decisions.

I Want It That Way (And You Don't Have to Tell Me Why)

"The world is divided into two types of people: those who are 'needers' and those who are 'wanters,'" says Dan Sullivan, founder and president of Strategic Coach.[16]

If I pause in the middle of this quote, you may have made a judgment about who makes better decisions. Who are you betting on? Now let's continue with Sullivan's argument:

"Needers compete for scarce resources and opportunities, while wanters are involved in the continual expansion of cooperation among abundance-minded individuals."[17]

If Needers are competing for scarce resources, that means someone is losing. And if someone is losing, fear will impact decisions. The Kellogg School of Management found fear-based decision-making leads to not taking care of yourself, underperformance, poor money decisions, and even bad food choices.[18] Needers not only sit in the cheap seats of scarcity, they're highly reactive and volatile. Not to mention, they're vulnerable to the manipulation of others' guilt trips and *shoulds*.

Wanters promote cooperation and collaboration. Wanters see the group as informing possible futures, expanding the view of what could be, and working to create that possibility. Because Wanters work in possibility rather than probability, their thinking is agile, even when data can be scarce.[19] Wanting moves you to look for freedom in your intrinsic motivation based on your values, not on pacifying fear (which will tempt you to compromise your values). Although necessity is the mother of invention, wanting is the spark that changes *we have to* into *what if we could?* and relaxes everyone. Wanters tap into the unending resource of creativity as they get to the other side of fear.

At twenty-four years old, I sat across from a mentor asking for guidance. I really loved speaking and teaching. I'd had a tiny opportunity at a conference, and I buzzed for hours afterward. This mentor regularly spoke at our church and larger conferences. So I asked her, "How can I get more practice? Can you help me learn how to do it better?"

"Oh, you shouldn't want that," and dismissed the idea with a wave of her hand.

That conversation crushed me for nearly twenty years. Many other messages throughout the years stunted and blunted my ability to name what I wanted, let alone think it was acceptable or truly needed.

I have a feeling you've been conditioned to ignore what you want for a multitude of reasons. When you're out of practice identifying what you want, wanting seems out of reach or even forbidden. But if you don't know what you want, how can you make an informed choice?

Practice being a Wanter informed by your values, so you are focused on what you want the most. When you are a Wanter, your decision-making is already on the path to joy.

And for more ways to practice being a Wanter, see the *Playbook*.

The Tools Nobody Told You About

Let's put all this self-awareness together. I'm going to give you a few reminders and my Decision Insight model. (Check out the Stories, Study Stacks, and Citations, and the *Playbook*, for more tools and resources.)

The Board: Your Outside Eyes

Making decisions in isolation is a recipe for disaster. I absolutely want you to trust yourself in making good decisions, and consulting others keeps you from fallacies and fixed thinking.

You only have two eyes that face one direction and your own limited knowledge. Annie Duke says that outside input expands your ability to "test alternative hypotheses and move toward accuracy."[20] Get your outside input from your Personal Board—wise friends, advisors, cheerleaders, and straight shooters who will show you what you can't see and remind you of who you are.* Author and decision-making expert Emily P. Freeman says these people will "tell it all and tell it true."[21]

Calling the board doesn't need to include suits and heels at the conference table. (My board holds most meetings through the Marco Polo app.) But calling the board *does* give you more informed choices.

Choices: Narrowing Down to Joy

You walk into the store and see six jam options—strawberry, peach, blueberry, grape, raspberry, and fig. Another store? There's an entire rainbow of twenty-four varieties glowing on the shelves, including mango-chipotle and elderflower-plum. Better, right? Research says no.

In this now-famous study by professor and choice expert Sheena Iyengar, the bigger display definitely got more buzz—60 percent of shoppers took a look—but only 2 percent bought anything. At the six-flavor display, 40 percent stopped by, and an impressive 30 percent of shoppers bought a jar.[22]

---

* For more, see "The Power of the Board" in "Stories That Didn't Fit" in Stories, Study Stacks, and Citations.

Iyengar calls this the paradox of choice: More options entice us but ultimately confuse us. You feel paralyzed, second-guess your selection, and delay making a decision. Then you end up walking away with nothing or are less satisfied with what you did choose.*

We think more options will bring more joy. In reality, however, Iyengar found that "more choice leads to less satisfaction or fulfilment or happiness." When making decisions, more choices bring more confusion. So, what's the Goldilocks Zone? Iyengar discusses the power of six options. So go with single digits. More than that, and you're in the law of diminishing returns.[23]

As you narrow options, you have more informed choices. And the surprise outcome is discovering the joy of limits. Wynton Marsalis, a master jazz artist and composer, celebrated the limits. "Jazz always has some restrictions. Otherwise, it might sound like noise." What separates noise from jazz is taking limits and using wisdom to create something new. He says how he puts together music isn't the "right answer," but a "useful combination."[24]

When those choices are distinct and limited, you will make better decisions that lead to more joy.

Decision Insight Decoder

In the ancient book of Proverbs, or *Mishlei*, the author records the intense advice of his father: "Do what I tell you—live! Sell everything and buy Wisdom! . . . She guards your life . . . Above all and before all, do this: Get Wisdom!"[25]

---

* When you are endlessly searching for things like flight options, or the exact right insurance plan, you are likely too focused on the outcomes and trying to control your love, safety, or belonging.

Joyosity

In the swirling of life, that advice feels like you have to climb to a mountaintop and sit with a guru in silence for ninety days. Ain't nobody got time for that. **Getting wisdom is a lifelong process that includes learning from each decision that comes your way.**

You need a coherent process to integrate the knowledge and insights you've gathered in this chapter. This means getting it out of your head and onto paper. To paraphrase information visualization expert Ben Shneiderman, models and visualization aren't about pretty pictures. It's the insights from the process that form the beginning of clarity.[26]

This is my Decision Insight Decoder for decision-making:

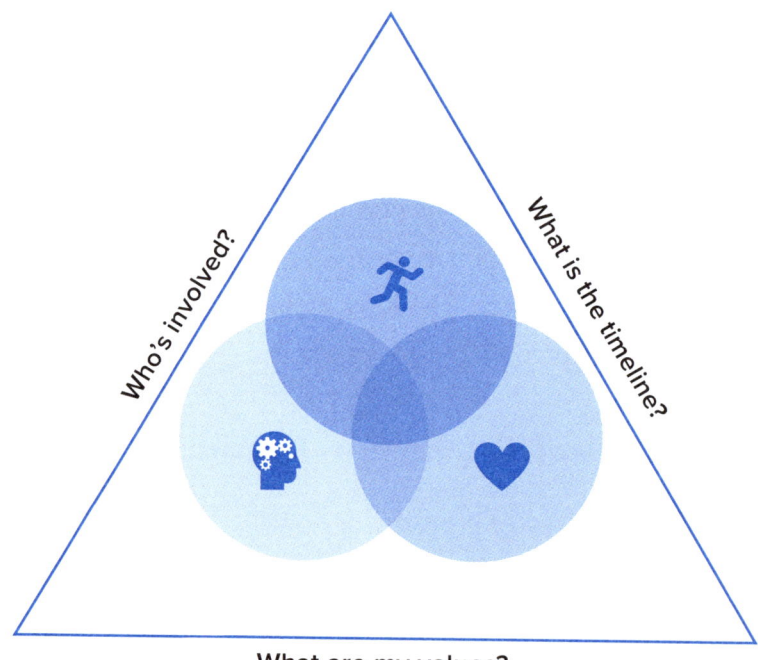

What are my values?

The Venn diagram represents balanced Centers of Intelligence. And as a Trailblazer, I have to work at bringing the Feeling Center into the process and not rely on my bias toward logic and independence. Connectors, you'll need to focus on productive thinking and not assuming it's all on you. Professors, focus on productive doing and engagement.

Ask these questions to balance the Centers and decode your decisions:

- How do I feel about it? How do I feel about the options?
- What's my data? What am I assuming? What don't I know?
- What are the possibilities? What action could I take?

The outer triangle integrates the remaining context needed:

- Who's involved? Who on the Personal Board can help?
- What's the timeline? Will this matter in ten years?
- What are my values? What do I want to do most? (This is the ultimate for Wanters, and aligning with your values keeps you from fleeting desires and focuses you on freedom.)

Draw this out and write all over it. Getting all the pieces out of your head and employing all the Centers of Intelligence bring insights and wisdom you will otherwise miss if you just endlessly ponder *What should I do?* You will reduce choices, find the right information, gather the right counsel, and maybe get a snack. Focus on the process, your choices, and your action steps—not the outcomes.

Joy by Agency, Not Control

"Peter's right. It's the only way," Catherine, the senior agent, states with measured conviction.

"Peter?" Rose, a civilian, whirls to look at Peter, the other agent. Her eyes plead, desperate for a different decision.

The foreign informant knocks on the door of the basement safehouse. The investigation, the mission, and the safety of millions seem to rest in the balance of this one decision.

Arms out, begging for Rose to understand, Peter insists, "We don't have a choice."[27]

At this point, I have to refrain from shouting at my phone. Watching *The Night Agent* as I churn away on the elliptical, I'm exhausted. Not by the workout, but the amount of times the characters claim they have "no choice."

If you start paying attention to popular culture, your friends' social media posts, and even your own language, you'll notice this "no choice" language everywhere. **The truth is you always have a choice.** You may not like the options or outcomes, but there is always a choice when you claim your own agency.

Agency is your ability to make your own choice, to own your responsibility and capacity to manage yourself. **You will experience more joy when you use your agency rather than feel helpless with "no choice."** You will also experience joy when you recognize that you have agency, but not control, over the outcomes. Because life will always be a game of incomplete information, owning your agency is part of the deep roots of resilience and joy.

Iyengar reminds us, "If you believed you have a choice, you benefited from it."[28] That is the power of agency.

The Wisdom of Tomatoes

Tommy Kail faced billions of decisions from the moment *In the Heights* touched his hands until his forty-four seconds on the Tony Awards stage.* You simply cannot make decisions only focused on the *one* outcome and also experience the joy of life. Attempting to control the outcomes is a recipe for pain and shame. Focus on the process. Possibilities and joy will follow.

---

* 2,044,140,000 if you're curious.

The Gist

Joyful leaders don't chase results. They choose wise processes. Informed decisions, rooted in values and agency, build lasting joy. Because how you choose is how you live.

Don't chase the fleeting. Choose the freeing.

—Jenn Whitmer

Connection

Do you have a Personal Board? List five people you want on your board.

How do you connect with people based on your Enneagram leadership style? Are you independent? Are you moving toward? Or are you withdrawing?

Where are you misusing or overusing your Enneagram leadership style strength?

. . . .

Curiosity

Do you think you are more of a Needer or a Wanter? Do you think it's OK to be a Wanter guided by your values?

Use SNAP to examine your stories about wanting what you want.

. . . .

Joy

Practice checking in with yourself at least once a day and ask, "What do I want?"

Find your Enneagram leadership style joy pump activity. Write a time on your calendar to do it.

Choose a decision you have to make right now. Are you caught up in resulting? Practice using the Decision Insight Decoder so you have agency.

Part 3

It's your place in the world; it's your life. Make it the life you want to live.

—**Dr. Mae Jemison**

Experience

Stop Rehearsing. Live in Joy.

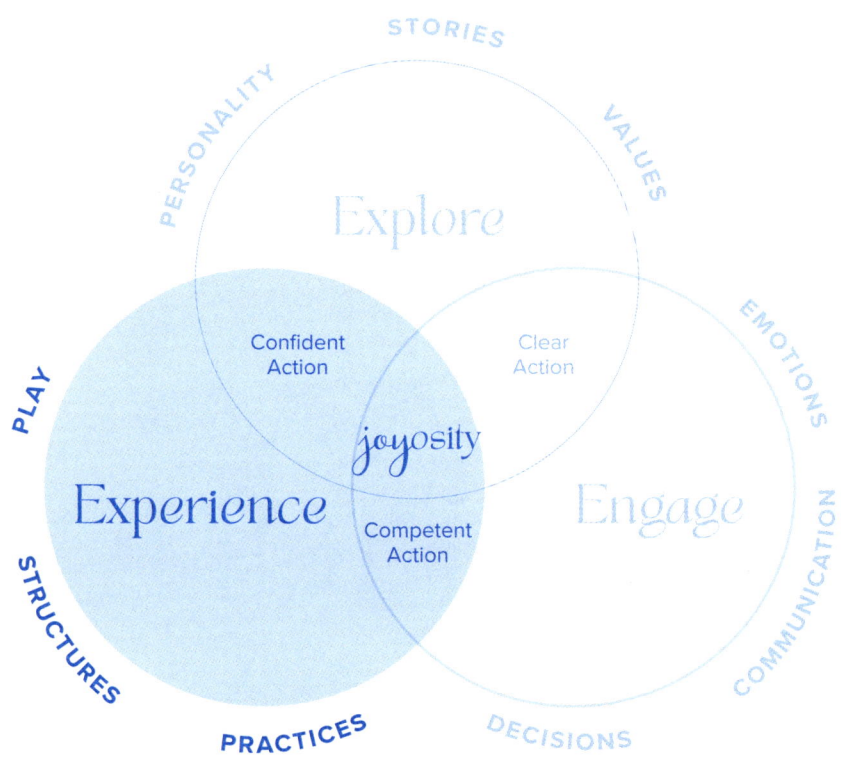

Aaron Peirsol touched the wall a full 2.4 seconds before Markus Rogan of Australia. Not only winning the gold medal in the 2004 Olympics Men's 200-meter backstroke, he set an Olympic record. Ripping off his cap and goggles, Peirsol expected to see that red "OR" next to his name, but instead "DSQ" appeared. Disqualified?

Officials disqualified the twenty-one-year-old swimmer for "an illegal turn." The US team filed a protest that began hours of video review, judge interviews, and tense deliberation. But during the excruciating wait, Peirsol realized something he'd been feeling for a long time: He'd done the work to get to his second Olympics. Day in and day out, he did the work. Setting a record or not, winning a medal or not, he was satisfied with the day-in and day-out work.

Reflecting on those tense hours on the *Rich Roll* podcast, he said, "The Olympics . . . are an amazing pinnacle of what sport is." But it's too much pressure to spend your life at the pinnacle, and most of the time, you're not there. If you spend all of your time at the most intense part of your career, Peirsol said, "You'd be missing out on your entire life . . . and that's really unfortunate."

Soon after Peirsol's revelation about his time and the pinnacle, the judges reached a decision—the disqualification was overturned; his gold medal and the Olympic Record were reinstated.[1]

Not only is staying at the pinnacle too much pressure, you want to enjoy a life that includes the practices and habits that get you there. The laps, the nutrition, the visualization, the sleep, the 4:30 a.m. alarms . . . the underwater work far away from the pinnacle.

Same goes for leadership. The unseen work creates your experience: practices that fill instead of drain. You need structures that hold up your best (or even above water) when life gets messy and there is no handbasket. And you need play that keeps you connected, productive, and in flow. Let's build a life of joy beyond the pinnacle.

You can't think your way out of stress; you must practice your way through it.

Your Inbox Isn't a Hippo

Practice Your Way out of Stress

> When we just sort of focus on the small things, the big things often accidentally end up taking care of themselves.
> —Paul Thomas Anderson, director and screenwriter

In 2019, the city of Chennai, India, hit "Day Zero." Eleven million people turned on the tap in the morning and not a drop of water came out.

You could see the cracked dusty floor of all four of the city's reservoirs, completely dry. There was no water for showers, dishes, cooking, or tea. Hotels and restaurants shut down. Overwhelmed hospitals couldn't sanitize equipment. Those who could, paid the equivalent of an average weekly salary to receive water delivered by private tankers. The rest queued up for hours in over a 100°F heat with multicolored jugs, cans, and plastic water bottles to receive a ration of water from the inland.

How does a coastal city on the Bay of Bengal, prone to flooding, not have a drop of water? Chennai became an "extremely water-stressed" city by using more than 80 percent of its water supply each year. An interconnected set of causes exacerbated the stress into crisis: lower than average rainfall; a population spike from 500,000 to 10 million people; unregulated development of water-intensive industries such as textiles and concrete; and an increase of polluted waterways.

Chennai continued to function, but barely. Economic productivity dropped 6 percent. Production stalled, spirits sagged, and the whole city limped forward—spent, overwhelmed, and one empty jar away from collapse.[1]

How often have you felt like the city Chennai? A crusty ditch, bone-dry from overextending yourself, with zero margin, and even polluting your own water source? You may still be showing up, but your people are lining up with empty buckets, and you've got . . . dust.

As a leader, you are a reservoir flowing into culture. That reservoir not only serves you, but also the others in your life: your family, your friends, your team.

To protect against a Day Zero (or heal from one if you've lived it) and cultivate consistent joy, lay down the idea of mountain-sized changes and one-size-fits-all solutions. You need tiny practices.

Practices are easy to dismiss. They aren't hacks or absolute formulas. They're part of a slow, steady flow that fills your reservoir as you and your circumstances change. The world isn't static, and neither is your inner world. They're dynamic and complex.

To sustain the joy you need as a human and the engagement you want as a leader, you must first tend to yourself with tiny practices—specific and intentional. These tiny actions fill *your* reservoir. Tiny practices shape strong leaders and forge transformed people.

Tiny Practices. Big Changes.

"Practice" can feel slippery. A little too woo-woo. We get weird about "practices," as if they are unexplained fairy dust to sprinkle over your life or require a full day sitting cross-legged on a tree stump. Rick Rubin, creative, artist, and record producer, says, "A practice is the embodiment of an approach to a concept."[2] An even broader definition comes from Peter O'Hanrahan, body therapist and Enneagram specialist: "A practice is anything you undertake with intention and breath."[3]

Practices are tiny actions that apply a healthy idea inside a moment of your life. That means your actual life—walking around, getting coffee, sending emails, running carpool. Take this as a menu, and find the ones you need right now. In the next chapter, we'll talk through practices that refill you consistently. In this chapter, we'll start with the most pressing threat to your joy—plugging a gaping hole in your reservoir.

Backing Up the Bus

Brad Baker led hundreds of leadership events, camps, and retreats during his forty-plus-year career in Young Life, usually with an inevitably long bus ride.

Once for a ski trip, Brad took 250 Memphis teens to Colorado, a trip he'd taken countless times. They packed five coaches and headed for the Rockies. The trip was thrilling, chaotic, loud, and exhausting. Everyone piled back onto the buses for the overnight trip home on I-70.

Brad was in the lead coach, in the front seat, just behind the driver. With the interior lights off, the teenagers snored, heads lolling, limbs akimbo in the seats. Brad dozed too.

Until he felt a jerking—start-stop, start-stop—that finally woke him. Groggy, he peered out the front window. But he couldn't see brake lights. In fact, he couldn't see any headlights from oncoming cars either. Brad turned to the driver, "Hey, where are we?"

The driver, calm as anything, replied, "Well, we're getting onto the on-ramp to the bridge to cross the Missouri River."

Brad blinked. Brain still fuzzy, he inhaled. *The bridge doesn't have an on-ramp.*

Brad's eyes widened. "STOP!!! STOP THE BUS!!!"

The bus wasn't on the interstate. They were on a *boat slip*, about twenty feet from the banks of the Missouri River.

The driver slammed on the brakes, lurching to a halt. The other four buses in the caravan did the same.

So there they were, on a road just wide enough for the buses, feet from the Big Muddy, far below the bridge that would take them back to Memphis.[4]

Before the caravan can continue on their way, fuel up, or even hit a rest stop, what's the first problem they have to solve? They've got to back up the last bus. That is the most urgent, pressing issue. No other moves will be effective until that last bus shifts into reverse.

Your most urgent pressing issue is closing the stress cycle.

Stress, Stressors, and the Stress Cycle

Stress: The physical and emotional response to a challenge or demand or threat.

Stressor: The perceived threat that sends your body into a stress response.

Stress Cycle: The phases of *threat*, *response*, *release*, and *balance* that your body uses to manage threats and return to homeostasis.

Stress is psychological and neurological.[5] In a stress response, your heart pounds, your blood pressure soars, and you breathe heavily. Your muscles coil, ready to run or fight, and your mental attention narrows to right-here-right-now. Your brain shuts down anything that isn't vital to fighting the challenge at hand, including organ systems like the digestive, immune, and reproductive.[6] Who cares about growing or healing when you need to slay this stressor?

In their book, *Burnout*, Dr. Emily Nagoski and Dr. Amelia Nagoski write, "Your *entire body and mind* change in response to the perceived threat."[7]

That *"perceived* threat" is the *stressor*: the thing that sends your body into the stress response. The challenge or demand in front of you can be a physical or sensory experience that will, or you believe will, hurt you. Stressors from the outside include discrimination, parenting, finances, unreasonable expectations, misaligned culture, client demands, performance pressures, and a multitude of others. And then there are the ways you stress yourself from the inside through flashbacks, self-image, body pressures, internal stories, and what-if scenario-building.

It can be anything, from something you hear—the creaking floorboard when you're home alone—to situations—budget deficits and the asshat at work—to your own mind—the fear of the bully in sixth grade. A stressor is anything that makes your body say: "Threat detected. DEFCON 1. Lock it down."

Your body is designed to manage stress through the *stress cycle*. It is programed to move from calm and balance to stress intensity and back to homeostasis again.

Imagine it like this. You're at the zoo, and the glass at the hippo exhibit disintegrates. The water pours out everywhere, and a hippo opens its jaws large enough to engulf a six-year-old whole and shows off its gigantic canine teeth. You're in its territory, and the 9,000-pound aggressive omnivore stares at you. (Are you running yet?)

Your body floods with adrenaline and cortisol that shut down everything else (emotional regulation, contextual thinking) so it can focus on the immediate stressor.

You hightail it across the zoo, but you're not fast enough and get crushed by the hippo. (So sad. We'll miss you.)

Or you dodge and outrun the hippo, and it charges along to find a local swamp. Panting and free, you're safe! You see your family rushing from the other end of the zoo, somehow still holding their ice cream. Hugs all around, you recount your ordeal and sigh a breath of deep peace. Your heart rate slows, your stress hormones dissipate, and your body returns to homeostasis. All is right with the world.

That's the stress cycle: **threat, response, release, balance**. Your brain struggles to know the difference between the hippo charging at you and that asshat at work taking credit for your idea again. Your brain says, "*Threat!*" and your body goes into response mode to protect you.[8]

Let's go back to our hippo for a moment. (Don't worry, it's not real. You don't have to hide the book in the freezer.) You're outrunning the hippo, bobbing and weaving through the zoo. You jump over a culvert, but the hippo trips into it, falls flat, and gets wedged in. It's totally stuck and can no longer chase you.

You're kind of safe, but confused. Your body has stopped midstress-cycle. All that adrenaline and cortisol are stuck, blocking the rest of the other body functions. Your mind knows you are safe, but again, your body still exists in the phase of threat response. It's like you're the middle bus in the caravan by the Missouri River: You're trapped, cycle incomplete.

Your body isn't made for constant calm. Stress naturally occurs, and you're designed to manage it. You want to be able to move *through* the stress cycle, fully and completely, and then be prepared—from a place of calm—to handle the next challenge. Without your body completing the cycle, the stress builds and builds and builds, shattering your wholeness and stealing your joy.

The Nagoskis explain: "Stress is not bad for you; being stuck is bad for you."[9] You can't get unstuck from the middle of the stress cycle by thinking, any more than you can think your way through digestion. You can't think your way out of stress; you must *practice* your way through it.

Seven Practices to Get from Threat to Balance

① Let's Get Physical

Intense physical activity is the most effective practice to close the stress cycle, because you're talking to your body with your body. Your body doesn't comprehend "presentation deadline" or "my teenager just got their license and drove away." Your body speaks the language of sweat, stomp, spin, and sway.

Even sixty seconds of intense activity that gets your heart rate up will do the trick. Jenny Evans, stress and resiliency expert, calls them microbursts.[10] My favorite microburst is a Sally Z.-style sixty-second dance party.* Other great options to try for one minute: star jumps, running up and down the stairs, head-shoulders-knees-and-toes as fast as you can, shadowbox the computer, or if you're a glutton for punishment, burpees.

At the same time, making physical activity a practice in your everyday life has even greater benefits. When you intentionally stress your physiology, it does more than make it easier to walk up that one hill in your neighborhood. **This intentional, positive stress trains your body to manage stress better.** Dr. Stacy Sims, exercise physiologist, explains it like this:

"[Exercise] creates changes from the central nervous system down to the smallest little thing in your cells to improve your *overall stress resilience* and metabolism. Meaning how your body handles food, how your brain reacts to stress, how your brain perceives an

---

* You met Sally (author of *Speaking Story*, speaker, and my speaker coach) when we talked about stories. Sometimes you just need to hit the sixty-second dance party button. Hers is yellow.

environment, and just moving really does help bring center and bring yourself back to you."[11]

You don't need a lot, and you definitely don't need to train for a marathon or even a 5K.* For most people, all it takes is twenty to sixty minutes of any activity that gets your heart pumping and passes the "talk test":** intense enough that you can still have a conversation, but not sing a little tune.[12] Just get your body moving.

A few years ago, Michael suddenly got laid off. My business was fairly new and just breaking even. We had two kids in college, two at home, a mortgage, and dying cars, along with all the shame and grief of the experience.

I had heard someone say on a podcast, "Grief is a walking emotion," so I encouraged Michael to walk.[13] And walk the man did. If he had a phone call, he walked. If he needed to run to CVS, he walked. If he needed to think through an idea, he grabbed a clipboard to write and walk.

He started averaging nine to eleven miles a day. He wore the soles of his shoes to holes every couple of months. We had no idea how that practice would prepare him for a more grueling challenge that lay ahead.

Years later, in a different organization, he faced a work environment that ticked all the boxes marked toxic. It nearly dragged him under. And still, he walked. Work only got worse, but he kept closing that stress cycle. Along with other practices, his walking practice saved him from burnout, depression, regular medication, and possibly losing his mind.

---

* I ran a 5K once. I don't need to do it again, thank you.
** This is actually the technical term. It's also why in *Pitch Perfect*, Aubrey trusts they'll "add their own cardio" so they can sing while they dance.

A simple, consistent practice of physical activity makes you stronger for that hill and for that hard conversation. Even more, it prepares you for the moments you never see coming. A simple practice of movement builds more than muscle. It builds the strength for you to stay whole when life tries to break you.

2 Ctrl + Alt + Breathe

Two-year-old Annalise was on her knees, quietly focused, building towers of colorful blocks in our living room.

Suddenly, her three older siblings barreled through the door after school. All clumsy feet, swinging backpacks, and zero spatial awareness, one of them destroyed her towers in a single swipe of chaos.

Annalise froze. Her lip quivered as she stared at her once-proud structures now scattered across the wooden floor. She touched a red block with a single fingertip. Then she stood up. Her little belly puffed out with an enormous inhale, and—I swear I hadn't taught her this—she said, "I go my room cahm down." She blew out the rest of her air, took another breath, and walked out.

While Annalise stayed in her room, the other kids gathered the far-flung blocks, returning them to the living room. About two minutes later, Annalise emerged and joined in the block collecting—not quite like nothing had happened, but ready to face it.

I'd heard a thousand times: *Take a deep breath*. But that's the day my toddler showed me the magic of breath work.

Most of us are shallow breathers, even when we're *not* stressed. And then when your brain raises the alarm, it shuts off that C-suite of your brain altogether because it's directing all the oxygen to the threat response. Sometimes you stop breathing entirely. It's possible you're doing so right now.

In 2008, Linda Stone coined the term, "email apnea," because 80 percent of the people she observed either held their breath, stopped breathing, or hyperventilated while checking their email. Later, she expanded it to "screen apnea" because of the overwhelming stimulus of screens—texts, Slack notifications, sixty-seven open tabs, and a pop-up to save 15 percent when you're just trying to log in.[14]

To paraphrase James Nestor, author of *Breath*, our bodies can't handle the constant stimulus. Dr. Stephen Porges, psychiatrist and expert in the autonomic nervous system, explains that if you regularly stop breathing, you send "the nervous system into a chronic state of threat."[15]

It's like someone's knocking down your blocks all day long, and you need to breathe.

Although breathing is an automatic process, you can learn to shift the energy where you need it and reduce your body's perceived threat level. O'Hanrahan teaches that breath both directs energy to "mobilize" and to "relax and conserve."[16] Your natural breath pattern connects to your Enneagram leadership style (see chapter nine).

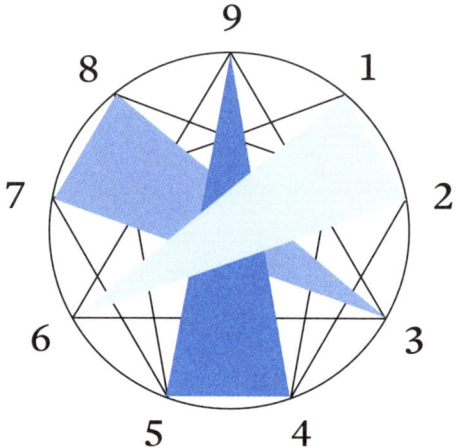

Trailblazers tend to breathe high in the chest, expanding that space of high energy. Inhales are natural, but you restrict the exhale. This keeps the energy high, but often creates struggle when you need to calm or relax. Exhales also mean release and vulnerability, and creating strength and energy feels far more comfortable to the Trailblazer.

Professors tend to breathe lower in the body, more around the belt. Your breath pattern is to constrain the inhale and emphasize the exhale. This place of exhale requires less energy, and you stay longer in that little space after you exhale, almost like you're unconsciously contemplating if the energy to inhale is worth it.

Connectors ironically have a lot of breath tension because they inhibit both the inhale and the exhale. The one you're inhibiting at the moment connects to what's happening right in front of you, particularly *whomever* is standing in front of you. You mirror energy through your breathing. Practically, while you're deciding, you hold your breath frequently.

Regardless of your type, you benefit most from simply asking yourself: *How am I breathing right now?* Then you can decide what kind of energy you need.

There are six foundational breathing techniques that shift your energy and complete the stress cycle. I'm including two here, and you can find all six in the *Playbook*.

Whoosh and Go

If you need a quick reset, or a little help to do a Taylor-style "Shake It Off" of built-up tension, whoosh and go. Take a fast but big inhale, expanding both your chest and belly. Then audibly sigh or let all the air out with a "whoosh."

Four-Corner Calm

A general way to bring balance back to your nervous system is with box breathing. Put one hand on your chest and the other on your belt. (If you want to do this in the middle of a meeting, just keep your hands where they are.) Inhale evenly into your belt hand to the count of four. Hold for four. Exhale evenly for four. Hold for four. Repeat at least twice or until you feel a bit of heaviness in your body. Two times is about thirty seconds; four is about a minute.

3 Look Up. Speak Words.

One of my leadership clients Tiarah decided to give up online ordering, self-checkout, *and* having her headphones in while she shopped. Every Aldi run and CVS pick-up now meant she talked to a real, live human. (You might be aghast right now but stick with me.) As a single woman leading in a hybrid work environment, she could

Joyosity

go days without speaking to another human in person. Convenience had stolen her connections.

There's a good chance that lack of connection or even loneliness is leaving your stress cycle open. Loneliness isn't solitude—it's a *feeling* of being isolated and alone. Loneliness sets in when you don't have enough "meaningful connections."[17]

To combat loneliness and close the stress cycle, you need about eight to twelve minutes of connection. Hop on the phone with a friend. Walk with your neighbor. Get a coffee with your work buddy.

You can also connect with strangers. By ditching her AirPods, Tiarah had consistent connections with clerks at the store or with neighbors in her condo unit. Connection, even with strangers, boosted her mood and closed the stress cycle. Her experience matches what research has found about initiating conversations with strangers: We assume people don't want to be bothered and will respond negatively, but that isn't true! People generally welcome the interaction. And the study found the initiator felt less awkward and more optimistic overall after practicing for just a week.[18]

These micro-moments of connection not only act as mortar to your community and career bricks, they also absorb stress to bring you more joy.

4 Undignified Laughter

She fell over on her side, tears streaming down her face. She could only wheeze with laughter. My Aunt Karen laughs easily, but this night in the middle of a game of spoons, her laughter incapacitated her, and the rest of us joined in. Just thinking of that night makes me start to giggle.

You've got one of those memories too. When you or your brother or your cabinmate laughed so hard you couldn't breathe. Not only is laughter a way to close the stress cycle, so is the memory of it.

I'm not talking about that stoic, golf-clap type of, "Oh, that's funny." I mean the real deal that comes from your belly that is completely and wonderfully carried away—the laugh until you cry, pee, or fart (which is my friend Ginger's favorite).

Laughing with others builds more positive social connections because now it's a shared memory that says you belong.[19] To paraphrase Sophie Scott, a cognitive neuroscientist specializing in laughter, laughter is a social behavior. It's not just about humor; it's bonding.[20]

The physicality of laughter also closes the stress cycle. Much like the physical effort of walking up a hill, laughter stimulates oxygen production. Along with the oxygen, endorphins, dopamine, and serotonin flood your system to stabilize your mood, relax your muscles, and bring satisfaction. So yes, that deep belly laugh will bring you back to calm.

Laughter doesn't only have to be spontaneous. If you start the physical act of laughing, your body will eventually join in, and you'll laugh for real—either by physical response or just from the sheer ridiculousness that you're making yourself laugh. Any way you get there—remembering the time your Aunt Karen fell to the floor laughing, watching your favorite *Saturday Night Live* sketch, or making yourself laugh—you're closing the stress cycle.

5 The Ugly Cry

"The cure for anything is salt water: sweat, tears, or the sea."[21] The Danish author Isak Dinesen probably didn't know the science, but she absolutely knew the feeling: Tears are release. Like its sunshinier sibling of undignified laughter, this isn't the melodramatic single tear that slips from your eye and glides down your cheek. This is the snotty-nosed, red-faced, ugly cry—the sobs that bring hiccups and spit strings. You probably even have a special place for sobbing (the shower, the car, the pillow).

When you cry, your brain releases oxytocin to signal that you can trust again, as well as other hormones to relax you and relieve pain (and remember that you *feel* emotions in your body).[22] You're not removing the stressor, but you are getting yourself back to homeostasis so you can solve the problem.

Yet we often try to hold back tears for a myriad of reasons. For example, the middle of a pitch meeting isn't really a safe place to sob. I think we also don't like that out-of-control feeling that comes with the big cry. Although women who cry experience some stigma, I think the social pressure for men to not cry is more harmful. Trying to not cry, or believing crying is shameful, reduces the mood-boosting benefits of the ugly-cry catharsis.[23]

Ugly cries won't last long. You can't sustain the ugly cry for more than eight to ten minutes, and you don't need more than that. You want just enough to get to the big sigh. The key is to not hold it in and to let the tears flow. Sometimes you know you need to cry, but the tears feel stuck. You need a little character crying support. Grab a novel that moves you, a playlist of sad songs, or that one episode of *Grey's Anatomy* which undoes you. Mine? *A League of Their Own* or

Come from Away. Your body doesn't need to connect to why you're crying—you just need to cry to close the stress cycle.

6 The Booth Hug

Booth Andrews is one of the coolest people I've ever met. Her résumé includes roles like Executive Vice President, Of Counsel, Chief Executive Officer, Founder, and Board Member. But the reason she's so amazing? The Booth Hug. Legendary.

I've only been with her in person three or four times. But each time, Booth's mighty arms enveloped me in a hug that has lasted longer than a polite little squeeze. And each time, I've walked away with a deep sense of calm.

That's the power of affection. Affection, particularly physical touch, reinforces love, safety, and belonging (because you don't generally touch folks you don't feel safe with). That experience of physical affection says, "I got you," and releases hormones to reassure your body that you're safe from that charging hippo[24]—that it's OK to return to normal.*

If you are anywhere near middle age, you've been served some kind of ad that talks about cortisol and chronic stress. "How I lowered my cortisol with this one special $999 hack!" The hack doesn't work, but the problem of chronic stress and cortisol overload is real, particularly in middle age.

Most of your friendships probably consist of texting memes and saying we should get together but never do. If you're a parent, you probably don't have little kids laying on you anymore. Regular adult

---

* "Do you want an ear, advice, or a hug?" I try to ask my kids (and my friends!) when there is a hot mess o' stress in front of me. And I've learned to ask myself too. My friend Diana asks if you'd like a snack or a sing-along.

friendships—that include a long enough time together where you can hug—get interrupted by dance classes and work trips. Researchers call it social strain, and it keeps your cortisol elevated.[25] Affection is an antidote (and it's free).

There are many options for affection, but two key components are time and attention. When you experience a Booth Hug, you're the only person in the room. And her solid hug lasts at least twenty seconds. This is way longer than social comfort typically allows, and that's the point. The twenty-second hug begins the release of hormones, slows your heart rate, and lowers your blood pressure.[26] It also brings attunement, the physical experience of trust and connection, and being fully present and in sync with another person.[27]

A bear hug might be hard to come by. You can also pet your cat or other furry friend to feel that sense of affection and attunement.[28] Just ten minutes of that attention, repetitive movement, and warm cozy weight says to your nervous system, *you can slow down now.* Corporate worship and prayer can also bring a similar effect on your stress cycle.[29] When you believe you are connected to a loving God, Creator, or higher power, time meditating, singing, and praying provides affection, as well as connects you spiritually to others who feel the same.[30] You're a part of a real, albeit invisible at times, community that your body recognizes as safe.

Again, the key to affection is time and attention, even if you can't get a Booth Hug.

7 Create Your Way Back

BIG FEELS get squeezed out of us by the rush to move on, the pressure to perform, and the fear of being too much. One place in modern culture has always made space for the full spectrum of expression: the arts.

Singing, performing, crafting, drawing, painting, dancing, storytelling—they're called outlets for a reason. They blow the doors off and say, "Come on in and *feel!*" They make a space to release the fear and the pain that stressors bring your way. Like the way a regular practice of movement builds resilience, a regular creative practice regulates your nervous system.[31]

Write poetry, curate a road trip playlist, act it out on the stage, craft a song, play the piano, pick up a paintbrush . . . all of these creative activities are like a little back door into closing your stress cycle.[32] Baking, woodworking, cooking, tinkering, knitting, restoring furniture, collecting, sewing, and coloring are included in this category. You are working out the stress, even if no one ever sees your creation.

One reason so many of us have such piled-up stress cycles? Our culture has left behind creative hobbies in favor of passive entertainment or the need to "monetize" our hobbies and have a "side hustle,"[33] which makes everything, again, about productivity and profit. We don't have the release of the regular creative outlet, and on top of that it's a product that must be good right away. Your nervous system is back to running from that hippo.

The arts are *practices*. You don't need to be trained or skilled for creative expressions to bring calm. You just need to breathe and do it with intention.

Joyosity

You can't avoid stressors: The calendar invite for 4:30 p.m. on Friday comes in from your boss. Or the phone rings, and the caller ID shows the name of a hospital near your aging parents. Or the brake lights fill the stretch of interstate ahead of you when you had no margin to get to the meeting. None of these is a true physical threat, but they tear a gaping hole in your joy.

Signs You're Stuck in the Middle Bus

When you've left the stress cycle open too many times, it shows up physically. These are four signs that your stress cycle is wreaking havoc on your body:

1. *You feel weird in your body.* You keep getting sick, have chronic pain, or suffer a repeated injury. Because the stress cycle is part of your biology, your body is saying, "Hey! I'm feeling open and exposed here!"*
2. *You're a volcano.* You erupt with an outsized response to the current situation, but it matches what's happening inside your body.
3. *You play hide and no seek.* Even though someone has called, "Olly olly oxen free," you're still under the bed. You're consistently retreating because it "just feels like too much." You numb out or regularly cancel plans.
4. *You are on the log with Pete and Repeat.* You check if you put your wallet in your bag, and then you go back and check it again. Or you're biting your cuticles, twisting your hair, or any repetitive picking at your body. You keep reading and rereading the same paragraph but don't take in the information.

---
* Maybe it's perimenopause; maybe it's the stress cycle.

Your brain keeps repeating concerns because it's holding too much.

These seven practices are the way you back up that last bus to help you return your body to homeostasis, where it feels safe and cozy and ready for the next stressor to come bounding your way. This isn't an exhaustive list, but the practices are simple enough to encourage you to close the stress cycle on a regular basis. If you don't regularly close the stress cycle, that hole in your reservoir widens, inching you closer to a Day Zero when all the joy has drained out.

The Gist

Practices are tiny actions that apply a healthy idea inside a moment of your life. You can't avoid stress, so you use practices to build capacity and regularly close your stress cycle.

You can't think your way out of stress; you must practice your way through it.

—Jenn Whitmer

Connection

Look through "Create Your Way Back." Choose a practice to try that connects you to something you've enjoyed in the past. Put it on your calendar four times to practice it.

How can you get more micro-moments of connection in your days?

Curiosity

Where is immediate stress disconnecting you from either the purpose of your work or from other people?

Review the four signs that you're stuck in the middle bus. Are you experiencing any of these?

Write down the seven practices that close the stress cycle. For each practice, what activity feels the most fun or accessible to you? For example, take The Booth Hug: Does petting your dog for ten minutes feel good? Or Let's Get Physical: Do you want to try burpees, because you're a glutton for punishment?

Joy

Which stressors steal your joy on a regular basis? Go back to your Joyosity Explorer Map and look at the joy drainers.

Do these stressors cause you toil more than 10 percent of the time?

How can you deal with the stressors so they stay in Toil's Tiny Ten?

You can't outsource your joy.

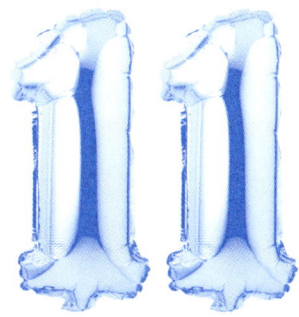

Wipe Out the Fuzz
Practices That Protect Joy

The input is automatic. But where is the output?
—**Emily P. Freeman,** *The Next Right Thing*

I'm a multi-beverage worker. As I write this, my desk has two twenty-four-ounce shiny Starbucks cups of water, a half-full gold Harry Potter mug of coffee, and a white Roy Kent mug with the leftover milk film from tea—and that's just from today. Typically, there's a smoothie and something bubbly too.

This excess of containers always makes desk clean-up an event. One day, I was packing up at a consulting client's office before a weeklong vacation. I gathered the empty Diet Coke can, multiple water bottles with lemon wedges, and coffee mugs. Stan appeared and asked me to come by his desk before I left.

I put down my favorite St. Louis Public Radio mug with the dregs of that morning's creamy coffee and waltzed over to Stan's cubical. We solved the problem and said goodbye. I grabbed my computer bag and jacket, and headed out the door, ready for a beach vacation.

That was March 11, 2020. My coffee mug had its own COVID lockdown.

Six months later, the company boxed up all our belongings and sent them to our homes. Nestled in with my kids' photos and my favorite TUL pens was the biohazard of that coffee mug. I have no idea what type of penicillin was growing in that mug.

What do you do? Throw it out, or boil and bleach it? Well, I loved that mug, so I kept it. And I just poured my morning coffee right in.

No! Of course not! Before anything was going in that mug, I boiled, bleached, and dishwasher sanitized—the whole nine.

Let's take a little leap: Imagine your life as that mug.

You could have pitched the mug, but you can't throw out your humanity. So often this world tells you to leave your humanity in a box, figuring it's just fine there. But green fuzz grows from neglect. And neglect harms your joy.

Your life fills with the everyday pressures that aren't urgent, but persistent. The looming deadline, the hard conversation that's coming, the constant barrage of *shoulds* and tasks, and the world of information we carry around in our pockets that, for some reason, we still call "a phone." This is beyond the immediate stress cycle we walked through in the last chapter.

Living our lives without regular practices is like pouring coffee into the mug caked with green fuzz. Or to combine the metaphors, if your reservoir is full of schmutz, there's no room for clean water to get in. We've become so accustomed to the fuzz, we don't realize it's slowly eating our joy.

Cultivating joy includes implementing practices to remove the fuzz of everyday pressures and pour in the fresh water you need. And here's where we're going deep, back to the Johari Window and the Unknown quadrant. Part of why the Unknown exists is the fuzz—you literally can't be aware of it because it's covered with gunk. This level of self-awareness is a deeper practice that isn't just knowing you'd like to feel joy, but working to experience it.

Research supports practices that provide regular cleanouts and bring joy into the present rather than delay it. These practices increase the regeneration of cells, produce new neural pathways, reduce blood pressure and anxiety, increase focus, and enhance creativity.[1]

Not just one more *should*, these are the very practices that ease the pressure of the rest of life. They are the practices that create space, safety, and support that open your door to joy. There is, of course, more in the *Playbook*.

Space: The Beauty Between the Beats

I love watching my kids tap dance, especially when Stuart and Sabrina tapped in high school. The sounds, the movement, and the power mesmerized me.

During a demonstration class, Miss Amanda explained that the spectacular moment of tap dancing wasn't when the tap connected to the floor—it's the spaces between the taps. You can't fill every sound from the music with your feet, or you're gasping after three minutes. It's the space that protects the performance from becoming a cacophony instead of a dance.

Joyosity

You need the space too. Space incorporates three practices—silence, stillness, and solitude. I know, when does that happen? This is the point. Our world is designed to compress you into productivity, crushing the life you want. This is why you need these practices to work together to give your soul the opportunity to breathe and clean out the fuzz.

Every human needs all three, but your Enneagram group—Body, Heart, or Head—will indicate which one you need most. As you read these, you might think, *I'm definitely avoiding that one.* Stay with it, because that's probably your most beneficial practice.

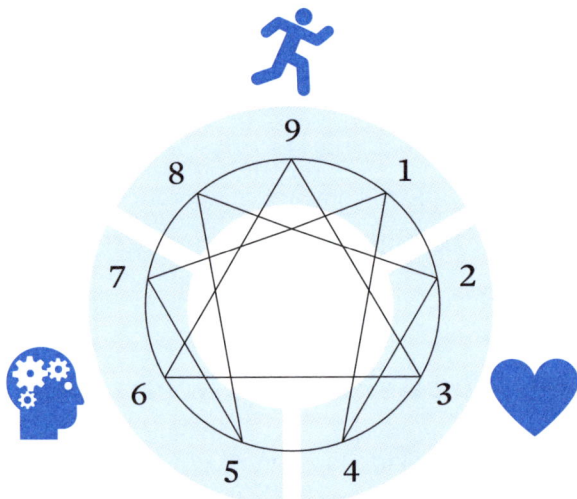

Stillness: Just Human Being

Stillness is the practice of just being, without solving or escaping. It's creating space by stilling your mind, body, and spirit.

In the whirlwind of our addiction to action and obsession with productivity, it's likely you're escaping. *If I just keep producing, I won't lose control, or have to feel or face issues I don't want to face.* In this process, you lose touch with yourself. **Practicing stillness creates space to belong to yourself.**

Stillness isn't vegging on the sofa for a *Great British Bake Off* binge with food delivery. Instead, stillness tunes you to your *being* and knowing yourself. Stillness doesn't have to be a lack of movement. It's an intentional focus on you as a human in the world, with presence, power, and worth.

Body Group: Eights, Nines, and Ones

Your practice is stillness. (If you just reopened the book after you slammed it closed, it's OK. Welcome back.) You'll resist this practice for many reasons, but the main one is because the Body Group connects to control, escape, and productivity. You're working for belonging, and you need to belong to yourself first. Stillness helps you develop intimacy with yourself. Chris Heuertz, Enneagram expert, author, and Eight, calls these "postures."[2] I think of them as approaches.

> **Eights:** Who am I when I'm not protecting?
> *Consent* to the stillness and open yourself up to vulnerability. Stillness lets you rest from solving and protecting for a bit so you can belong to yourself.
>
> **Nines:** Who am I when I'm not avoiding?
> *Engage* in stillness, not numbing. Stillness allows you to calm the fear of using your voice, recharge from the demands of others, and know you belong.
>
> **Ones:** Who am I when I'm not improving?
> *Rest* in stillness. Stop fixing and pause the *shoulds*, knowing the world will not end without you working to make right. In stillness you don't have to be good to belong—you already do.

Solitude: Standing Strong with Yourself

Solitude is the practice of removing yourself from the presence of others to be with yourself. After productivity, we're addicted to validation. *Am I doing this right? Is this approved? Is this significant enough?* Solitude returns you to your identity, fully away from the gaze and approval of others. **Practicing solitude creates space to love yourself.**

Solitude lets you connect to your emotions and needs, allowing you to separate yourself from the identity of others. Remember, this isn't isolating yourself. Practicing solitude means intentionally being with yourself, so you cultivate the self-possession needed to face life.

Heart Group: Twos, Threes, and Fours

Practice solitude. Many people in this group identify as introverts because it's exhausting to spend so much time chasing validation from others. Solitude restores your identity. You get to be you without needing approval from anyone else. All of that emotional energy you expend, all the emotions you carry, start moving through and heal in solitude. You can rebuild your energy with solitude and by loving yourself.

Twos: Who am I when I'm not needed?
Consent to solitude. Solitude allows you to pause filling up everyone else and finally validate your own needs and emotions. Find humility by recognizing your own needs and loving yourself in them.

Threes: Who am I when I'm not impressing?
Engage in solitude. In solitude, you can stop being the chameleon, becoming who others want you to be. Solitude allows you to find your authenticity and know you are worth love as you are.

Fours: Who am I when I'm not looking for validation of my identity?

Rest in solitude. You can stop trying to be noticed and seen because you see yourself. Solitude melts the extremes into equanimity. You discover you already have love in you for yourself.

Silence: The Quiet That Lets You Be Loud

Silence is the quieting of all *generated* sound.

We live in a noisy world—and not just the decibel level. More information is available and travels faster than at any time in human history.[3] It's zero effort to absorb data. The game fills the background at a restaurant, the Slack knock-brush notification sounds, the trash trucks rumble past, your roommate practices their presentation in the next room, the reporter announces the headlines . . . Constant input leaves no room for you. Silencing the noise means you can listen to yourself. **Practicing silence creates space to be safe with yourself.**

In silence, our bodies find homeostasis, our minds contextualize, and our souls release the issues we've been covering with the constant barrage of sounds that come from media, modern life, and even your own voice.

Head Group: Fives, Sixes, and Sevens

Your practice is silence. The Head Group invests in information gathering, advice gathering, and experience gathering. Threats to your perceived safety lurk everywhere, so you tune into anything that helps you push away fear: news alerts, music, TV in the background, phone calls in the car, podcasts while you clean . . . all of it keeps your thoughts churning. Heuertz writes, "Silence brings clarity to the overactive mind always convoluted by its hunt for answers, assurance, or access."[4] Practicing silence gives you space to quiet a racing mind, knowing you have security in yourself.

Fives: Who am I if I do not know?
Consent to silence. Lay down your demand for knowledge. In silence, you practice healthy nonattachment to knowledge and discover you're safe to be comfortable in a world with mysteries.

Sixes: Who am I if I'm not prepared?
Engage in silence. You face your anxieties and bravely release your vice grip on the illusion that you can control the outcomes. Practicing silence lets you discover you are safe "even if."

Sevens: Who am I when I'm not avoiding pain?
Rest in silence. Develop the presence of the present. What you've avoided with the noise will come up in the silence. It may be painful, but practice perseverance, and find joy in being safe with yourself.

Stillness, solitude, and silence do not have to be heavy. In fact, there should be a lightness to them. Remember O'Hanrahan's reminder: A practice is anything you undertake with intention and breath. You're creating space, not making it "work." When you try to make practice a performance, you lose its whispered magic.

The world opposes space, and with that, your joy. Create the space to clean out the mug so there's room to fill it up.

Safe Enough to Show Up

You've been rushing since your parents fussed at you to hurry up when you were two, and that hurry has covered your life in the fuzz. You're so used it, it feels safe, even though it's toxic. Creating safety for yourself includes using practices to communicate this narrative to your soul: "It's OK here. You can peek your head around and come out." Sometimes when you begin deeper practices of creating wholeness and joy, it's unnerving or downright panicky. These practices reinforce the safety of space, slowness, and awareness.

Writing: Put It on the Page

Write the fuzz out of your head, clearing your mind so it is a place of safety again. In the *Playbook*, you'll find practices like morning pages, journaling styles, intentional worrying, and your personal book of awesome.

Places: Your Restorative Spots

Your body keeps a map of places with emotional connections. Neuroscience research has found that you connect to physical places where you've felt confident, energized, relaxed, creative, or safe.[5] These restorative places reset your nervous system and absorb the fuzz you're trying to clean out. Here are five types of places to create safety:

Power Places

Author Shauna Niequist writes about her "magic desk" as part of her process of restoration after a turbulent period in her life. I would call it her desk of power because she wrote that the desk gave "the pain and the fear and the suffering a place to be outside my body. It became the safest place in the world to me." Anytime she had to face difficulty or challenge, she went back to sit at that tiny desk because, she says, "I felt powerful at the desk."[6]

Recharge Places

Michael has a gray wingback chair in our sunroom. He reads there in the morning, journals, and pets our insistent cat. He calls it his "recharge station," and returns to the chair for a reset any time of day. The chair is the place where he restores depleted energy.

Peace Places

I've made it a practice to not watch TV or work in bed. I've established a place where people don't need me. I can disconnect from the stressors and just be. Before I go to bed, my phone goes to bed in the kitchen, automatically setting to sleep mode.* My bedroom is the place where the outside world can't disrupt my peace from 10 p.m. to 6 a.m. (Just a note: If shock and objections just came up for you, that's OK. You get to choose your practices and place. Try it for two months and if you don't like it, pick something else.)

Thinking and Creating Places

During pandemical times, one of my leadership clients desperately needed a thinking space. She cleared out a closet, replaced the light with a higher-wattage bulb, and added a small chair. She told her family there was no disturbing her in the thinking closet. She would go to the closet when she needed deep work time—just herself, her laptop, and sometimes their pandemic puppy. She had a safe space to allow her mind to work through ideas and problems, and to focus long enough to come to conclusions.

Away Places

In the summer of 2022, Annie F. Downs, speaker, podcaster, author, and leader, suffered a pile of tragedies, including the death of her

---

* For more, see "Putting Your Phone to Bed" in "Stories That Didn't Fit" in Stories, Study Stacks, and Citations.

infant nephew. Devastated, she said these events "felt sadder than I knew what to do with." Over the next several months of grief in private, a public life of running a business, and launching her first *New York Times* bestseller, *That Sounds Fun,* Downs visited friends in New York City. At dinner, a friend floated the idea of spending more time in New York. After some considerations, she began living in both NYC and Nashville. What unfolded wasn't the original goal, but the city became her place where it was safe to grieve, a "whole other thing, this whole other place. This big, loud, constant city to walk and cry and dream."[7]

Rest Places

My friend Sarah's sunporch has been a place of rest for me for decades. She lives in Nashville, which is slightly inconvenient for me, but her porch has lovely plants, comfy furniture, and beautiful light. With her or alone, it's a place that's safe for me to release things I didn't even know I was holding.

Your power place might not be a "magic desk"—it might be a whiteboard. You might recharge at the museum or rest in your garden. You may get away to the lake or create in your basement. Establish *your* places at home, places at your office, places in your community, and places away from your everyday. Find places that welcome you back, where you can practice safety and restore joy.

Boundaries: Protect Your Attention

We could fill small libraries with the information we have about boundaries.* Psychologists Henry Cloud and John Townsend write

---

* I highly recommend *Boundaries: When to Say Yes, How to Say No to Take Control of Your Life* by Dr. Henry Cloud and Dr. John Townsend and *Set Boundaries, Find Peace: A Guide to Reclaiming Yourself* by Nedra Glover Tawwab.

that boundaries draw lines that "help us keep the good in and the bad out."[8] But how do you make keeping the good in and the bad out a practice? Let's remember Rick Rubin's advice: A practice is the embodiment of an approach to a concept. So, let's embody safety with the line that gets the fuzziest for you as a leader: your information consumption.

Pop quiz: Where do you get the most amount of information every day? Time's up. It's your phone. The smartphones that 91 percent of Americans tote around, and the apps on them, are designed to keep you using them, with little care for joy.[9] The average American checks their phone about every six minutes. We can't talk about making room for intense happiness without creating boundaries around the amazing and distracting tool that is your phone.

Email

Adults use their phones most to check email, likely for multiple email accounts clogged with tasks, shipping alerts, and your favorite author's newsletter. Rarely does an email require an urgent response.[10]

The easiest email boundary? Turn off all the notifications and badges for any email apps and web extensions. The sounds and previews crowd you, implying urgency that isn't there. They're called alerts, meaning *pay attention to me* rather than where you want your attention.

The next practice? Process email—don't just check it. Your email is not a to-do list. Block in your calendar one to six inbox processing times a day. During that time, open and read each message, complete the task or move the task to the right place, and file or delete the email. Then move to the next email. Remember, safety is about making room for slowness and awareness. Processing email brings your awareness to the task, improving your productivity, and protecting you against artificial urgency.[11]

Processing email means checking your work email while you're working, not when you first wake up, at the stoplight, or getting into bed. You might split your work time because you have a flexible schedule or work events, but boundary your work email to your working time.

[*Steps onto giant soapbox.*] THIS INCLUDES PAID TIME OFF. (I'm not shouting, just using a megaphone). [*Steps off soapbox.*]

Explicitly communicate your practice to your team. My website designer has an automatic reply to every email that gives the times she reads and responds to emails.

Don't let email crowd your attention and rob your awareness.

Notifications

Turn off as many notifications as you feel able to. With my coaching clients, I recommend that only phone calls, text messages, fraud alerts, and your calendar send you notifications. I have two group texts with my very best friends in the entire world—and both of those have alerts turned off. And all those places that text you with a discount for 15 percent off? Mute. No matter how many reminders apps give you (*"Are you sure? You don't want to miss the reply to your comment on that TikTok of Hobby Horse Competitions!"*), turn them off. I encourage you to err on the side of focus. You need far fewer notifications than you think.

You're practicing, not perfecting. Practice allowing room for your focus and what you want to give your attention to, not what the Shop app wants you to.

Do Not Disturb

This is my *favorite* phone boundary. Create specialized settings based on what you're doing. I mentioned earlier that I use the Sleep focus between 10 p.m. and 6 a.m. I also have a focus for workouts, speaking events, writing (special for this very book), vacation, and a general do not disturb. You can select the specific people who can reach you when, which apps go quiet, where the apps are on the screen, and more. You can set the focus to go on or off based on schedule, usage, or location.

Use this feature to create safety and focus for yourself as easily and automatically as possible.

Time Limits

Abby had a TikTok problem. She knew it was out of control. She also genuinely needed the app for her work as a social media manager. Deleting it wasn't a viable option. She used the time limit function to only allow the app on during her working hours from 9 a.m. to 6 p.m. She also added a time limit of four hours. This let her create content, respond to messages, and even research trends, but stopped her from mindlessly scrolling through cupcake content. This boundary keeps your time safe, but also protects your energy and attention.

Phoneless Times

In her book *The Unplugged Hours*, Hannah Brencher describes the power of a set time each day to put your phone away and choose what you do during that time. If you're anything like me, there's a lot of "double screening" happening—scrolling Instagram on your phone while watching a show on TV (and possibly having your computer in your lap) at the same time.[12]

I highly recommend creating a practice of no phones while you're eating with other people. For our family, that's usually around the supper table. Our kids have tried to thwart this practice at times, but it's an established boundary that provides safety for longer conversations and allows us to be present with one another. I extend this to restaurants, meetings, and even boarding airplanes. Brencher argues that setting boundaries for phoneless times isn't about being perfect, but about practicing presence and attention.[13]

There are so many more practices that help you create safety to be with yourself: meditation, reflection, yoga, and anything that allows you to be, in Rubin's words, "free to express what you're afraid to express."[14] These practices build experiences that prove you're safe with yourself (see self-efficacy from chapter four). When you connect to yourself, you can respond to life instead of reacting. That's how you clear out the fuzz that blocks joy.

Support: Fill Up on What Fuels You

You've created the mental space so you can deal with the fuzz. You've practiced safety to clean it out. But empty isn't the goal—full is. You want more than just survival. You need practices to support, nourish, and dare I say love, your neurobiology: sleep, movement, food, and community.

Sleep: Your Swiss Army Knife

In chapter eight, I told you about the question in my keynote "The $668 Billion Solution": What would you do with three more hours a week? Without fail, thousands of people across the world have answered: sleep. Telling, isn't it? **The number-one thing you can do to support yourself is sleep.**

When researchers study the connection between sleep and relationships, they have found people with inadequate sleep have lower emotional intelligence and less interpersonal effectiveness.[15] Lack of sleep creates toil-like conditions: impaired cognitive functions like memory, creativity, and decision-making. You're also more likely to make unethical decisions when you don't get enough sleep.[16] Matthew Walker, neuroscientist and author of the book *Why We Sleep*, says, "Sleep is the Swiss Army knife of health [bringing] vitality." Doesn't that sound like joy and wholeness?[17]

Yet we have this old story in our culture that sleeping equals lazy. Right now, take a breath then blink. Did you have a wave of shame about using oxygen or moisturizing your eyes? Not likely. When you need sleep, do you ever feel guilty, lazy, or weak? Change that story.

If you're going to cultivate joy, you need a healthy practice of adequate sleep. Most experts agree that adults need seven to nine hours of quality sleep on a regular basis.[18]

And you may have just thought, *I can get by with less*. Sure, for a time.

But you can't escape all the data about how a lack of sleep disables you. Trying to get by on less sleep is only adding fuzz back into your mug.*

Here's a quick test to gauge if you need more sleep: If you are still for ten minutes, do you feel sleepy? If so, your body is saying, "More

---

* For more, see "Riposa: Naps Are Delicious" in "Stories That Didn't Fit" in Stories, Study Stacks, and Citations.

sleep please!" If children, a schedule, or your own body doesn't allow for a full night's sleep, find a time to nap.*

If you want to start with just one practice, choose sleep. You'll have more capacity to close the stress cycle, to create space, and to just feel better if you get more sleep.

Movement: Follow the Fun

As the toxic work environment slowly wore me down, I'd stopped moving my body much. That trauma, compounded with a painful church exit, the mental health crisis of one of our kids, and launching a speaking business just months before a global pandemic . . . I felt uncomfortable and tired all the time.

One day I felt like the walls were closing in. Six people working and schooling at home was too much. I laced up my tennis shoes and walked out the front door. I strolled around our neighborhood. I walked the next day, and the next. It became a practice: Just move.

When our community center reopened, I started going to the gym. I stressed about what to do, but then I chose whatever felt like fun. Hitting the treadmill while reading a book? Great. Spinning on the elliptical while watching Netflix? Fantastic. A sunny walk instead? Perfect.

My ability to cope improved. My appearance didn't really change much, but my inner strength supported my life.**

We've already spent many words on the benefits of physical activity. This is the reminder to make it a practice. Make your weekly check-in a walking meeting. Join an adult kickball league. Practice

---

* If you have trouble sleeping, and you've tried good sleep hygiene, ask your doctor for help. Sleep difficulties could signal another problem. Sleep is worth it.
** After a while, I changed my practice with the goal of changing my body's fitness level. As I type this draft, my streak is 1,202 days in a row of closing all the rings on my Apple Watch.

yoga five minutes before bed. Pick movement that you can do and that feels fun.

Food: Nourish to Flourish

My friend Lee Ann Miller is hugs and butter. A nourishing soul, she feeds people, both heart and body. She often shares pictures of a plate of food in her Instagram stories with the caption "Made by Me. Held by D." She made the meal, and her husband, D, holds the plate. This is her reminder that you can have a beautiful plate for an everyday meal.

I'm not a doctor, dietician, or even a food blogger.* Go research for yourself why you shouldn't skip meals or how to make getting enough protein your side hustle. I'm saying this: Food is more than fuel. Food as a practice signals love for yourself, supporting your mind, body, and soul. Elevate a meal into a true practice: put it on a plate, sit at the table, and give it a flourish. Rebel against mindlessly eating at your desk or over the sink. Froth the cream in your coffee or sprinkle cilantro on your burrito. It doesn't need to be elaborate; just do it with breath and intention.

Community: If You Build It

Rachel Lovely got fired up one Monday in March 2025. The pregnant photographer posted a TikTok that went viral within days. She had read a quote, "Everyone wants to have a village, but no one wants to be a villager," and Lovely had *THOUGHTS*. She gives ten minutes of advice on how to build community—everything she's learned from

---

* But I do make amazing chocolate chip cookies. My secret is this: browned butter, dark brown sugar, and mini chocolate chips.

her mom who doesn't just build villages, but has created "a thriving metropolis."[19]

Lovely's video sparked conversation in the comments, moms' groups, and leadership circles. The concept of having a village, a community of supporters, comes from the adage "It takes a village to raise a child." And the truth is, it takes a village to be a flourishing, joyful human. You need varying levels of social interaction as you go through life, but you *always* need community—especially as a leader. The higher up you get, the lonelier it becomes.[20] You need to build your village, as a practice of support.

We've already discussed the "it's not that bad" problem and the Bootstrap Myth. I'm adding to those the "I don't want to be a burden" nonsense, perfectionism, and efficiency traps.

Delighted You Asked

One year on Thanksgiving break, I got a text from an unknown number: "It's Jena. We have extra dessert. Can we bring it over and hang out?" It took me a minute to recognize who it was. Jena and Tim were new in St. Louis. We'd met several times but hadn't hung out yet. She, Tim, and their three kids arrived at our house, and over cherry crinkle, we began a lasting friendship. Tim and Michael both led teams in large corporations and traveled weekly for work. Jena and I also had overlapping interests and experiences. Over the next few months when our husbands were gone, we'd gather whatever food would work for a meal and feed the seven children together. We'd talk about everything. We've relied on each other through cross-country moves, tornadoes, grief, job losses, trauma, and more. I can truly say, *I'm so delighted she asked.*

Practicing community means asking. That vulnerability builds deep connections. This is true in all areas of your life: giving a ride to the airport, covering a meeting, picking up a kiddo, or grabbing a cup of coffee. Specifically, as a leader, when you ask for help, your team has the opportunity to develop new skills while you get support.

You're not a burden. You are a human who needs interdependent relationships. Ask. People will be delighted.

Let's Do It Together

When I was a kid, I often hung out at Emily's house. Her mom, Gayle, was a force of both fun and work. She never worked alone. If there was laundry, we all folded it. Grocery errand? Everyone, grab a bag. Yard work? Gloves all around. And I loved it. The conversations, the jokes, the advice—I learned so much while folding someone else's tighty-whities.

As a practice of community, consider what you can do with others. Run errands together. Work in the same conference room. Take a lunch break together rather than eating at your desk alone—either in person or over FaceTime. In my leadership coaching group, I host "Get 'er Done Time": It's a two-hour block of time on Zoom where we jump on, share what we're working on, go on mute, and work. It's about just doing it together.

Oh, You Too? I Thought It Was Just Me

At the end of a workshop day, I had the team reflect. This team of twelve had only been working together for six months, and their beginning was, let's say, rocky. Conflict and lack of clarity had broken trust and made working together challenging. (Hence why I was there!)

I asked, "What's one thing you know now that you didn't know this morning?"

One woman, labeled as "difficult" by some, stood and shared some self-discoveries. And then she turned to another team member and recounted a story from earlier in the day. With a shaky breath, she said, "I really thought I was the only one who struggled with that. I've felt like such an outsider on the team. But you sharing that story helps me believe I can be a part of this team."

Fight perfectionism with regular conversations about your struggles. You need the village that says, *Oh no, you're not the village idiot for feeling that way*.

Trust the Process

One day, the fifteen-pound weights didn't feel heavy anymore. I lifted them with straight arms in a lateral raise, all the way up to my shoulders. A few workouts of only lateral raises didn't create that strength. I had consistently done a mix of exercises for months. It wasn't an efficient process, and I could have been doing 126 other things that felt more productive than investing time at the gym. Building a functional, strong body takes time that never feels productive, yet produces more than I expect.

Community is the same. Our faster-is-better, judge-you-by-your-résumé world doesn't value the time community takes. But you need it. Find a networking group; create a mastermind; show up regularly at the same café to work; send the text message. Organizing schedules may take black-belt-level calendar-ninja skills, but it's worth it to build support.

Broken Leg or Broken Soul: Know Which One to Protect

Tuesday, July 23, 1996: The Magnificent Seven were chasing Russia, determined to be the first USA Women's Gymnastics team to bring home Olympic gold.

Eighteen-year-old Kerri Strug stood at the end of the runway to vault, legs wrapped in ACE bandages. She sprinted down the runway into a roundoff onto the springboard, launching herself into a back handspring onto the vault. After a somersault and two twists through the air, Strug landed on her heels and fell back on the mat.

In severe pain, Strug told her coach, the legendary Béla Károlyi, "I can't feel my leg."

"Shake it out. Shake it out," Károlyi told her. "Give me one last good vault."

"Do I have to do this again?" Strug pleaded.

"You can do it. You can do it," Károlyi cheered.

She tried again, "Do we need this?"—asking about the points needed to win gold. Károlyi answered: "Yes."

"I don't know yet." Strug paused. "I will do it. I will, I will."[21]

She raced down the same runway, completing the same sequence, except this time she stuck the landing on one foot—before collapsing to the floor. She scored 9.712. Team USA had the gold. During the medal ceremony, Károlyi carried Strug, with a temporary cast, to the podium. She numbly raised her arm to wave at the roaring stadium.

In 2016, Strug said, "I think people want me to say there was a special, magical moment during the vault . . . It might be disappointing to hear, but there wasn't." She just had to do another rep. "When

I landed, I didn't think I'd done anything special. I was supposed to land the vault. Anything else would have been unacceptable."[22]

When official scores posted days later, they revealed that the United States would have taken the gold by 0.309 points without Strug's final vault. But the injury meant Kerri Strug would never compete again.[23]

On another July Tuesday, twenty-five years later at another Olympics, Simone Biles, the most decorated gymnast in history, prepared to vault. The twenty-four-year-old was determined to lead her team, but in training she'd struggled with "janky gymnastics."[24] Biles had the twisties—a dangerous and disorienting experience of losing spatial awareness and the mind-body connection midair. Biles couldn't tell the difference between the ceiling and the mat or correct her body position. A life-threatening landing had become a real possibility. Around the gym, the other competitors noticed too.

Biles ran through her one chance to warm up a vault before the competition. Her teammates' concerns escalated, "Are you OK?" Biles, trying to mind-over-matter the whole situation, shut them down. She chalked up her hands, mind racing with options. She stepped to the runway, completely undecided about what she was going to do when her palms hit the table.

She bit her lip, lifted her arms in the salute, and rocketed down the runway. Biles completed the handspring onto the springboard, and her palms hit the table. Instead of a tight body expertly twisting through the air, her brain opened up to nothing. She loosely rotated, having no idea where she was above the mat. She landed on two feet, listing to her left, and immediately took a giant leap forward. The announcers gasped, and crowd was silent.

"Oh, America hates me. The world is going to hate me. I can see what they're saying on Twitter" were the first thoughts Biles had when she landed.[25] The message for decades had been *Gold or don't come back.* But Biles knew she'd scraped by without an injury, and the twisties don't resolve overnight. She walked off the mat to her coach and said, "I'm done. I'm not doing any more. I survived that, but I don't know if I can survive much else."

"Are you sure?" Cécile Canqueteau-Landi, Biles's coach, asked.

"Yes." Resolute, Biles turned to Jordan Chiles, the vault alternate, "Gear up. You're in."[26]

Biles faced vitriol for her decision, including constant comparisons to Strug. She was devastated, knowing her team had lost a competing leader. But she also knew that caring for herself by withdrawing was best for the team.

If an injury pulled her during competition, Team USA couldn't substitute another gymnast. Biles's decision to protect herself also allowed the team to compete with a full roster. Though the team lost the gold for the first time in a global competition since 2010, with Biles cheering and leading from the bench, they ultimately salvaged a silver medal by two points over Great Britain.[27]

After withdrawing from the Tokyo Olympics to protect her body, her mind, and her team, Biles returned to the world stage in 2023. She won her eighth national all-around title and qualified for her third Olympics in Paris 2024, where she earned four more medals.[28] By slowing down to care for herself, she could continue a successful career and lead a new conversation about the impact of mental health on performance.

For decades, Strug's career-ending vault was replayed as the ultimate example of courage. The machinery of medals and money labeled competing through pain as "strength," praising the performance and ignoring the price. The reality was that Strug was trapped in a system that required her to sacrifice her body for a scoreboard that made other people money.

Biles shattered the lie that sacrificing your life is the cost of success. Though some scoffed and others applauded, she protected herself over being useful to the system that feeds loneliness, burnout, and hustling for your worth. She saved her team, her long-term performance, and quite possibly her life. Even if she hadn't come back to win, Biles embodied the freedom of recognizing the limits of your humanity. That's the strength required to cultivate joy.

You can't lead well—or for long—if you drain your reservoir to get results. Your reservoir holds the gifts you give world. But if you don't protect it, if you neglect it, if you deplete it, what is left of you? My friend Jeanne Hartfield, a speaker and spiritual mentor, calls this a "reservoir mindset." Resilient joy grows with regular practices that fill you. Then the world gets the overflow, not the last muddy drops.

It's easy to twist this into *I fill up so I can give, and that makes me worthy*. You don't need to do anything to earn joy. **Fill your reservoir because you are already worthy of joy.**

The Gist

Practices fill up your internal reservoir. These practices are how you lead yourself into joy. Don't get overwhelmed by doing everything. Start small and practice.

You can't outsource your joy.

—Jenn Whitmer

Connection

Which practice—stillness, solitude, or silence—do you need based on your Enneagram group? Find five minutes in the next forty-eight hours to practice it.

Ask yourself the question from your Enneagram type. For example, if you're a Five, spend three minutes in silence considering the question, "Who am I if I do not know?"

· ·

Curiosity

What do you need most right now: space, safety, or support?

Which practices from the chapter feel unattainable? Use SNAP to examine your story around that practice.

· ·

Joy

Where are you sacrificing self-care for your work?

Of the practices in this chapter, choose one that feels both doable and a little bit challenging. How can you try it at least once in the next week?

Joy doesn't grow in scattered steps. It rises from a steady structure.

Three-Layer Biscuits

Steady Structures That Sustain Joy

> You don't suddenly become a person who keeps their word. That kind of person grows out of a lot of corresponding actions, a long history of keeping commitments . . . They make the habit bonfire bigger and bigger.
>
> **—Ryan Holiday**

When I first met Michael's Uncle Mark, he hit me with a pop quiz. Mark, in overalls with a walrus mustache, pulled me aside and motioned toward the oval dining room table.

"Now, when I'm hiring a cook for the rig . . . " he began in his Southern drawl. Mark ran an oil rig, essentially a floating city in the middle of the Gulf of Mexico with hundreds of laborers needing three hearty meals a day.

". . . I put in front of 'em a bag of flour, a can of baking powder, a block of butter, and a jug of milk. And I ask, 'What are you gonna make?'"

And then . . . silence.

Not great with awkward silence, I blurted, "Well, you need salt. But with all that, I'd make biscuits."

Mark threw his head back, slapped his knee, and shook my hand. "You've passed, darlin'."

Pleasantly confused, I said, "Well, great? I guess?"

Still chuckling, he nodded. "Lots of people come with the right knowledge, even the right ingredients. But staring at the ingredients ain't gonna get hot biscuits to a canteen table full of 220 hungry men at 5:30 a.m."

Mark said, "You gotta know how to put them together systematically, over and over again, in all kinds of conditions to get the job done."

At seventeen, I didn't realize that Mark's wisdom holds far beyond the biscuit quiz.

Cultivating intense happiness as a leader requires more than collecting the right ingredients—the self-awareness, the skills, and the best practices. If you don't integrate them, *reliably* and *consistently*, you'll never get biscuits on the table when the weight of life tries to pull you under.

The waves of circumstance will *wipe. you. out*. People will fail you and take your breath away. One practice may give you a breath, but the tide will pull you under again. You need more than ingredients to run the kitchen when the rig shakes.

Joy doesn't grow in scattered steps. It rises from a steady structure.

Three Layers That Hold Up

"You're doomed! You're never going to top that."

Everywhere the *New York Times* bestselling author Elizabeth Gilbert went, people said this to her. All the Debbie Downers chirped that she'd never beat the success of *Eat, Pray, Love*.

In a TED Talk, Gilbert quips that no one ever warns chemical engineers like her dad that they'll end up depressed alcoholics, exhausted, anxious, and in an early grave. She says that reputation is reserved for creative workers, and we've accepted as a culture that artistic work requires suffering.

Based on all the data, we've accepted suffering as normal for leaders too. We've internalized the idea that work is toil and just be glad you've got a job. We've bought the lie that if you work hard and hustle, when you get to a certain level, then you'll have ease and joy. But then you're devastated when what got you to that level doesn't work anymore and isn't sustainable.

Rubbing her hands together, Gilbert asked the audience the same question I have for you: "Are you guys all cool with that idea?"

I'm not. It's destroying us. Gilbert isn't either. She said, "I think it's odious . . . dangerous. And I don't want to see it perpetuated into the next century. I think it's better if we . . . live. I would prefer to keep doing this work that I love."[1]

I want that for you—to do the work you love through all the ups and downs, without sacrificing yourself to the exhaustion and anxiety demanded by productivity and profit idols.

You can cultivate joy and reject the fallacy that pervasive, crushing anxiety is the cost of success. Later in the talk, Gilbert shared her stubborn determination to cling to a structure as the way to keep doing the work she loves. Do you want to keep doing the work you love and protect your joy when things are what they are? Then you need steady structures that put practices into automatic, repeatable patterns. You need to establish structures unique to your values and personality, flexible enough to shift with new seasons and strong enough to sustain you when the sea of life is rough.

You live *one* life, and the waves at the conference room table will impact you at the supper table. You have different spaces and roles and relationships that make up your life, but they are not separate. As you build steady structures, the integration must consider the totality of your one, continuous, whole life.

Steady structures have three layers: systems to free you, rhythms to steady you, and rituals to ground you.

Systems: The Gears That Keep You Moving

"Why do you people keep sending me the same emails?" I felt this in my soul when LaShonda Brown said this on the *Joyosity* podcast.

Brown, a tech educator and educational video producer, loves her twenty-hour workweek. I mean who wouldn't, right? But she didn't get there overnight. Frustrated by getting the same emails with the same questions, Brown decided to do something different. Rather than go back and forth explaining instructions and answering all the follow-up questions over email, she made a video. And the first generation of Bootstrap Biz Advice began.

"I mean it's hours back and forth in email or even Slack—when a two-minute video sharing your screen is faster and more effective," Brown said.

"How do we know when it's time to use a system? What does that look like in real life?" I asked Brown on the podcast. She didn't actually crack her knuckles and rub her hands together, but she was *ready* with the answer.

"When you are repeating yourself. And you're answering the same question over and over—that should have been a system," Brown declared.[2]

Systems keep you from reinventing the wheel. For our purposes, a *system* isn't the inner workings of your computer or the tech tool you use. Diana Wei Fang, CEO and a systems architect, calls a system "anything that interconnects to best serve you."[3] Ever the adder-onner, I expand on Diana's definition: A system is anything repeatable and interconnected that enables your favorite self to do your best work.

Basically, a system is *When I do xyz, I do it this way*.

What Systems Do for You

Don't you hate chasing down that one file or form? How much frustration does that cause you? Creating systems prevents the extra hunting and gathering. Jenny Blake, *New York Times* bestselling author and business strategist, says, "Stress is a systems problem."[4]

Systems aren't impersonal machines. They're a living process, like your circulatory system delivering the oxygen your cells need at the moment. Steady systems integrate your values into the details of your day.

Blake calls this "systemize the spirit." She has a value of generosity that she wanted to express in her business through gifts, but it wasn't happening. She knew she was the bottleneck that prevented the team from getting gifts into clients' hands. So, they created a new Gifting Database and six-step system: Make the card with the idea, get missing info like addresses, choose a gift and write a message based on their internal spending tiers, place the order, track and confirm once the gift has arrived, and archive the task. All the team members can see the process, they can order similar gifts in batches, and no clients are forgotten.[5]

Harvard Business Review studied how CEOs spent their time and found that reliable systems "keep the CEO from continually having to override decisions."[6] Systems reduce the sheer number of decisions in your life you make because you "decide once," a key principle of Kendra Adachi, the Lazy Genius.[7]

"I'm trying to decide which outfit to wear" might be the most common sentence my friend Camille and I say to each other. She leads a large area in an international nonprofit and attends what feels like 101 weddings and 15 galas every year. I speak at different organizations around the country and "business casual" isn't universal. To reduce the number of outfit decisions, we both choose a seasonal airport outfit. We decide once: "This is the outfit I'm wearing for this season if I'm getting on a plane," from the earrings down to the shoes (no metal on the boots because even in TSA PreCheck, metal detectors are finicky). Systems like this let you decide once.

Systems save you time, reduce decision fatigue, and keep your best work moving automatically.

Why and a Whiteboard

When you start crafting a steady system, for the love of all that's holy, do *not* start with a tech tool. A system is *integrated*, so before you decide on the tool, you have to know why you need the system and what you want it to do.

Here are a few questions to ask yourself as you're building a system (you can find more on the process in the *Playbook*):

- What decisions/activities/questions repeat?
- Where do my appointments and time commitments live?
- How do I track to-dos, tasks, and deliverables?
- Who needs to know, and how do I share information?
- Where, who, or what is the bottleneck?

With the answers, get the system out of your head and documented in one place before you choose any tools, technology, or automations.

Don't open a device and start tapping away. Go to a whiteboard or grab some Post-its. When you're designing the system, you need to move individual stages around. Analog works better than digital here. The *ahas* come as you're physically moving notes, making connections, and clarifying the steps that get you to the goal.

I have a corporate client that quadrupled in size and became a hybrid workforce in the span of eighteen months. As the company grew from twelve team members and few clients to nearly fifty team members and multiple clients, the easy communication in the group quickly disappeared, replaced by conflict and confusion.

Red flag! New system needed.

They chose a simple system to begin with. For internal communication: Slack. External communication: email. Collaboration, brainstorming, kickoffs, or decision-making: synchronous meetings together, either on Zoom, over a phone call, or in person. Updates, status checks, information sharing: asynchronous video recording, a Slack poll, or an interactive checklist.

This simple communications system significantly reduced the confusion in their communications. Caitlyn, the COO said, "It was like the gunk was cleaned out of the gutter, and everything started to flow."

As you consider systems, the **goal is always to serve the people**. Not the other way around.

Tiny Time-Saving Systems

I'm not a lover of restrictive and rigid systems; however, systems put you in a smooth track, like a pinball finding the chute that drops straight into the jackpot. That's the feeling you're going for.

Sometimes, a system is as simple as a text automation. We have 5,162 email addresses in our family—school, job, personal, iCloud accounts . . . you name it. I got fed up with typos, going to my contacts app, or worse, searching for an old email to copy an address, so I made automatic text substitutions for email addresses. When I type "jcc," my work email address magically appears. Type "mle," Michael's shows up.

My friend Kwame Christian (we met him in chapter eight), is an attorney, speaker, author, and runs three companies. He and his wife, a family practice physician, have two young sons. The dude is busy. If you send Kwame an email, you immediately get an autoreply that tells you he's not in his inbox regularly and a list of whom to contact for what purpose. This system honors his value of good communication without bogging him down in responding to every email, or losing business.

Our friends Jeff, an SVP and general counsel for a global financial institution, and his wife, Christina, a freelance technical writer and editor for the aviation industry, own a lake house they generously share with friends. They have a Google Doc with all the important details for the house, including trash, sheets, locking up, great restaurants in the tiny town, and where to park so you're not stuck at the bottom of the steep driveway.* No starting over, no scramble—the system works for every guest.

A system is anything repeatable and interconnected that enables your favorite self to do your best work. Start small and always design steady systems for your joy.

Rhythms: The Dance of Your Time

"Why are we clapping this again?" Peter complained. "We can read the notes. Let's just sing it."

Dr. Arnold Epley, with exacting ears and mysterious whims, led the Chamber Singers: six women, six men—all nearly professional musicians. Or so we thought. We were indeed superb musicians and sight readers. But as first-year undergrads, the difficulty level had sky-

---

* Ask me why they added that one. Short answer: me.

rocketed. Rehearsing this piece, we were disjointed, off beat, and far from harmony and flow.

Dr. Epley, a self-proclaimed cranky old fart, had patience for inexperience but exactly zero for entitlement. Dr. Epley ran his long fingers through his floppy, salt-and-caramel hair and sighed like a man mourning the death of harmony itself.

"Mr. Meenington," he began, voice deep and heavy, as he lowered himself onto his stool. "While you may believe you can just 'sing it,' the cacophony assaulting my ears is evidence to the contrary. Let me enlighten you *why* we're clapping the rhythms."

Dr. Epley began his weary tirade by reminding us how harmony works. "And you, collectively, aren't in harmony. It doesn't matter that half of you have perfect pitch," as he swept his eyes around the room. (For the record, I wasn't in that half.)

"Robert Shaw always said, 'The right note at the wrong time is the wrong note,'" Dr. Epley made eye contact with each of us. "Let me say it again: The *right* note. At the *wrong* time. IS the *wrong* note."

Dr. Epley's wisdom changed the way I approached music and thought about my time in general.

Rhythm *and* rhythms matter.

In music, the beat is the steady pulse of the music. Rhythm is the arrangement of patterns of sounds and silences over the beat. The downbeat brings beat and rhythm together. It's the accented beat, a reliable anchor in the flow where it's easy to regroup. In dance club music, you'd call it the beat drop.

In the structure of your life, rhythms are the way you spend your time *over* time. The pattern of practices you put together around downbeats gives structure to your life and days. And just like in music, rhythms have movement and breath in them. Things can get a little shaky, and you may wobble. But then you find the downbeat, and you're solid again.

Some people prefer *routines* to rhythms. That feels too restrictive for the complexity and variability of life. So we've got rhythms.

A rhythm is the sequence of actions or pauses that you repeat regularly. This can be the rhythms of your day, your week, your month, or even your year.*

Rhythms breathe and bend. They aren't inflexible and rigid, etched in stone for all of time. Nor are they fragile habits you carelessly discard when the riptide takes hold. Rhythms provide the groove and keep you in alignment.

Rhythms (and next, *rituals*) are more embodied than a system. A system can be delegated, outsourced, or automated. Rhythms require you to show up for yourself and hit the downbeats.

Just like in practices and systems, we can't go through every possible option in this book. So here are a few guiding questions to help you think about rhythms in your one, continuous, whole life:

- What practices do you want to make habits and downbeats in your life? Daily, weekly, monthly, annually?
    - Daily meditation, reading, or walk? Weekly mentor phone call? Monthly planning time? Quarterly silent retreat? Annual fishing adventure?
- What tasks, practices, or activities do you want to make time for? (Go back to your Joyosity Explorer Map and what brings you space, safety, and support.)

---

* Clap, clap, clap, clap. Go ahead. Do it out loud.

- Naps, networking, book club, car detailing? Pickleball league, volunteer group, religious services, watercolor class?
- What are your regular responsibilities? What are the typical commitments that you need to fulfill?
  - Daily carpool pickup? Saturday soccer games? Weekly dashboard review? Monthly status meeting?
- Can you negotiate or delegate any of your responsibilities, commitments, or obligations?

Anytime you create a new rhythm, come back to these questions. I try to revisit my rhythms every ninety days. I changed my rhythms to write this book. When my kids were all at home and we had a new sports season or dance schedule every few months, I often needed to adjust the rhythm. My friend Addie is a farmer, so she adjusts her rhythms based on the season. Planting season in the spring with her four kids in softball and baseball requires different rhythms than the summer growing season with no school.

Once you have these answers, you can lean into the right downbeats.

The Downbeats: Design Your Week

You know the last week of December when you don't really know what day it is and you're just full of cheese? And then after a while, you're just ready to get in a groove? That groove you're wanting is the downbeats.

But most of the time, you probably feel more like Steve.

Steve was off-kilter. A senior director of compliance in a fast-paced manufacturing company and responsible for a team of ten, he also had three elementary-aged children, and his wife, Felicia, was a corporate attorney. Every morning, he woke up and dealt with whatever came at him—team questions, kids' needs, all the usual suspects. At work, his team felt overextended, but the system said they "should" be able to handle the work. His calendar was often triple-booked with meeting invites, and recently, he'd missed picking up his youngest daughter.

When I started coaching Steve, I asked him, "What's your typical week like?"

"Uh, busy. Really full. And actually, every week is different," he replied, as if reviewing an invisible calendar. "I don't have a typical week."

"I think that may be part of your problem," I offered. "Your life is running you rather than you running your life."

You may be living that way too. Even if you have rhythms, the dance studio, the school calendar, or the work conference schedule set them for you. And then your weeks simply happen to you, even if you plan them. To create your own downbeats and rhythms, start with the Designed Week.[8] Here's how:

Remember You Write the Rhythm

Remember "Joy by Agency" from chapter nine? You will experience more joy when you use your agency. Before you start sketching the week's rhythm, remember that you're in charge of your life.

Managers, Makers, and Musicians

To set up your weekly rhythm, you need to choose if you are a Manager, a Maker, or a Musician.

Managers divide their days in short blocks of time, like an Outlook calendar, usually thirty minutes or an hour. They might string together blocks of time, but typically they are moving from one task or meeting to another. Even outside the typical nine-to-five model, Managers think based on the clock.

Managers built the business, project-management, and time-management world. So if you're nodding your head like this makes perfect sense and everyone does it this way, you might be living in a Manager's schedule world, and you're a Manager-girl.

Makers work best in at least half-days. The work of a maker involves creating. Makers don't always consider themselves creators, but their work takes focus, wrestling ideas into an output, and a type of flow (more on that in chapter thirteen). The work takes time to settle into. And they often spend a lot of time thinking, staring out the window, reading, writing something down, and crossing it out. That 2:30 p.m. meeting ruins the flow.

Paul Graham, Y Combinator cofounder and coder, puts it like this:

"I find one meeting can sometimes affect a whole day. A meeting commonly blows at least half a day, by breaking up a morning or afternoon. But . . . there's a cascading effect. If I know the afternoon is going to be broken up, I'm slightly less likely to start something ambitious in the morning."[9]

If you feel a little seen reading this, you might work best as a Maker.

Musicians have full days of similar activities or a type of work. There are three types of days: onstage days, backstage days, and offstage days. *Onstage* days include doing the work that is your best work: creating, preparing, practicing, and performing. *Backstage* days are the tasks and meetings required to do the best work: client meetings, expense reports, email processing, calendar checks, laundry, and the like. *Offstage* days are rest days: days that you don't actively engage in work. It doesn't mean you just veg on the couch with the remote (although it can), but it means you are not working.

Emily P. Freeman has used *theme days* to group similar types of work in one day.[10] With one of my coaching clients, we grouped her days as a musician by client: Rather than days dedicated to a type of work, days of work were dedicated to a specific client. You don't need to be a performer to be a Musician in the way you approach your Designed Week. But if you're longing for an entire workday to focus on doing one type of work, well, you may be more of a Musician.

If you're thinking, *I want to be a Musician, but I live in a Manger's world*, you're not alone. Many leaders face this challenge. Everything reinforces the Manager's approach, from the time-management industry to every calendar system. The other challenge ties back to the first principle: You may not have full control of your schedule, but you still get to design how you want to spend your time. Remember, you write the rhythm.

Design "As If"

Imagine you have the final say over every bit of your time. (Well, you do, but we don't live like that.) Just like designing systems, you're starting with pencil, paper, and a grid of your week.*

---
* See the Designed Week in the Lounge.

As Steve worked through this, he realized he wanted to work more like a Maker. His role focused on strategy, yet he rarely had more than a thirty-minute block to think. Also, he wanted more connection with his wife besides kid school drop-offs and the birthday dinner at Aunt Julie's.

He created a Designed Week. On Sunday nights, Steve and Felicia had "calendar committee" meetings to review the week's responsibilities and exceptions. After the kids were in bed, they'd reconnect in the kitchen or on a short walk—no TV, just a few minutes of real conversation. The den was off-limits because flopping on the couch meant flipping on a show and zoning out.

At work, Steve blocked off three half-days: Monday and Wednesday mornings, and Friday afternoons. He reserved these for strategy, industry reading, and deep focus—no meetings allowed. The rest of the week had themed blocks: admin, one-on-ones, site visits, and status updates.

He told his team about the experiment, explaining the boundaries and why they mattered. When meeting invites rolled in, he asked for purpose, agenda, and if they truly needed his presence. Often, the answer was no. As Steve climbed out of the weeds, his strategy sharpened, and his team stepped up. They started carving out their own focus blocks, and the overwhelm began to lift for everyone.

After a few months, we were setting goals for the next ninety days. I asked Steve again, "What's your typical week like?"

"Currently, I've got my half-days flowing well at the office. But it's May, which means I need to set a new rhythm with the kids' summer schedules. Felicia and I decided we'd both take PTO next week to look at the summer together and then go to our daughter's award ceremony."

The difference from "I don't really have a typical week," to this *I'm conducting this show*—well, I had to sit on my hands to not clap! I pointed out this evolution to Steve.

"I forgot how chaotic it felt before. I don't have less to do. I just feel like I'm the one deciding how I want to do the work before the work comes to me."

That's the feeling of a rhythm with clear downbeats. Rhythms help you anticipate the flows of life and sustain you when life rains on your parade . . . or movie set.

Dealing with the Rain

People say, "The weather just always works for Nolan." Except Christopher Nolan, the director of award-winning films like *The Dark Knight*, *Dunkirk*, and *Oppenheimer*, completely disagrees. Early in his career, Nolan decided he wasn't going to fall into the trap of chaos in the name of creativity. Through process and rhythms, he consistently comes in under budget on his films.

On set, he establishes the framework and the rhythm of shoots. Here's where the weather comes in. He says, "I'm very unlucky with the weather. But I made a decision early on that whatever the weather is, until it's unsafe, I will shoot." His daily rhythm is to review the storyboards with the crew and take the weather as it comes, "whether it's pouring rain or the sun is out. And beautiful things can come from that."[11]

Beautiful things come when you write your rhythms, the way you spend your time *over* time. Rhythms steady you in the rains and waves of life, even if you wobble a bit.

Rituals: The Door Between

The door opens with a click as Mr. Rogers steps inside, singing, "It's a beautiful day in the neighborhood, a beautiful day for a neighbor." He slides off his sport coat, smiles, and continues to sing as he opens the closet, hangs up his coat, and retrieves his knit cardigan. He sits on the bench unlacing his dress shoes and trading them for sneakers. With the final strain, "Please won't you be my neighbor?" Mr. Rogers has crossed the threshold from the outside world of work into the domain of home.

Although you have one whole, integrated life, you do move among many spaces, roles, and groups in that one life. If you're lurching from one to the next, you'll feel like that pinball ricocheting from bumper to bumper instead of gliding over the threshold, fully present for the next moment.

Rituals are a sequence of activities that mark the transition from one activity, posture, or experience to another.

Rituals should be included in your rhythms, but they help you mentally, emotionally, and physically move smoothly through phases of your day and your life. They are tiny doorways that sustain your joy as you move through them.

Rituals are unique to *you*. I'll give you a few that every leader needs to sustain joy. First, let's start with the right questions you need to create rituals:

- What are the different roles you play during the day?

- How much time and what practices do you need to process feelings and events of the day?
- What types of energy shifts do you need?
- What practices do you need to transition well?

Again, rituals change as life happens. When our four kids were young, both Michael and I had schedule-driven, paying jobs with obligations outside the nine-to-five hours. We also had time-intensive volunteer leadership roles in our church. There was no way—between slopping oatmeal in breakfast bowls, supervising lunch-box and school-bag packing, getting mascara brushed on my lashes, and checking I had on shoes and not slippers—I could have a ninety-minute morning ritual. Becoming a unicorn wrangler would have been more realistic.

Rituals should feel joy-giving, even if you resist them some days. They need to fit into your real life, not a fantasy life. When my mornings meant searching for missing tap shoes while asking Michael, "What do you mean you have to fly to Germany tonight to introduce two people?" my rituals focused on tiny habits.[*] Often taking five minutes or less, rituals don't need to be long, formal, or complicated—they just need to bring ease and joy to the transitions.

Start at the End

When the sunset hovers over the horizon, Jewish and Islamic traditions welcome the new day. That messes with a mind steeped in Western concepts of time. But when it comes to rituals, it's the wisest perspective.

---

[*] Yes, that really happened one day. Also true: "I have to fly to DC right now so I can help a delegation of Vietnamese catfish farmers speak before Congress." WILD.

Regardless of whether you live for the crack of dawn or would like the day to begin around 10:45 a.m., your perfect morning ritual means nothing if you can't get your poop in a group the night before.

Shut-Down Rituals

In the late '90s, I was a new wife, Mary Kay team leader, youth group leader, and teacher, none of which had a clear starting or stopping point. I felt like my desk: scattered with sticky notes of to-do lists breeding overnight. Then, one Monday-night meeting, my Mary Kay national sales director changed my life.

In her Bordeaux-colored sales director suit, Renee said to fifty eager consultants, "At night, you're the boss. In the morning, you're the employee." At twenty-three, my mind was blown. Decades later, Renee's voice still echoes in my work shut-down ritual.

The line between work and home can become a dot to you, especially if you commute to and from the kitchen table. The shut-down ritual closes the workday and sets you up for success the next day. Here's the basic outline:

1. **Review and adjust your task list from the day.** Anything you didn't finish, decide what happens with it. Does it move to the next day, another day, or do you delegate it?
2. **Record a win.** Write it down! Small or big, write down the win and how you feel.
3. **Review your schedule for tomorrow.** I have multiple digital calendars. But each evening, I write down the next day's schedule in my planner so I know the flow of the day. If you don't have a consistent start time every day, this helps determine what time your work begins (and when you need to wake up).

4. **Set your top three for the next day.** Renee also said you can't do more than three big things in a day. Write down your three must-do tasks for the next day, and rank your number-one task, number two, and number three. (Based on the schedule, some days I can accomplish only one task.) Then add the rest you want to get to if you can.

5. **Gather the junk.** Close the clutter. If you're like me, at the end of the day you've got two coffee mugs, a water bottle, and possibly a plate, along with Post-it notes, open books, and papers around the desk. It's likely you have 116 tabs, five apps, and three PDFs open as well. Start by closing the tabs (I know. Breathe.) and saving files. If you're terrified you'll lose the tab, open a Google Doc and copy/paste the links. Not only will your computer work faster, you'll retain the information better.[12] Then take eighty seconds to toss the trash, bookmark the book, and gather the dishes to take to the kitchen.

6. **Close the door.** At a client's open-concept office, Lori's cubicle had a handwritten open/closed sign on it. When she left for the day, she flipped it to "closed." She'd also switch it to "closed" during the day when she needed to focus. If you have a door for your work area, close it. Especially if you work from home, close the door—literally or figuratively. Put away the trappings of work so you can move to your home space, even if it's the same table.

The work shut-down ritual reduces anxiety, promotes better sleep, and allows you to transition smoothly, joyfully, and fully present into a different area of your life.[13]

Evening Rituals

As a kid, I spent a lot of time with my grandparents and cousins on Lake Lotawana. Grandma cleaned the kitchen after supper and turned off all the lights except the one over the stove. The signal was clear: The day is done.

Evening rituals serve two purposes: They prepare you for the next day and signal to your body, heart, and mind the day is done.* And I'm telling you, with full-throated enthusiasm, this ritual is the secret sauce to better sleep and peaceful mornings.[14]

When you create your evening ritual, ideally, you'll include these components. (More details in the *Playbook*.)

1. **Put your house and phone to bed.** Take five to ten minutes to close the blinds, set the morning coffee items out, gather up a few stray items, and put your phone on the charger (see boundaries back in chapter eleven).
    - 1a. If you have kids, do a check-in about the morning (lunch, permission slips, etc.). My kids would roll their eyes, but my mantra was "I don't work for you in the morning." It helps them prepare and unwind and makes space for connection too.
2. **Pick your clothes and pack your bags.** Self-explanatory, but easy to skip. If you plan to wear something, look at it. The worst is waking up in the morning to discover your power outfit is too snug or has a tear on the collar. (If it's been living on "the chair" for the last week, just give it a sniff.) Same goes for your bags: Your briefcase, tote, lunch box, wa-

---

* When I was a young mom, I found The FlyLady. Her signal that the day was finished? Shine the sink.

ter bottles, gym bag . . . pack it up. All of this alleviates the strain on your working memory; it's already done.

3. **Care for your body.** Early in the pandemic, Austin Channing Brown went all-in on her skin care routine. The speaker, *New York Times* bestselling author, and new mom, expressed how hard self-care is on Brené Brown's podcast, *Unlocking Us*. Austin told Brené, "I roll that jade over my face. I have eleven steps . . . Brené, I'm in it." But those ten minutes let her connect with her body and glide into rest.[15] Brush your teeth, stretch, wash your face, take your vitamins, put on cozy pajamas. Do something that cares for your body and prepares you for rest.

4. **Care for your heart and mind.** Wordle makes me happy, and it's my little unwind. One client responds to a one-word journal prompt. My friend Maya uses a meditation app. Sara goes through a nightly liturgy. Skip the news and scrolling TikTok. Choose something that calms and replenishes your heart and mind.

Sometimes at the end of the day, you're weary to the bone, and these rituals feel like one more thing. Try viewing rituals as pouring in and restoring your energy. If you can't do it all one night, don't. Ask yourself, "What do I need most right now?"

Establish these end-of-the-day rituals over time. As you do, you'll find habit overtakes your weariness. Mornings may not be perfectly smooth, but you're ready to absorb the bumps.

Open the Day

Just like the end of the day says it's time to stop, opening the day signals it's time to start moving. Some people love long morning rituals that feel like a slow revolving door to ease them into the day. Others prefer an automatic sliding door that they quickly move through. You get to decide. Following the same principles, opening rituals mirror closing rituals.

Morning Rituals

Morning rituals include the practices you need to shift your energy from sleep and rest to movement and activity. If you've done your closing rituals, you aren't prepping for the day at the same time you're trying to open your eyes. Here are the components of a morning ritual:

1. **Care for your body.** Your body needs to warm up to the day. Eat breakfast, walk the dog, work out, comb your hair, or shower. (Please brush your teeth.) Tell your body: We're moving on up.

2. **Care for your heart and mind.** The end of the day is an emptying and releasing. The opening of the day is filling up and claiming. My friend Zack taps shuffle on a playlist of music with positive, spiritual messages about himself and the world. My client Simone cares for her plants. Eliza, COO of a large nonprofit, reads five pages of a book. Choose a practice from chapter eleven or from the ones in the *Playbook*. You're filling up your reservoir with what you want to pour out the rest of the day.

3. **Open the house.** Open the blinds, turn on lights, feed the gerbil. Prepare your space for activity. If you're ready, get

your phone. Do *not* jump into email, work tasks, or mindlessly scrolling social media! (Boundaries. Chapter eleven.)

4. **Greet your people.** If you live alone, send a quick text or voice message to friends or family. If you live with others, a simple sleepy smile and soft *good morning* are enough. Morning greetings build connection.

Morning rituals are a soft, kind opening to the day. And some mornings, it's still a mess. Morning rituals can be a do-over at any time. If the morning goes badly, restart. Even if you don't have time for all the steps, call a mulligan and find a way to pour into your body, heart, and mind.

Start-Up Rituals

Karena checked her email in the car every day. By the time her twenty-minute commute to the office finished, she'd be through her inbox.[*] In a coaching session, I asked her my favorite question: "How's that working for you?"

"Well, I'm caught up. I know what's happening," Karena said, but her eyes shifted.

"How do you *feel* when you get to work?" I asked.

Karena considered. "Well honestly, I feel frenzied. Like I'm behind."

"Are you actually caught up? Or just full of information and other people's needs?"

Karena went from zero to whack-a-mole, mistaking reactivity for efficiency. The start-up ritual establishes you as the leader of your workday. If you did your shut-down ritual, you're starting with a clear

---

[*] Yes, this is unsafe. Please do not treat this as a how-to guide. It's a confession of a bad habit, not a recommendation. If you're tempted, consider this your official "don't."

vision. This ritual carries you from home to work, preparing your space and mind.

1. **Set the stage.** If you need multiple beverages (of course you do), get them. What light do you need? Do you have a fan or heater you flip on? Prepare your space for work.
2. **Big loud purpose.** At a conference, speaker and author Judi Holler pulled index cards from her hot pink blazer and read her dreams to us. Inspired, I made my own "Judi Holler" cards with handwritten dreams and intentions. I read the cards aloud while standing or walking in my office. Besides integrating multiple modalities—hearing, seeing, moving—I believe your voice holds power. Saying good things about yourself and your work changes your mindset and your physical being. In Dr. Masaru Emoto's famous water and sound studies, positive words created more aesthetic ice crystal formations, versus negative words that created chaotic patterns.[16] Positive, out-loud words change the energy. Remind yourself of your purpose, values, and what connects you to joy in your work.
3. **Review your top tasks and appointments.** Revisit the big three from the boss (you) and decide *when* you're doing them. Review your written schedule and refresh your electronic calendar (no email yet) to see if anything has changed.

Some mornings, I'm swallowing my last bite of cottage cheese as I switch on lamps forty-two seconds before a Zoom call begins. Days like that happen, and they're rarely as joyful and productive as I want. You can always do a start-up ritual reset, just like with the morning ritual.

Three-Layer Biscuits

Use the same ritual questions to stay present during other transitions. Some are calendar-based—weekly, quarterly, and annual rituals. Other rituals mark shifts in season or stage—fall to winter, summer break to school, vacation to regular life, or rites of passage.

It's tempting to feel the shamey *shoulds* right now and quit or try to *do. it. all.* This is a menu, not step-by-step IKEA instructions. Start with what you're drawn to. If you want to do it the "right way" (I see you, Enneagram One), there is no right way. Stuck in option overload? Start with the work shut-down ritual.

Rituals are a sequence of activities that carry you over the threshold from one activity, posture, or experience to another. You can't sustain joy if the pinball flippers are always knocking you to the next bumper. You will have more joy when you intentionally ease into the next space, leaving behind what you don't need and moving your presence to what's next. Mr. Rogers again shows us how:

"Often when you think you're at the end of something, you're at the beginning of something else," Mr. Rogers says as he sits on the bench to switch his sneakers back to dress shoes.

He returns his cardigan to the closet as he sings, "It's such a good feeling, to know you're alive . . ." With his sport coat back on, he pauses by the door to say, right to you, "There is something of yourself that you leave at every meeting with another person. I'll be back next time. Bye-bye."

Build It Before You Need It

Aisha landed a dream role: vice president of strategy for a 150-person company. The CEO wanted a comprehensive and consistent strategy that also established a healthier culture.

She was so ready. We'd built her systems, rhythms, and rituals, clarified her Enneagram type and values, and strengthened her skills. Her team warmed to the cultural changes, and their productivity and engagement increased. The company's board praised both the strategy and the results.

Then, two unexpected storms rolled in. A major supplier hiked prices, and a significant buyer sold her business to a private equity firm, which promptly cancelled its contract. The CEO panicked, and trying to make the finances look good, he made every short-term cut possible.

The stress mounted. Executive meetings deteriorated from lively discussions to passive-aggressive power plays. Compliance rules changed almost daily. The tracking systems generated conflicting reports from the same contracts and budgets. The CEO abdicated decision-making, and authority became a guessing game. You've seen this movie before: Without steady structures, people revert to bad habits under pressure that dissolve into dysfunction and toxicity.

Aisha clung to her rhythms and rituals to manage the pressure.

"I did *not* want to walk today," she told me in a coaching session. "Well, I wanted to walk away from everything. But not take my regular walk."

"Did you?" I asked.

"Sure," she huffed. "This job was supposed to be amazing, and now I have to take a damn walk every day so I don't puke during meetings." Aisha took a breath, "But while I was on my 'stupid walk for my stupid mental health,' I saw a twisted and splintered tree."

"What's important about the tree?" I asked.

"The tree gets battered by the weather, and it can't move. But I can," she smiled. "I can move. I don't have to fix this toxic place that won't change. I don't have to *stay* here."

Through her steady structures, Aisha realized she was sacrificing her life for a place that wouldn't change and would watch her break without blinking. Months after she left for a new organization, she told me, "My rhythms and rituals kept me alive."

The best time to create steady structures is now. Don't wait until Monday or the first of the month. Take the first small-scale but steady step to design your life for joy.

The Gist

Your joy won't survive without structures. When life hits hard (and it will), it's not talent or willpower that keeps you in the Joy Ratio. The systems, rhythms, and rituals are the steady structures that uphold you when you can barely hold yourself.

> Joy doesn't grow in scattered steps. It rises from a steady structure.
>
> —Jenn Whitmer

Three-Layer Biscuits

Connection

For a few days, jot down the tasks and activities that you repeat. How can you solve one of them with a tiny time-savings system?

Where are you the bottleneck?

· ·

Curiosity

Are you a Manager, a Maker, or a Musician? Is your work culture a Manager culture? Or more of a Maker or Musician culture?

Do you have a work shut-down ritual? If you don't, create one. If you do, is it working for you? Do you need to adjust it?

· ·

Joy

Download your Designed Week grid. Record how you spend your time currently. Mark what feels like joy and toil. (If it feels overwhelming to do your whole day, start with just your workday.)

Look at your time. How much time are you spending in activities that feel like joy? How much time are you spending in activities that feel like toil? And how much time are you in the Messy Middle? Are you in the Joy Ratio of 35-10-55?

All work and no play doesn't make you dull. It makes you dangerous.

The Serious Business of Play

Productivity and Performance Through Play

> Play is the cheat code to business success.
>
> —**Gary Ware,** *Playful Rebellion: Maximize Workplace Success Through the Power of Play*

"I'm done. I can't do this anymore."

May 31, 2010, Novak Djokovic decided to quit tennis at the French Open. At twenty-three, he'd survived war-torn Serbia as a child and exploded onto the world tennis stage in 2003. Even being ranked number three in the world, winning a Grand Slam, and considered a contender to take home the Wimbledon Championship Cup, he wanted to zip up his racket forever.[1]

Joyosity

He broke the news to his coach, Marián Vajda. With Djokovic sobbing uncontrollably on the floor of the room, Vajda just let him cry.[2,3] After a while, Vajda changed the conversation.

"Let's look back. Why did you start? Do you really like holding a racket in your hand?"

Djokovic paused. "I love holding a racket. I still like playing for the sake of playing," he realized.

Vajda dipped his chin, "Well. That's your source."[4]

Djokovic calls that his turning point: "I wasn't feeling the joy." Finding how to just play again was his way back. "After that moment, I felt I was freed."[5]

He still struggled three weeks later at Wimbledon, but then he led Serbia to its first Davis Cup title in December 2010, starting his winning streak. That season collected forty-three straight wins, the Australian Open, the US Open, Wimbledon, and its own Wikipedia page.[6] He finished 2011 as the number-one men's player in the world.

When he reflected on that season, he said, "I started to play freely. I became the kid that I was when I started playing. Before, I was playing to achieve. Now I was playing for joy."[7]

When was the last time you played? Or when was the last time you felt like your work tasks included something that felt energizing and enjoyable?

Uh, I'm an adult. I don't play.

Welp. Shall I nod at you like Vajda, and ask, Maybe that's why you're exhausted and unproductive?

Remember my prison of homework in second grade? I couldn't play until work was finished. This is a huge cultural lie. Play isn't a just a break from work. Play is the vehicle of work. Play, like the rest of this experience section, provides an essential *how* of staying in the Joy Ratio. Stuart Brown, PhD, psychiatrist, clinical researcher, and founder of the National Institute for Play, says it straight: "The opposite of play is not work. The opposite of play is depression."[8]

Play powers productivity and cultivates joy.

Let's create a working definition of play, its benefits for adults, and how to find your unique play style. Then we'll focus on the power of play at work to produce flow and productivity, keeping that 35 percent of the Joy Ratio crystal clear.

Play Is a State, Not a Game

In my first months as a school administrator, we were deep in our first-ever accreditation process—think IRS Form 1040 with every schedule attached. I was the director of assessment and feedback; Dana, my partner in this project, was the director of curriculum and instruction. She loves details like I love brainstorming.

One night, I sat on my blue couch with my laptop while she ran laps at her community center. I read the standards; Dana, with all the institutional knowledge in her head, told me where the evidence lived on the server. We laughed as we brainstormed, I hunted files, and she ran.

Suddenly, Dana gasped, "Oh my gosh!"

"What's wrong?" thinking she'd bit the dust on the track.

"I've been running for an hour and a half."

Dana wasn't a long-distance runner, more like a thirty-minute run/walk girl. That night she unknowingly ran her first 10K. Time had disappeared for both of us.

Accreditation doesn't sound like play, yet our couch-and-10K collab had all the play properties.

The Eight Wonders of the Play State

There is no standard definition of play. It's too confining for something inherently a little wild. A host of play experts—from Stuart Brown, PhD, and Gillian Ferrabee to Gary Ware and Scott Eberle, PhD—suggest characteristics, phases, or properties of play as a state of being, not an activity.[9] Here are eight of those characteristics:

1. **Apparent purposelessness:** Mihaly Csikszentmihalyi,* the original expert on flow, uses the term *autotelic*: The act alone possesses inherent value without needing to serve any other purpose.[10]
2. **Voluntary:** You choose to do it. If you're scared of forced fun, that's not what I'm suggesting.
3. **Inherent attraction:** There is something that makes you go, *Mmmm, interesting*. Even if it's not new, it's attractive, novel, or fun.
4. **Freedom from time:** You feel time bends, either rushing ahead or stretching endlessly. You're suspended in another state where time doesn't exist.
5. **Diminished consciousness of self:** You stop thinking about how you look, how your little toe aches, or the gaze of other people. Your internal critic sits silently in the corner. Gillian Ferrabee, play expert and former director of the Creative Lab at Cirque du Soleil, calls it "electric ease."[11]

---

* Pronounced "chik-sent-mee-*hai*-ee" if you're wondering.

6. **Improvisational potential:** You're not focused on one strict way, so you are open to fresh ideas and combine information from all the arenas of your life.
7. **Continuation desire:** You want a way to keep it going, either editing the experience or finding a way to continue.
8. **Risky:** The stakes stimulate you in some way. There is a positive anticipation paired with low-level danger—physically, emotionally, socially, or cognitively—that trigger all those feel-good brain chemicals.[12]

Scott Eberle, PhD, play expert and social historian, describes play as a cycle of stages. In healthy play, you're eager, then surprised by discovery, which creates a good feeling. Then a new understanding occurs that brings confidence, which produces poise or balance. And then you're ready to begin again.[13]

Where do you see these properties in your life? Not what other people say is a game, but when you're in a state of play?

Play Your Way to Mastery

The principle "play is the work of the child" guided my career in education. This truth, from Dr. Maria Montessori, Italian physician and educator, shaped how I taught, coached, and led learners of all ages. For decades, I experienced firsthand the power of play to produce results. Stacking blocks becomes the foundation of engineering and problem-solving. Pretend play rehearses collaboration and communication. Montessori named the profound process of achieving *mastery*—practicing, experimenting, and refining skills through joyful engagement.

Play is the state where curiosity and joy build skill.

This truth doesn't expire with age. Slipping on work shoes doesn't override your neurobiology: Play is the work that builds mastery. Even as an adult, play is still your most powerful method to explore new possibilities, test ideas, and strengthen your unique skills. When you find how you naturally create, compete, explore, or connect, you harness the same force that powered you in childhood.

This is one reason that a lack of play takes such a toll. You're not just losing a bit of fun—you're denying the process that develops your best abilities, makes you an effective leader, and sustains your capacity to adapt under pressure.

The risks of life without play aren't always obvious. History shows that the consequences can be devastating.

The Serious Business of Play

The Danger When Play Disappears

On August 1, 1966, the absence of play lay at the heart of a tragedy in Austin, Texas, producing a new understanding of why play is vital.

University of Texas students poured out of classrooms into the press of the midday heat. As they crisscrossed the Forty Acres, booming noises and metallic echoes came from around the Main Building. At first, no one connected the sounds to gunshots cracking through the air from the observation deck of the Tower.

That Monday, architectural engineering student Charles Whitman had climbed the twenty-seven-story tower and barricaded the observation deck before indiscriminately killing fifteen people and wounding thirty-one more. After an hour of Whitman's sniper shooting and dodging the bullets from hunting rifles firing from the ground, three officials had made it to the observation deck. Finding Whitman, they "opened fire and Whitman slumped dead onto the observatory floor."[14] Later, the police would discover Whitman had fatally stabbed his wife and mother the night before.[15]

What became known as the Texas Tower Massacre unexpectedly drew Stuart Brown, PhD, into his first scientific study of play. After extensive investigations, a blue-ribbon committee of experts—representing dozens of disciplines from toxicology to neurology—came to a unanimous conclusion: Whitman's pathology was shaped by a "*lifelong lack of play.*"[16]

Brown continued gathering the play histories of convicted murderers, other violent felons, serial killers, mass shooters, and grievance killers. Across this subset of people, one pattern emerged: **every single individual had significant play deprivations, deficiencies, and deficits.**[17]

Lack of play caused poor emotional control, ineffective stress management, fixed mindsets, black-and-white thinking, and an inability to form deep connections with others. Expanding his pool of subjects, he compiled rich play histories of socialites, artists, Nobel Prize winners, and businesspeople. He concluded that the absence of play was as important as the presence of abuse in predicting violence.[18]

In short, Brown found that all work and no play doesn't make you dull. It makes you dangerous.

Although severe, these grim examples of lack of play show what happens when play is controlled, squashed, and shunned. You probably aren't living on that extreme. You do wrestle with quieter, slower losses like stifled innovation, exhaustion, and disconnection. More toil. Less joy.

Without play and fun, work shrinks into a thin pencil line—a whimper of activity—instead of bursting into a full-color masterpiece of meaningful work. Lack of play shows up as absenteeism, lack of creativity, fragility, overwork, and bullying behavior.

1. **Absenteeism:** For the *It Pays to Play* report, Sir Cary Cooper, organizational psychology expert, and his team studied thousands of workers across industries and career levels. Play at work impacts whether or not employees show up. Of the employees who reported not experiencing play or fun at work, 58 percent of had eleven or more sick days in three months, or about one day a week.[19]

2. **Creativity and collaboration drop significantly:** When comparing people who played at work regularly versus those who didn't, creativity dropped by nearly twenty-five points and collaboration by twenty points. Cooper's study

connected this lack of fun directly to a significant drop in overall well-being. For you this might look like a lack of curiosity about work or projects, feeling "stuck in a rut," or rigid thinking that reaches for an either/or answer.[20]

3. **Unhealthy soothing behaviors:** Adults that don't have enough play grab for comfort—that extra glass (or two) of wine at night, excessive working out, or just "get me to the couch and Netflix."[21]

4. **Fragility:** Micromanagement that produces a lack of play also creates a lack of agency. When you don't play, you lose an internal sense of being a resilient problem-solver. That email demand pops into your inbox, and you tumble into an anxiety spiral. Feeling helpless to change or generate options is a sign of lack of play.[22]

5. **Overwork:** Without play, the trend is to create an environment of working well beyond your expected or contracted time. The IRS classifies full-time work as thirty to thirty-nine hours per week. Cooper's study found 71 percent of employees working those hours rated play in the workplace as important. The rate drops to 65 percent of folks with higher salaries working fifty or more hours each week. Cooper concluded: "The danger here is that those higher earners are becoming slaves to the task."[23] This isn't discretionary effort. These are the subtle, or even overt, messages that overwork is expected: The uncommitted *only* work forty hours a week.[24]

6. **Office bullies and toxic friends:** Because play is a biological imperative, when real play is absent, the brain and body

figure out another way to play. In searching for real play, controlling and manipulative behaviors arise as fake play. Eberle describes fake play as when the bully "does not show the 'play face' that evolution has given us as a universal invitation. We know what is on the bully's mind by reading his intentions in his feral grin. The bully's rictus provides the age-old cue: Glee tinged with cruelty is not play."[25] Fake play can expand into full-blown narcissistic behavior. When there isn't enough real play, people engage in narcissistic play in any relationship.[26]

Play deprivation is far from harmless. Missing play as an adult might not make you a headline, but it corrodes joy, weakens resilience, and builds a fragile life. Without play, danger grows, fed by the myth that play is childish and separate from work. Let's look at what happens when you stop treating play as frivolous and start seeing it as fundamental to real work.

The Payoffs of Play

Jeff Harry had a quarter-life crisis that changed his career.

In third grade, Jeff saw the movie *Big* and decided the toy industry in New York was the only career for him. With a bellyflop into bubble-bursting reality, he discovered working in toys was miserable.

"No toys, no fun, no high fives, no joy, no play," is how he described his days.

Jeff skedaddled out of New York to San Francisco and found a job on Craigslist teaching engineering to kids using LEGO. Seven people, playing with LEGO for a living. *Score!*

Those seven folks played their way to 400 people and the largest LEGO-inspired STEM organization in the country, teaching 100,000 kids a year. The big tech companies in Silicon Valley started paying attention. Jeff's little Craigslist job had exploded into ways to foster all the things big companies wanted: creativity, innovation, collaboration, and more.[27]

At work, play creates the environment for joy in tangible ways. Here's a baker's dozen of those ways:

Positive Affect: Researchers found a direct connection between play and better work relationships. When you play together, people feel seen, heard, valued, and appreciated.[28]

Collaboration: Great collaborations feel crackling, not like a status meeting. Play is the fastest way to form collaborative relationships that improve group decisions and flow.[29]

Creativity and Innovation: Your brain's play circuits link the cerebral cortex and the cerebellum. When those circuits activate, they create a high-speed train connecting the cortex up front—where all the strategy, problem-solving, and emotional intelligence live—and the cerebellum in the back, with instincts and reflexes. You're firing on all cylinders, engaged with the environment, increasing creativity and innovation.[30]

Keeps You Sane: Playing protects your mind from difficulty, stress, and even trauma. A US Air Force pilot imprisoned in North Vietnam played a full eighteen holes of golf every day in his imagination. Released after years of physical and mental trauma, he asked to play a round of golf. Even emaciated, with scores of health issues, he played a marvelous game. The mental play kept his mind intact.[31]

Changes the Mood: Some play alters your mood as well as the group's (like the lunchroom Helens from chapter six). Brown found the act of play releases tension in the body with all those feel-good hormones, changing the energy of the room.[32]

Strengthens Relationships: If you've been working with someone long enough, you can slip into a negativity-bias rut: *Why can't Karl ever send the file on time*? Or *Why does my wife always finish other people's sentences*? Soon, that's all you see. When you play together, those issues rightsize. Brown says play "refreshes and refuels long-term adult relationships."[33] It's not just individual relationships; play promotes cooperation, tolerance, cohesion, and attunement, making teams stronger too.[34]

Establishes Norms: Play shows us the rules of morality and justice. It establishes the rules of engagement with each other and the cultural norms of your relationships.[35]

Sticky Culture: When people play together, it directly increases what academics call "positive organizational citizenship behaviors" without manipulation.[36] No guilt trip required, you want to come to work and give a little extra. Retention is four times higher in positive playful cultures, and 80 percent of those employees also recommend their company versus the 4 percent in unfavorable cultures.[37]

Higher Performance: When you have a playful posture, you're better at your work. Researchers found that adults who had a playfulness about their work had more effective "work outcomes, including task evaluations, perceptions, involvement, and performance."[38]

Improves Productivity: When work feels like play, you are five times more productive because your brain has less mental strain.[39]

In a state of flow, play integrates information faster than other types of repetition. Dr. Karyn Purvis, developmental psychologist, said, "It takes 400 repetitions of an act . . . to get one new synapse. Or twelve repetitions with joy and laughter because there's a release of a chemical dopamine."[40]

Increases Communication Across Differences: Play is the opening act to a cooperative society of complex and diverse humans. Nate Jones, a master mechanic for elite race car drivers, brought his Kids Motorsports Education to a juvenile detention center. What began with crossed arms and established racial factions ended with laughter, cooperation, and fun. The guards were gobsmacked. One boy even asked to stay past his release date so he could be in the next car assembly and race.[41] Play diffuses differences. McKinsey & Company found the same results in tense relationships and hostile workplaces: Play "lowers the level of violence and increases communication."[42]

Manages Discomfort: Play teaches through *experience*—not a lecture—that all good things also involve difficulty and discomfort. A playful approach to life and actual play trains you to manage *through* discomfort to the good stuff on the other side.[43]

Radical Acceptance of Reality: Play isn't a blink-it-better magic trick, but it does ease the tension of facing reality. Gary Ware, author and play-based facilitator, calls it "radical acceptance of reality."[44] Jessica Morgan, improv trainer and Upright Citizens Brigade (UCB) alum, calls it the foundation of improv: Everything is an invitation.[45*] Play offers the opportunity to hear someone else's reality, accept current circumstances, and build new solutions.

---

* UCB is a comedy and training institution founded by Amy Poehler, Matt Besser, Ian Roberts, and Matt Walsh.

Joy*osity*

Aren't you raising your hand for these benefits? They're all the buzzwords of healthy and happy work. If play is this effective, why is it so rare? Brown explains, "I've found that in trying to encourage playfulness in adults it's much less about teaching something new than it is stripping away the obstacles to playfulness."[46]

Let's name the obstacles to play.

What Will Block Play

"Stand up and make a circle."

When I begin an off-site or workshop with this line, the responses range from excitement—*Oh good, we're not going to have a lecture all day*—to a side-eye—*Oh no, what is this going to be?* In the debrief after the activity, there's always an emotional journey from skepticism, to surprise, to understanding its purpose and impact. One exchange with Dan, a CEO of a large Midwest manufacturing operation, sticks with me:

"When we started, I felt unsure. Well honestly, I felt vulnerable and childish." He continued to describe Eberle's cycle of play stages, from vulnerability to balance.

I asked him if we could go back to how he felt at the beginning, "When you were walking to the circle, did you feel childish or childlike?"

He nodded and thought for a moment. "I think at first, I felt childish. But then it was childlike. And a little freeing."

Side by side, childish and childlike feel different. But as adults, we've conflated the two. *Childish* is playing boss against boss (mom against dad), zero self-control (tantrums) when things don't go their way, and department turf wars (I-was-here-first fights) over who has the power. You're left exasperated. Childish behavior leaves you anxious and unproductive because it's unpredictable.[47]

In contrast, *childlike* behavior brings delight, wonder, and the energy of children chasing dandelion puffballs for hours. When you're willing to be childlike, your vulnerability fuels discovery. You are curious, open, and tolerate ambiguity, change, and uncertainty.[48]

Children are most like us in their emotions and least like us in their logic. And that's what play provides: a break from the rigid adult logic that keeps you stuck. Your fear isn't childlike wonder. Instead, you're worried about being labeled as ignorant, naïve, or unsophisticated—you're scared they'll look at you and think you a fool. That fear keeps you buttoned up, but that armor blocks the profound connection of joy.

Researchers continue to discover that the journey from childhood to adulthood isn't as linear as we once thought.[49] You didn't wake up one day, head to an office to fill out paperwork, and get an adult card. But a workplace that doesn't welcome play slices at your wholeness, sending the message, *We're serious here. Stop being childish and do your work.*

Jana Mohr Lone, philosopher and educator, writes, "Childhood and adulthood are just ideas people thought of, and then they put boundaries around these names to create [a story] that isn't actually real."[50]

That story and those fears obstruct productive states of play. Gary Ware calls it going from the "playground to the proving ground." Some barriers are internal, others external. Here's a breakdown of the most common play-blockers, especially at work.[51]

Internal Blocks to Play
The stories you're telling yourself

- Comparisonitis
- Fixed mindset
- Guilt
- Outcome obsession
- Perfectionism
- Unreasonable self-expectations
- Self-consciousness

External Blocks to Play
The messages and systems around you

- "It's for children"
- Bias
- High-control environment
- Lack of psychological safety
- Micromanagement
- Measurement obsession

Lifestyle Blocks to Play
The drains to your energy and attention

- Excessive screen time
- Disorganized or overly cluttered spaces
- Switchtasking*
- Extreme exhaustion
- Lack of planning
- Uncontrolled notifications
- Unmanaged stress cycle

In earlier chapters, you've already learned how to work through many of these barriers, but it can still feel like a maze. Play *is* the path through the blocks. The best way to play through is to find your unique play style.

---

* Your brain can't actually focus on more than one task at a time. What you're doing is rapidly switching tasks. You're not multitasking; you're switchtasking.

Play Like an Expert: The Play Personas

What was your favorite childhood toy or activity that you returned to again and again? Pause right now and just skip down memory lane. While you're there, do you remember your cousin or next-door neighbor playing in a way that just baffled you? *That looks like zero fun. What are you even doing*?

Everyone plays, but everyone plays differently. What excites one person exhausts another. (Dana? Loves herself a spreadsheet. Give me a whiteboard.) In Brown's research, he found eight styles of play. I've built on his work from my experiences with clients to bring these eight personas to life for you.

The Collector	The Competitor
The Creator	The Director
The Explorer	The Kinesthete
The Jester	The Storyteller

You have one dominant style with two supporting styles. Your special trio forms how you naturally lean into play. This trio draws you to activities at work that feel effortless, energizing, and exciting.

For now, just focus on finding your leading style. For each persona, you'll find a strength, a set of ideal activities or skills, and a specific action to bring the style to life. In the Lounge, there is a quiz to help you find your lead style. Once you have your play style, put that into your Leadership Personality Dashboard that we talked about in chapter three. And of course, there is more in the *Playbook* on how to apply play styles.

The Collector

Your Strength: You thrive on gathering, organizing, and curating information or experiences.

At Work: Use your ability to track details, create systems, and bring order to chaos. You're great at project management, research, and structuring workflows.

Try This: Curate resources for your team, create an organized knowledge base, or track progress toward key goals.

The Competitor

Your Strength: You're energized by challenges, clear goals, and measurable success.

At Work: Set benchmarks, track progress, and use friendly competition to motivate yourself and others.

Try This: Create a personal or team leaderboard, set achievement milestones, or turn tasks into games with rewards.

The Creator

Your Strength: You bring ideas to life through imagination and hands-on creativity.

At Work: Use your innovative mindset to solve problems, design engaging presentations, and improve processes.

Try This: Infuse creativity into projects—brainstorm visually, sketch ideas, or experiment with new solutions.

The Director

Your Strength: You thrive on organizing, planning, and making things happen.

At Work: You're a natural leader who turns chaos into order by managing people, projects, and logistics.

Try This: Set up clear action plans, delegate roles effectively, and lead meetings with a structured agenda.

The Explorer

Your Strength: You love discovering new ideas, experiences, and perspectives.

At Work: Bring curiosity to problem-solving, embrace innovation, and inspire teams to think outside the box.

Try This: Research new trends in your field, experiment with fresh approaches, or seek out professional development opportunities.

The Jester

Your Strength: You bring humor, energy, and levity to every situation.

At Work: Keep morale high, ease tension with laughter, and create a culture where people feel comfortable and engaged.

Try This: Start meetings with an icebreaker, add humor to presentations, or use playfulness to build team camaraderie.

The Kinesthete

Your Strength: You learn and thrive through movement and physical activity.

At Work: Bring energy to your environment by incorporating movement—stand-up meetings, walking brainstorms, or hands-on projects.

Try This: Use a standing desk, take movement breaks, or engage in active team-building exercises.

The Storyteller

Your Strength: You connect ideas and people through compelling narratives.

At Work: Use your storytelling skills to communicate vision, engage audiences, and make information memorable.

Try This: Frame key messages as stories, create engaging presentations, or use anecdotes to inspire your team.

Remember Montessori's principle: Play is the work that builds mastery. Once you're playing in your style, you can hone your play. This doesn't mean getting better at Spades. Play at its highest level is your craft, your expert skill, and your fast track to joy. Pearl S. Buck, humanitarian, Pulitzer Prize–winning author and the first American woman to win the Nobel Prize in Literature, wrote, "The secret of joy in work is contained in one word—excellence. To know how to do something well is to enjoy it."[52] That excellence comes from embracing what makes you unique. Remember Jade Simmons, the powerhouse performer and keynote speaker from chapter five with her unforgettable definition of purpose? On the *Joyosity* podcast, she called this your "differentiator" at work—the special, authentic way you integrate all of yourself.[53] Your personality, values, life experiences, and unique play style fuse to set you apart. While others strive to fit a mold, your signature presence propels you forward in your career and leads you to more fulfillment and joy.

Putting Play to Work

In June 2018, Brianna Castle and Rachel Skibicki swayed back and forth on the swings in the Hatch, looking at the multicolored Post-its that littered the whiteboard wall. While swinging, they pondered the missing link in the idea.

"What if you could just swing through the drive-thru?" Brianna asked. "Like Tarzan, swing by, grab your order, and go?"

"And Tarzan-yell your order, so it's exactly what you want, with all the right drinks and sauces!" Rachel chuckled.

Brianna planted her feet on the bright-green fake grass. She turned to Rachel. "What if the Tarzan-yell was in the app. Because it's unique to you?"

Rachel stopped her swing. "And you could make your order and pay in the app too? And just say your name?"

The Chick-fil-A One® drive-thru mobile order pickup was born.

The converted warehouse known on Chick-fil-A's corporate campus as "The Hatch" houses its innovation center. Full of functional and flexible spaces, the atmosphere embodies play, collaboration, and the wild work of change. One room indeed has an airstream parked on fake grass with swings surrounded by walls made of whiteboards.

Pale oak plaques etched with paper airplanes fill an entire wall in the Hatch. Under each airplane is the name of an innovation born in there, with the names of the idea's leaders. On one trip to lead a training, I snapped a picture of Castle and Skibicki's plaque—their mobile order system, which is hands-down my favorite restaurant app (verified by Bob G. at my Brentwood Chick-fil-A and my order history).

I've imagined this story of Castle and Skibicki's process, but I do know this: They developed this successful innovation through Chick-fil-A's playful approach. Back in 2018, restaurant apps were a new technology, and most were clunky at best. Mobile orders represented 6 percent of Chick-fil-A sales at the start of that year. This innovation was so profitable, at the end of the year, it was up to nearly 20 percent.[54] The playful approach pays off.

Play as Flow

The same energy behind Chick-fil-A's success fuels what psychologists call *flow*. Throughout the book, we've talked about the way we "flow" together. And you may have noticed *flow* popping up in this chapter on play. That's because the properties of play and the conditions of flow are almost identical. In his book *Flow*, Csikszentmihalyi describes flow activities that are all forms of play.[55]

The one difference that moves you from play to flow is an adjustment in naming the point of the activity. Remember, a core characteristic of play is *apparent purposelessness*. To expand play into flow, add a small amount of direction to expand the benefits.[56] This shift brings play into the productivity of your work. Intentionally using your play style to inform the Joy Ratio brings you into greater flow.

The Play Approach

Play is more than gamification and is definitely *not* forced fun. Play can be a game, activity, mindset, or approach, as long as you have several of those properties of play. Ferrabee calls play "high-level contingency testing in a low-stakes environment."[57]

To bring a playful approach, do not start with a high ropes course. Ask a simple question:

"How can we play with this?"

This simple question opens the door to a new mindset for you and the rest of the room. You've lowered the stakes while still moving toward solutions. Experiment with your atmosphere, your meetings, your celebrations, and even the way you arrange your roles and tasks, to connect to your play style with playful problem-solving. This approach will bring more joy into your work.

Play to Solve Problems

On each table sits one marshmallow, twenty strands of spaghetti, one yard of white string, and one roll of masking tape. Around the tables are working groups ready to complete the task: build the tallest freestanding structure possible in eighteen minutes. Ready? Go.

Time's up! Let's look at the results.

- In last place, recent MBA graduates: 10-inch tower
- In third place, lawyers: 15-inch tower
- In second place, CEOs: 22-inch tower
- The winners, recent kindergarten graduates: 26-inch tower[58]

Yes, the six-year-olds bested the adults. Are they better at geometry and physics? No. They *played* their way through to solutions.

In all your life, you face an array of problems, from simple to complex. I could never give you all the play activities that work for every circumstance, but here's a specific play activity to use as a problem-solving technique.

Top of the Brain

Your brain handles complexity better just below your consciousness. It uses what researchers call *dynamic logic*. The journal *Brain Sciences* describes how the subconscious takes a set of vague representations and transforms them into precise, conscious thoughts.[59] Top of the Brain leverages dynamic logic and the brain's play circuits.

This activity works best with a partner or a small group of no more than twelve people.

> **1 Pick a one-sentence problem.** Isolate and name the problem. If it's a complex problem, focus on one component of

the larger issue. The easiest frame is using an "I don't have" or "I need" statement. *I don't have enough leads. I need more help.* It could also be a choice. *Do I use Zoom or Butter?* Define the problem clearly in one sentence.

2. **Pick a play activity.** Use your play persona to help guide this. I highly recommend an activity with some type of tactile or movement component. Puzzles, an improv game, darts, a card game like Happy Salmon, or a simple game of catch all work.

3. **Put the problem on the top of your brain.** Imagine the problem sentence at the top of your brain, like a hat with words on the top of your head that you can't see, but you know is there.

4. **Play.** Participate in the play activity. It can be three to ten minutes long. You're not discussing the problem—talk about other things, fully get into the play, and keep imagining that problem-statement hat. If your hat slips off, just put it back.

5. **Reflect.** Once the game stops, talk about what came up as you played—the ideas, thoughts, considerations, possibilities that came to you. Share them with your partner or team, regardless if they are "logical" or not.

The activity uses all your Centers of Intelligence and brings surprise solutions that may feel obvious in hindsight. *Why didn't I think of that earlier?* Well, it was imprisoned by rigid thinking that the play unlocked.

How Play Puts You Back Together

Pauly's thick New York accent was the first thing you noticed. The next thing? His ever-present FDNY hat. A twenty-year veteran New York City firefighter, Pauly seemed an unlikely student in Improv 101 at UCB's training center.

Jessica Morgan (whom we met early in this chapter) opened the class in the summer of 2017 with an easy, active game of Enemy and Protector. In a more playful mood, the participants sat down for introductions and goals.

When the circle turned to Pauly, he gave a wave that lived somewhere between a hello and a shrug and said, "Look, I'm a pretty happy guy, alright? But talkin' about my story? Eh . . . it's tough, ya know? It's just . . . a lot. And I don't wanna dump that on folks. But people ask. So . . . I think I gotta figure out a bettah way to tell it."

Jessica smiled warmly and nodded, "That's perfect, Pauly. Do you want to tell us a little now or wait until we know each other better?"

Pauly rubbed the back of his neck and flashed a half-smile, "Yeah, sure. Uh . . . I responded to the North Tower on 9/11."

The room inhaled. Everyone understood the weight of the trauma and pain Pauly carried.

Jessica nodded, more slowly this time, "Well. Pauly, thank you." She turned to the group. "The foundation of improv is *everything's an invitation*. Even the heavy stuff." She chuckled lightly. "Even the awkward moments when we're not sure how to respond. We don't have to pretend it's easy to play our way through."

Pauly bobbed his head and a lopsided grin tugged at his mouth, "So, uh . . . do we win prizes for the biggest downer of a story?"

Joyosity

After eight weeks of improv and playing with his story, Pauly practically bounced into the final night of class.

"So I'm on the E train, right? And the lady next to me sees my hat, asks if I'm a firefighter. We get to talking—and, long story short, she asks about the Towers," he paused. "And I could tell her my story . . . without all the weight, ya know? Like, it mattered. It mattered a lot. But it was . . . I dunno. Healed."[60]

We've spent a whole chapter on play and flow, and not just so you can create innovative products, boost engagement scores, and keep your best employees. Practicing play and experiencing flow might even give you wins on par with Djokovic's Wikipedia-owning season. Playing more in your life will protect you from stagnant ideas, overwork, and becoming the office bully.

But more than that, play is in the healing business. Play restores. It rebuilds. Play ushers in joy.

The Gist

You've been lied to—play isn't the opposite of work. It's the secret sauce to doing your best work without exhaustion. It's a biological necessity for everyone, but everyone plays in their own unique way. Find that, and it's your productivity power. Play activities keep you in the Joy Ratio, all while increasing your resilience, creativity, and connections.

> *All work and no play doesn't make you dull. It makes you dangerous.*
>
> —Jenn Whitmer

Joyosity

Connection

Who else plays like you?

Use play or a playful approach in your work or home this week to connect with people.

. . . .

Curiosity

Think back to your childhood. What was your favorite toy? Did you like to play by yourself or with other people? What were the rules about play when you were a child? When was play encouraged or discouraged?

Which of the eight play personas feels like your lead style? If the descriptions aren't enough, use the quiz from the Lounge. Put that in your Leadership Personality Dashboard.

. . . .

Joy

Review the eight wonders of the play state. List the activities at work that feel like play to you. You can use your play persona to help you.

Look at the blockers to play. Identify which ones are holding you back from playing more.

Your RSVP to Joyosity

The Choice That Changes Everything

> And even if something looks like a solitary sport, it's a team effort.
>
> —Diana Nyad, author and journalist

Stepping on the wooden gangplank in polished boots and clutching the hand of her young son, Giuseppina Dell'Aria embarked on a ten-day journey that would change *my* life.

Giuseppina and her family had lived in the mountain village of Calascibetta, Sicily, for generations. But poverty, a devastating 7.5 earthquake in 1908, political corruption, and instability in the Kingdom of Italy made everyday life increasingly difficult. Millions of Sicilians were emigrating to America, imagining a new life for themselves. Giuseppina and her husband, Calogero, began to wonder if they should too.

Saving lira for three steerage fares, packing all their belongings into one trunk and two canvas bags, arranging for a new life in the

United States—those were the easy parts. But leaving the safety and comfort of family, community, language, even the very landscape of the green mountains of Sicily . . . How do you leave the only place you've ever known, even if it's slowly destroying you?

The planks beneath her creaked with each step. Filippo jumped into Calogero's arms when he joined them after securing their trunk. The waters churned with the boat's wake as the shore of Sicily, familiar and flawed, slipped away.

Nearly a century later, I wasn't stepping onto a gangplank, but I sat clutching the arm of that white couch, getting fired.

There's more to that July meeting in chapter one.

Remember, we were stuck in a cyclical, toxic culture. Mentally, physically, and professionally, I was a mess but persevering with a "when this happens, it will be better" mindset that only made everything progressively worse.

When our head of school eliminated my position, I sat in shock as he described that he would take on my responsibilities—the same role he "didn't really understand"—the role I was paid thirty hours a week for, although I worked fifty. With his next breath, he rehired me for a one-year position as special assistant to the head of school.

I referred to it as my Banishment to Elba. Required to work off site, I could come to campus for approved meetings with specific staff or as a parent. True to his history, he answered none of my questions about student achievement concerns, teacher support capacity, or the excellent performance reviews he'd given me every single year. I cleared out my office and decamped to the second floor of my home, grasping for familiarity and safety. Because educators solve problems with degrees, I enrolled in a master's program in communication and culture (y'know, as one does).

But the truth is, I had always "played school." Education wasn't a job; it was the only path I'd ever imagined. So on that white couch, in the stranglehold of shock, toxicity, trauma, and overwhelm, I felt trapped. Choice, agency, change—not one felt within my grasp. I needed to accept this role and persevere with the only things I had left: his shaky promises of reformed behavior, and my relentless, undying optimism.

For the first weeks of the school year, work was "fine." The constant low-level anxiety and waves of grief remained, but it was "manageable." The truth? I was gaslighting myself. I was languishing, and nothing was improving.

That year at the Dellario family Christmas, my aunts walked through the door with lasagna, meatballs, and treasures from their recent trip to Calascibetta. They brought marriage certificates, birth certificates, and stories of how they had crashed a local wedding reception—all the fun stuff. But everyday life in Sicily still challenged residents. The locals had described how hard it was to find work and afford housing.

"What would have happened to all of us if Calogero and Giuseppina had stayed in Sicily?" my aunt wondered aloud.

I looked around at the four generations laughing, eating, and generally enjoying life. These precious people. We were the legacy of courage, of choosing joy through the discomfort of change.

And like a 2x4 to the head, I realized I didn't have to stay the same, and staying the same was worse.

So, I walked in the footsteps of my great-grandmother—a woman I'd never met, yet I knew we shared the same dimple in our cheek, the same brown eyes, and a quiet valor for change. With that, I resigned from the only career I'd ever imagined, known, and wanted.

The status quo pretends safety. It's a quiet acquiescence to the path of least resistance. Ron Tite, author, creative director, and founder of Church+State, calls it the "greater resignation."[1] It's decay dressed up as devotion, and a resignation from joy.

I want to protect you from the trap that snared me: *If I just stay the course and persevere, all will be OK.* But I was falling prey to the fear of change. I hadn't learned yet that joy extinguishes fear.

You don't have to leave your company or change industries. But you do have to leave your comfort zone, because the status quo will never save you.

The High Cost of Resignation

What does this look like for you? Let's just imagine for a bit. You decide, "It's fine." Staying the same will be enough.

Work continues to be a slog. Your anxiety continues to climb. You notice your physical health declines. You live emotionally disconnected. There seems to be only languishing and struggling. You perpetuate the myths that only what you can measure matters, that it will always be this way, that work comes first, and that despite all the evidence to the contrary, it's not that bad.

Without meaning to, you signal to your team, your community, and the children watching you the same story the greed-centric machine taught you: Productivity buys your right to exist, profit matters more than your humanity, people are expendable if they slow the grind, and exhaustion is a virtue. And joy? Well you might earn joy once you've sacrificed your very life to the system.

Are you OK with that?

"Culture is defined by the worst behavior tolerated," Dr. John Amaechi, OBE, psychologist and consultant, reminds us about workplaces.[2] That applies to you as an individual too. Your life's culture, the way you flow with yourself and others, is defined by the worst behavior you tolerate for, or from, yourself.

You don't have to stay the same. You can cultivate joy instead.

The Magic and Mess of Change

"I loved my job. But I couldn't keep doing it," Carrie Campbell, senior vice president of events for the Boston Red Sox, said of a turning point in her career. "I couldn't survive that way."

Fresh out of college, Carrie fell into hospitality and fell hard. She started out as a temporary executive assistant for the owner of the historic Hampshire House in Boston—the real-life setting for *Cheers*. Within weeks, they said, "We're hiring you." A couple of years later, the Fairmont Copley Plaza hotel came calling for the Carrie Campbell magic.

She poured herself into the work of weddings, catering, and events: long hours, big wins, learning on the fly, and saying yes to *all. the. things*. At the Fairmont, she encountered new ideas—culture training, leadership development, and employee engagement.

That place taught her how to lead, but she worked as if the job she loved also demanded her life. After years of hundred-hour weeks and blurry boundaries, Carrie hit a wall. She realized, "I love this work. I love hospitality. But I can't keep working like this."

So she started changing.

Carrie began learning how to lead without abandoning herself. She drew boundaries, asked for what her team needed, and cared for herself. She knew she had to have her own joy before she could give it to anyone else.

Then, she helped change an entire organization.

Not long after the four-star Boston Harbor Hotel recruited her, *Forbes* took away a star. This devastating downgrade could have spiraled into rage and blame. Instead, the general manager said, "We're going to fix this. Together." They dug into the issues. They wrestled first for purpose, then overhauled guest service protocols, empowered frontline staff, and transformed the culture from "policy first" to "people first." They trained everyone—from the experienced GM to the newest night-shift dishwasher—on self-awareness, mindset, connection, and play. The hotel went beyond regaining a star; it became a *Forbes* five-star property and a AAA five-diamond resort.

Now, it was time to build in joy from the start.

In the early 2000s, the Boston Red Sox were looking for a new revenue stream. What could the Red Sox offer at Fenway Park for the 284 days a year without a home game? After an experiment with Bruce Springsteen, then Boston, in concert, they knew the answer: events. The Red Sox had been paying attention to the success just four miles down the harbor. They wanted their own Carrie Campbell magic to develop their events into something special.

Carrie was determined to build this department with empowered staff, clear communication, and systems that made sense, but not at the expense of the people.

"When I looked at 'Where do I start?' I thought about the staff. Where does the joy get sucked out? What makes them cry in the shower on Sunday night?" Carrie said about bringing the personal and professional lessons she'd learned at the Fairmont and Boston Harbor.

Fifteen years later, Special Events significantly benefits the Red Sox and the city of Boston. Fenway Park hosts hundreds of private events each year as well as the Fenway Concert Series, Football at Fenway, other sporting events, and college graduations. The economic ripple is impressive. Concerts alone generated nearly $43 million for the Red Sox in 2024. Around Boston, the concerts supported local part-time and full-time jobs, poured more than $45 million into local businesses, and collected more than $8.6 million in state and local taxes.[3]

The Carrie Campbell magic continues, rooted in her core belief: "Pouring into people is the most important business decision you can make."[4]

The Joy You're Capable Of

What if you believed you could be a Carrie story and create your own magic? What would choosing joy in your one, whole life look like, even if things are what they are? What if you decided your life wasn't up for sacrifice—that success comes through putting your humanity at the center—and that not only are you willing to work for joy, but you believe you're worthy of it?

Then what?

You explore with joy. You discover your deep motivations through the Enneagram. You notice your stories and rewrite them. You identify and live by your values.

You engage through joy. You connect with people with your emotional intelligence and highly skilled communication. You use curiosity in conflict and wisdom in your decisions.

You experience joy. You close the stress cycle and develop practices that care for your mind, body, heart, and soul. You have steady structures of systems, rhythms, and rituals that sustain you. You play just for fun, but play like an expert to build connections, solve problems, and heal.

Joy isn't a far-off goal to earn. You're living in the Joy Ratio every day.

Breathe that in for a moment. The rooted, wild lavender of joy.

Perhaps a cascade of doubts just tumbled in: *I can't do that. I don't know where to start. I've tried before. Even if I could change myself, making changes at my workplace? Not likely.*

But what could happen if you believed a new story?

The Growth Path to Your Favorite Self

My friend, you're already on the growth path. There are four distinct phases you'll walk through:

1. **Unconscious Incompetence:** You don't know what you don't know. And you don't even know if joy is possible. You're living unaware and wondering why it's all so hard.
2. **Conscious Incompetence:** You know that you don't know how to do this yet, *and* you know that joy is possible. So you start applying ideas and trying them out, but it feels all kinds of awkward. Since you're reading this book, you're probably here. Hang on, this is where the tide shifts.
3. **Conscious Competence:** You know how to do this. You're starting to apply these ideas regularly. You feel more competent, but you're still having to think about it, to apply effort to choose your best practices of joy. You don't just believe joy is possible—you're starting to experience it.
4. **Unconscious Competence:** Your skills are automatic, and the idea of toxic and dysfunctional habits are a distant memory (most of the time). Joy is your regular experience, even when things around you aren't changing.

You don't have to become an entirely different person to live in the Joy Ratio. You're becoming who you want to be. That's not faking it—that's choosing your favorite self.

In the words of Miles Davis, "Sometimes you have to play a long time to sound like yourself."[5]

Want to know what your favorite self sounds like? Work toward the Joy Ratio:

Joy's Magic Third

In 35 percent of your time, look for the markers of the deep roots of joy:

1. You feel lucky, favored, or fortunate to do the work.
2. You feel connected because of your work. You feel a sense of belonging.
3. The work has purpose. It impacts other people.

Toil's Tiny Ten

Keep the bite of acid and rock of toil under 10 percent. This includes:

1. The work that drains you.
2. The work that feels meaningless.
3. The work that doesn't interest you, or you don't have the skills and resources to enjoy it.

The Messy Middle

In the remaining 55 percent, you are managing the Messy Middle. You use all your engagement skills, plus the practices you've honed, the structures you've built, and the play you've discovered, to cultivate joy.

Every bit of the Joy Ratio requires you to practice self-awareness with the Enneagram and apply it with grace. Remember to get your Joyosity Explorer Map and Leadership Personality Dashboard in the Lounge. You'll learn to put all your self-awareness tools in one place and gain insights that allow you to create change toward joy.

Be the Change That Brings Joy

The quiet valor of change rarely swims alone.

My brilliant friend and fellow TEDx speaker Jacqueline Kerr, PhD, is the founder of Leading Real Change. Her research as a behavior change scientist has informed the work of James Clear and others who write about habits and change. When I asked her how leaders like you can sustain individual changes and create bigger changes in their workplaces and communities, she offered three important steps: **Start small, find fellow formers, and carry compost.**

Start Small

"Change doesn't succeed through grand declarations. It begins with small experiments," Kerr said.

She suggests choosing one small start that you can beta test for yourself. Maybe it's your shut-down ritual, email boundaries, or finding your Enneagram type's impact on your leadership. Once you've experienced the wins, share the benefits with others and invite people to bring their ideas.

Start small and share your story.

Find Fellow Formers

"Find the other people with a pioneer mindset and form a network," Kerr encouraged. Lasting change for yourself, and then larger system changes, come when you connect with other people who also want to shape the culture.

Going it alone creates too much pressure. There are too many people invested in the status quo. You need a network just to maintain your own positive change.

Joyosity

You probably already know a couple people who want positive change. They're the other people who bring new ideas (and probably vent about the stubborn system). Try your small experiments together. As you notice the positive results, you'll begin to create what Kerr calls an "emergent system." I call it building your Joyosity Team. Your small but mighty group grows into communities of professional practice that eventually become influential in the system.

I've watched this happen when one team experiences growth and happiness, and all the looky-loos come over the fence and say, "Hey . . . how are you doing that?" In *Revenge of the Tipping Point*, Malcolm Gladwell gives us the Magic Third of change. When your network becomes about a third of the whole, you move from being outsiders to influencers. In a group of nine, that's just three people. Sharing Sukhinder Singh Cassidy's experience, Gladwell wrote, "One person, she said, felt lonely. Two felt like a friendship. But three was a *team*."[6] Find your fellow pioneers to form your Joyosity Team.

Carry Compost

"Find the strengths of the old system, what success can you use as 'compost' to fertilize new growth," Kerr said.

Not everything is all bad. As much as some days you want to *burn it all down*, find the parts of the old way that matter. Use the compost to ease yourself into change and help people recognize something familiar.

Kerr's research shows that when you use previous successes as compost during change, "It's not so different that it feels threatening." (Remember self-efficacy from chapter four.) Compost helps you sustain your individual change and have leaders who continue to invest in positive change.[7]

Are You Audacious Enough for Joy?

My great-grandmother Giuseppina probably knew the journey in a steamship would be an arduous ten days. She had all the information—timetables, baggage allowances, port locations—but literally nothing changed until she placed her first polished boot on the gangplank.

Because here's the truth: Information ain't transformation.

You have pages of data, examples, and tools you need to cultivate the lavender of joy. But it matters not one bit if it all stays in your head.

Joyosity requires action.

Don't close this book and continue making the same choices that lead to dysfunction, languishing, toxicity, and burnout. Be curious and choose your first step. Then take it. Put your polished boot on the gangplank toward Joyosity.

Joy is what will save you.

Extra!

Extra!

The Joyosity Resource Lounge

Need a download? A framework? A next step? Here's where the work of joy keeps working. And for deeper exercises and expanded support, get the *Joyosity Works Playbook*.

Tools, Quizzes, and Downloads

You can download these at jennwhitmer.com/lounge.

Joyosity Explorer Map
The Joyosity Explorer Map will guide you to understanding the deeper purpose and story you tell yourself about your work.

Leadership Personality Dashboard
Understand how the major personality tools work with the Enneagram as the foundation. Input your scores from all those other professional developments and see them in one dashboard.

Values Identifier

You can't lead with confidence if you're unclear on what matters. This free guide helps you identify and define your top five values so your choices stop feeling like darts in the dark.

Feeling It! Name-Rate-Find

This is your download for all the 200-plus feeling words, the rating scales, and the body scan.

Twenty Helpful Phrases in Difficult Conversations

In tough conversations, it's helpful to have some phrases to fall back on without blowing up the moment. Use these phrases to help you get started, to manage the back-and-forth in the middle, and to make sure you've closed a hard conversation well.

Getting Started

• Can we talk? • I am struggling with something, and I'd like to talk with you about it. • I feel like something is off between us. Is there anything I've done that you'd like to talk about?	• I have made a mistake, and I'd like to talk with you about it. • I'm feeling ____ by something that happened. Can we talk? • I care about you and our relationship. Because you are important to me, I want to share an observation.

In the Middle

• Can you say it again? I want to make sure I understand. • Here's what I hear you saying . . . (Repeat back what they're saying.) Is that right? • Can I clarify something? • Here's what I remember happening . . .	• Here's the story I'm telling myself right now . . . • Tell me more about that. • How do you feel? • What are some reasons you think that?

Closing Well

• Have I answered all your questions? • How can we work together to make a plan? • Do you feel like we've resolved this issue?	• Thank you for listening to my perspective. • Are we OK? • I forgive you.

Joyosity Leadership Stance Quiz

Seven quick questions to discover your signature stance as a leader so you can overcome your greatest leadership difficulties and unlock your innate leadership powers.

Play Persona Quiz

Your natural play personality shapes how you solve problems, stay in flow, and lead with ease. Take the "Find Your Play Style" quiz to discover how your unique play style will bring more creativity, confidence, and productivity.

Designed Week Grid

Design a week that works for you. Download the Designed Week Grid to track your time and create a rhythm that fuels your life.

Just Breathe

Get six breathwork techniques to help you calm, focus, and recharge and explore short videos showing you exactly how to do them.

More

Joyosity Works Playbook

If you are ready to really put Joyosity to work, the *Joyosity Works Playbook* is for you. You've seen me mention it throughout the book—it's time to get your own copy. Grab your copy at jennwhitmer.com/books.

Enneagram Navigator Session

We've only dipped our toe into the Enneagram here, and you might still be wondering, "What's my type?" That's where a Navigator Session comes in. I'll walk you through a process to discover your true type, understand why you do what you do, and give you practical tools to live and lead with clarity, confidence, and joy. Learn more at jennwhitmer.com/enneagram.

Say It Like This: Enneagram Communication Guide

Still feeling stuck in conversations—even after dabbling in the Enneagram here? This guide includes descriptions of each Enneagram type's communication style, including what to work on for each type and how to communicate better with each type. Use the code ECG75 for 75 percent off, and find it at jennwhitmer.com/enneagram-communication-guide.

Book Jenn and the Joy: Speaking, Coaching, Consulting

Do you feel that? That's the breath of fresh air coming your way. Be the hero that brings Jenn to your event and watch your audience connect, laugh, and gain practical tools to create positive, profitable cultures. See Jenn in action and read more about her keynotes and workshops at jennwhitmer.com/keynote-speaker.

If you want a guide to walk with you, find out more if coaching in the Joyosity Leadership Lab or other coaching experiences is right for you. You'll work out the principles of Joyosity in your real leadership and life. Head to jennwhitmer.com/coaching.

Stories, Study Stacks, and Citations

If you're the one who reads all footnotes . . . this is your moment. Here are the references, context, and all the nerdy goodness.

Stories That Didn't Fit

Stories Shape Results

Parakeeto, a company specializing in data systems, uses data to help agencies improve performance. It's not a place where you'd expect a lot of storytelling. CEO and cofounder, Marcel Petitpas, believes that measurements, metrics, and systems are all about the story.

"We have a saying at Parakeeto: 'The data can only tell you what the data is. It can never tell you *why* the data is.'" Marcel brings his clients through a group storytelling process to have a conversation about the data that includes the numbers and the story underneath. Once the team understands what the data means (the story of the data), then they decide what actions to take. As he told me on the *Joyosity* podcast, that's when performance changes.[1]

The Bootstrap Myth

The myth (note that *myth* means false idea) preaches that you can achieve the outcomes you want all by yourself through hard work, effort, and wits alone. You're not a victim of circumstances—you rise above without support or resources.

But the phrase is quixotic in its origin. In 1888, JD Steele published the science textbook *Answers to the Practical Questions and Problems in the Author's Scientific Text-Books*, as a manual for teachers. Question 29: "Can a man standing on a platform-scale make himself lighter by lifting up on himself? He cannot; because action and reaction are equal and opposite." Steele disproves the fiction of Baron Münchhausen, whose tall tales included pulling himself (and his horse) out of a swamp by his own hair. Back to Steele's textbook: Question 30: "*Why can not a man lift himself by pulling up on his boot-straps?* See last problem."[2] The task is impossible.

Yet the overstory of US culture is that if you pull yourself up by your bootstraps, you can go from rags to riches. In "Pursuing the American Dream," Pew Charitable Trust reported that only 4 percent of people move from the bottom quartile of income to the top. Additionally, those who do achieve that Hollywood ending rely on shared resources, partnerships, and the combined efforts of community.

So why does the Bootstrap Myth live rent-free in the minds of Americans and shame us every day? I blame Horatio Alger novels of the 1890s.[3]

The Power of the Board

Stacey Abrams, attorney and former US representative from Georgia, tells the story of her early days in the House when she would practice the old "anyone could do it" deflection. She believed this demonstrated her humility.

"You need to stop giving your power away," came a sharp caution from an experienced female legislator one day. Abrams, curious, asked what she meant.

The mentor replied, "If these men think you're smarter than they are, let them. That means they'll come to you for advice, and you can help. But it also means they might follow your lead. But if you keep saying you're nothing special, they'll start to believe you."[4]

Putting Your Phone to Bed

If you're screaming, *What if something happens and you get a call in the middle of the night?!* Here's the answer and my encouragement: My ringer is on, and the phone is on the charger. I have a sleep setting on my phone so that no alerts, including texts, come through. I've set it up so that if I get a call from any of the important people who would need me—Michael, our kids, our parents, or my sister and sister-in-law—the phone will ring. It's loud enough to wake me up, even from the kitchen. If anyone else calls twice, the phone rings. I'm not willing to give up my peace for the *very slim* chance there is a genuine emergency between 10 p.m. and 6 a.m. And if there is a problem, they can find me.

Riposa: Naps Are Delicious

My grandfather came from Italy as a child, and I remember he practiced *riposo* most days. After lunch, he would grab a *pennica*—an "I'm going to close my eyes for a moment" snooze—for twenty to thirty minutes. My deep love of naps comes from Grandpa Dellario. Naps are delicious. I like a full hour and a half nap, but even a twenty-minute *pennica* feels delightfully indulgent.

Study Stacks of Great Resources

Books

The Enneagram is ancient, complex, and deep. We have only dipped into the baby pool in this book. (Don't worry, more to come from me!) In addition to my Enneagram certification and continuing education, these books have informed my Enneagram knowledge.

Allender, Scott. *The Enneagram of Emotional Intelligence: A Journey to Personal and Professional Success*. Baker Books, 2023.

Case, Sarajane. *The Honest Enneagram: Know Your Type, Own Your Challenges, Embrace Your Growth*. Andrews McMeel Publishing, 2020.

Chestnut, Beatrice. *The Complete Enneagram: 27 Paths to Greater Self-Knowledge*. She Writes Press, 2013.

Cron, Ian Morgan, and Suzanne Stabile. *The Road Back to You: An Enneagram Journey to Self-Discovery*. IVP, 2016.

Heuertz, Christopher L. *The Enneagram of Belonging: A Compassionate Journey of Self-Acceptance*. Zondervan, 2020.

Heuertz, Christopher L. *The Sacred Enneagram: Finding Your Unique Path to Spiritual Growth*. Zondervan, 2017.

Palmer, Helen. *The Enneagram in Love and Work: Understanding Your Intimate and Business Relationships*. HarperSanFrancisco, 1993.

Riso, Don Richard, and Russ Hudson. *Personality Types: Using the Enneagram for Self-Discovery*. Houghton Mifflin, 1996.

Stabile, Suzanne, ed. *Forty Days on Being a One*. IVP, 2014.

Stabile, Suzanne, ed. *Forty Days on Being a Two*. IVP, 2014.

Stabile, Suzanne, ed. *Forty Days on Being a Three*. IVP, 2014.

Stabile, Suzanne, ed. *Forty Days on Being a Four*. IVP, 2014.

Stabile, Suzanne, ed. *Forty Days on Being a Five*. IVP, 2014.

Stabile, Suzanne, ed. *Forty Days on Being a Six*. IVP, 2014.

Stabile, Suzanne, ed. *Forty Days on Being a Seven*. IVP, 2014.

Stabile, Suzanne, ed. *Forty Days on Being an Eight*. IVP 2014.

Stabile, Suzanne, ed. *Forty Days on Being a Nine*. IVP, 2014.

Stabile, Suzanne. *The Journey Toward Wholeness: Enneagram Wisdom for Stress, Balance, and Transformation*. IVP, 2021.

Books Recommendations

If you want more great books on the Enneagram, from authors I've mentioned in this book, or other great resources, I've got you! You can download the most current list or get clickable links at Joyosity Recommends: jennwhitmer.com/recommends.

Connection Apps

These apps have helped me stay connected with friends, extended family, coaching clients, and even my children and husband. They provide ways to feel like you're talking in real time when you can't. The $free.99 version of these apps are all great. (But ask yourself if you really need the notifications!)

- Marco Polo: Video messaging app
- Voxer: Voice messaging app
- Slack: Collaboration app

Improv Warm-Ups

Especially if you're not practiced at playing, you need a little warm-up before jumping into purposeful play. Typically you need to bring the energy up, but also to let loose a little. Both of these activities can be done alone or with others.

1. **Skips and Sass:** Start saying the phrase *skips and sass* over and over. Exaggerate the sounds, beat box them, say them faster and faster, add accents, anything—just keep repeating it until it all blends together, or you're giggling. Typically this takes less than two minutes. This activity feels like pure silliness (which is fine!), but it also physically prepares your body to engage and activates those play circuits.

2. **Crazy Counts:** Alone or with others in a circle, count down from six while shaking your right hand, then count down from six with your left hand, then with your right leg, and finally with your left leg. If you're in a group, try to make eye contact with everyone in the circle. Then start again with the right hand and count down from five. Repeat the pattern

until you get to 1-1-1-1. As you get comfortable with playing, here are variations:

Variation One: Voice

Choose a funny voice or accent for each countdown. For example:

    6-5-4-3-2-1: French Queen

    5-4-3-2-1: Mountain Man

    4-3-2-1: New Yorker

    3-2-1: Helium

    2-1: Whisper

    1: Shout

Variation Two: Time

Lengthen the exercise, counting down from a higher number. Or shorten it by starting at four or three.

Citations

Your Printed Invitation

1. Mazur, Caitlin. "40+ Worrisome Workplace Stress Statistics [2023]: Facts, Causes, and Trends." Zippia. February 11, 2023. https://www.zippia.com/advice/workplace-stress-statistics/.
2. Ibid.
3. Great Place to Work. "*Fortune* 100 Best Companies to Work For® in 2025." Accessed April 16, 2024. https://www.greatplacetowork.com/best-companies-to-work-for/.
4. Waldinger, Robert J. and Marc S. Schulz. "What's Love Got to Do with It? Social Functioning, Perceived Health, and Daily Happiness in Married Octogenarians." *Psychology and Aging* 25, no. 2 (June 2010): 422–31. https://doi.org/10.1037/a0019087.

Chapter One: Has Anyone Seen Joy?

1. McGregor, Lindsay. "It isn't just you – work really has become more dysfunctional." LinkedIn, February 22, 2024. https://www.linkedin.com/pulse/isnt-just-you-work-really-has-become-more-lindsay-mcgregor-uh48c/.

   American Psychological Association. "2023 Work in America™ Survey." Accessed August 28, 2025. https://www.apa.org/pubs/reports/work-in-america/2023-workplace-health-well-being.

2 UKG. "Mental Health at Work: Managers and Money." 2023. https://www.ukg.com/resources/white-paper/mental-health-work-managers-and-money.

Chapter Two: Languishing in Leadership

1 Gunnarsson, Jóhann Heiðberg. Death From Overwork: The Current State of *karoshi* in Japan. Bachelor's Thesis, University of Iceland, June 2022. https://skemman.is/bitstream/1946/41105/2/Death%20from%20overwork%20current%20state%20of%20karoshi%20in%20Japan.pdf.

Lim, Hyun Sul. "Karoshi: Death from Overwork." *Journal of the Korean Medical Association* 45, no. 6 (2002): 741-749. https://doi.org/10.5124/jkma.2002.45.6.741.

Adminamrc. "Karoshi and Karojisatsu in Japan." Asia Monitor Resource Center. October 1, 2004. https://amrcentre.org/karoshi-and-karojisatsu-in-japan/.

Totsuka, Etsuro and Toshio Ueyanagi. "Prevention of Death from Overwork and Remedies for Its Victims." Karoshi Hotline. August 1991. https://karoshi.jp/english/reports-overwork1.html.

BBC. "Japan's Dentsu Advertising Agency Charged Over Employee Suicide." July 8, 2017. https://www.bbc.com/news/world-asia-40541609.

Soble, Jonathan. "Chief of Dentsu, Japanese Ad Agency, to Resign over Employee's Suicide." *The New York Times*. December 16, 2016. www.nytimes.com/2016/12/28/business/dentsu-japan-resignation-employee-suicide.html.

Sato, Nan and Fisher Phillips. "Japan's Workstyle Reform Act – What Is the Compliance Deadline for Your Organization?" JD Supra. January 7, 2020. https://www.jdsupra.com/legalnews/japan-s-workstyle-reform-act-what-is-91110/.

2 US Bureau of Labor Statistics. "Table 4. Quits Levels and Rates by Industry and Region, Seasonally Adjusted." Last modified July 29, 2025. https://www.bls.gov/news.release/jolts.t04.htm#jolts_table4.f.1.

3 Harter, Jim. "U.S. Engagement Hits an 11-Year Low." Gallup. April 9, 2024. https://www.gallup.com/workplace/643286/engagement-hits-11-year-low.aspx.

4 Headspace. "2024 Workforce State of Mind." Accessed November 15, 2024. https://get.headspace.com/2024-workforce-state-of-mind.

5 Mazur, Caitlin. "40+ Worrisome Workplace Stress Statistics [2023]: Facts, Causes, and Trends." Zippia. February 11, 2023. https://www.zippia.com/advice/workplace-stress-statistics/.

6 Ibid.

7 Whitmer, Jenn. "Ep. 54 How Culture, Productivity, and Joy Go Hand in Hand with Moe Carrick." YouTube video, 28:31. September 11, 2024. https://youtu.be/yhVKXqA5xI0?si=jO-QpfC2EVOHHSrxh.

UKG. "Mental Health at Work: Managers and Money." 2023. https://www.ukg.com/resources/white-paper/mental-health-work-managers-and-money.

8 Gallup. "Employee Engagement & Experience." Accessed May 31, 2025. https://www.gallup.com/workplace/229424/employee-engagement.aspx.

9 DDI. "Confidence in Leadership Takes a Nosedive." *Global Leadership Forecast 2023*. Accessed December 11, 2024. https://www.ddiworld.com/global-leadership-forecast-2023/leadership-quality.

10 Ibid.

11 Deming, W. Edwards. *The New Economics for Industry, Government, Education*. MIT Press, 1993.

The W. Edwards Deming Institute. "Myth: If You Can't Measure It, You Can't Manage It." August 13, 2015. https://deming.org/myth-if-you-cant-measure-it-you-cant-manage-it/.

12 DDI. "Confidence in Leadership Takes a Nosedive." *Global Leadership Forecast 2023*. Accessed December 11, 2024. https://www.ddiworld.com/global-leadership-forecast-2023/leadership-quality.

13 Spheeris, Penelope, director. *Wayne's World*. Paramount Pictures, 1992.
14 Compelling Truth. "What Is the Difference between Joy and Happiness?" Accessed January 4, 2025. https://www.compellingtruth.org/joy-happiness.html.
15 Johnson, Matthew Kuan. "Joy: A Review of the Literature and Suggestions for Future Directions." *The Journal of Positive Psychology* 15, no. 1 (October 2019): 5–24. https://doi.org/10.1080/17439760.2019.1685581.
16 Garton, Eric and Michael Mankins. "Engaging Your Employees Is Good, but Don't Stop There." *Harvard Business Review*. December 9, 2015. https://hbr.org/2015/12/engaging-your-employees-is-good-but-dont-stop-there.

Barker, Eric. "How to Become 40% More Productive by Adjusting Your Work Hours." *Entrepreneur*. April 9, 2019. https://www.entrepreneur.com/en-za/growth-strategies/become-40-more-productive/326884.

17 Great Place to Work. "*Fortune* 100 Best Companies to Work For® in 2025." Accessed April 16, 2024. https://www.greatplacetowork.com/best-companies-to-work-for/.
18 *Happiness at Work Statistics: Market Data Report 2024*. Gitnux. Accessed April 30, 2024. https://gitnux.org/happiness-at-work-statistics/.
19 Housman, Michael and Dylan Minor. "Toxic Workers." Working paper, Harvard Business School, 2015. https://www.hbs.edu/ris/Publication%20Files/16-057_d45c0b4f-fa19-49de-8f1b-4b12fe054fea.pdf.
20 Ibid.
21 Kohler, Lindsay. "Why Joy Should Be Your New Key Performance Indicator." *Forbes*. May 31, 2024. https://www.forbes.com/sites/lindsaykohler/2024/05/31/why-joy-should-be-your-new-key-performance-indicator/.
22 Lovich, Deborah and Rosie Sargeant. "Enjoying Work Matters More Than You May Realize." BCG. February 13, 2024. https://www.bcg.com/publications/2024/joy-at-work-matters-more-than-you-realize.

Kohler, Lindsay. "Why Joy Should Be Your New Key Performance Indicator." *Forbes*. May 31, 2024. https://www.forbes.com/sites/lindsaykohler/2024/05/31/why-joy-should-be-your-new-key-performance-indicator/.

Chapter Three: Don't Let Your Personality Drive the Bus

1 Church, Allan H. "Managerial Self-Awareness in High-Performing Individuals." *Journal of Applied Psychology* 82, no. 2 (May 1997): 281-292. http://dx.doi.org/10.1037//0021-9010.82.2.281.

Bass, Bernard M. and Francis J. Yammarino. "Congruence of Self and Other' Leadership Ratings of Naval Officers for Understanding Successful Performance." *Applied Psychology* 40, no. 4 (October 1991): 437-454. https://doi.org/10.1111/j.1464-0597.1991.tb01002.x.

2 MIT Sloan Management Review. "Self-Awareness: A Key to Better Leadership." May 7, 2012. https://sloanreview.mit.edu/article/self-awareness-a-key-to-better-leadership/.
3 Eurich, Tasha. "What Self-Awareness Really Is (and How to Cultivate It)." *Harvard Business Review*. January 4, 2018. https://hbr.org/2018/01/what-self-awareness-really-is-and-how-to-cultivate-it.
4 Luft, J. and H. Ingham. "The Johari Window, a Graphic Model of Interpersonal Awareness" (PDF). Proceedings of the Western Training Laboratory in Group Development. University of California, 1955.

Luft, Joseph. "The Johari Window: A Graphic Model of Awareness in Interpersonal Relations." September 1996. Columbia University. https://static1.squarespace.com/static/572d003b40261d2ef97e5b0b/t/5ca20f5d6e9a7f566fc3ef14/1554124637198/The-Johari-Window.pdf.

5 Jung, C. G. *Aion: Researches into the Phenomenology of the Self*. Translated by R. F. C. Hull. *The Collected Works of C. G. Jung*, vol. 9, 2nd ed. Princeton University Press, 1959.

6. Whitmer, Jenn. Personal notes from "Enneagram Stances," conducted by Suzanne Stabile. Nashville, TN. September 17–18, 2021.
7. Mansky, Jackie. "There Was the Magazine Quiz. Then Came the Internet. What Now?" *Smithsonian Magazine*. February 11, 2019. https://www.smithsonianmag.com/arts-culture/magazine-quiz-internet-what-now-180971463/.

   Fazeli, Seyed Hossein. "The Exploring Nature of the Assessment Instrument of Five Factors of Personality Traits in the Current Studies of Personality." *Asian Social Science* 8, no. 2 (January 2012): 264. http://dx.doi.org/10.5539/ass.v8n2p264.
8. Lynn, Jonathan, director. *Clue*. Paramount Pictures, 1985.
9. Franklin, Benjamin. *Poor Richard's Improved, 1750*. Founders Online, National Archives. 1750. https://founders.archives.gov/documents/Franklin/01-03-02-0176.
10. Forrester, Brent, writer. The Office, season 9, episode 4, "Work Bus." Directed by Bryan Cranston, featuring Rainn Wilson, John Krasinski, Jenna Fischer, et al. Aired October 18, 2012, on NBC.
11. Heuertz, Christopher L. *The Enneagram of Belonging: A Compassionate Journey of Self-Acceptance*. Zondervan, 2020.

Chapter Four: Cut! Rewrite! Action!

1. Sondheim, Stephen and James Lapine. *Into the Woods*. New York: Theatre Communications Group, 1987.
2. Champion, Mary Clare. "Understanding Child Narrative Development Through the Lens of Lessons and Dialogue in Mother-Child Interactions." PhD diss., University of Tennessee, December 2005. https://trace.tennessee.edu/cgi/viewcontent.cgi?article=1842&context=utk_graddiss.
3. Kegan, Robert. "Making Meaning: The Constructive-Development Approach to Persons and Practice." *The Personnel and Guidance Journal* 58, no. 5 (January 1980): 373-380. https://doi.org/10.1002/j.2164-4918.1980.tb00416.x.
4. Hall, Kindra. *The Story Edge: How Leaders Harness the Power of Stories to Win in Business*. HarperCollins Leadership, 2024.
5. Furnham, Adrian. *Lay Theories, Everyday Understanding of Problems in the Social Sciences*. Pergamon Press, 1988.
6. Yeager, David S., Gregory M. Walton, Shannon T. Brady, et al. "Teaching a Lay Theory Before College Narrows Achievement Gaps at Scale." *Proceedings of the National Academy of Sciences* 113, no. 24 (May 2016): E3341-E3348. https://doi.org/10.1073/pnas.1524360113.
7. Mason, T.B., K.E. Smith, A. Engwall, et al. "Self-Discrepancy Theory as a Transdiagnostic Framework: A Meta-Analysis of Self-Discrepancy and Psychopathology." *Psychological Bulletin* 145, no. 4 (2019): 372–389. https://psycnet.apa.org/doi/10.1037/bul0000186.
8. Sherif, M. and C.I. Hovland. *Social Judgement: Assimilation and Contrast Effects in Communication and Attitude Change*. Yale University Press, 1961.

   Wood, Joanne V., W.Q. Elaine Perunovic, and John W. Lee. "Positive Self-Statements: Power for Some, Peril for Others." *Psychological Science* 20, no. 7 (July 2009). https://doi.org/10.1111/j.1467-9280.2009.02370.x.
9. Williams, David M. and Ryan E. Rhodes. "The Confounded Self-Efficacy Construct: Conceptual Analysis and Recommendations for Future Research." *Health Psychology Review* 10, no. 2 (June 2016): 113–128. https://doi.org/10.1080/17437199.2014.941998.
10. Lipton, James, host. Inside the Actors Studio, season 12, episode 11, "Dave Chappelle." Aired February 12, 2006, on Bravo.

Chapter Five: Eagles on Posters Don't Fly

1. Disney Institute. 2019. "Disney Customer Service 101: Why Courtesy Is Not Always Our First Priority." *Disney Institute* (blog). *Disney Institute*. February 19, 2019. https://www.

disneyinstitute.com/blog/disney-customer-service-101-why-courtesy-is-not-always-our-first-priority/.

Whitmer, Jenn. Personal notes from Poetics Retreat, Walt Disney World Resort, Orlando, FL, January 12–15, 2023.

2. Whitmer, Jenn. "Ep. 72 Purpose Unleashed: Successful Leadership with Jade Simmons." YouTube video, 25:00. January 15, 2025. https://youtu.be/GgtlQKm3ejo?si=gZrJkCBfHOZpJWTX.

3. Whitmer, Jenn. "Ep. 58 How Values Build Your Leadership with Ken Black." YouTube video, 24:29. October 9, 2024. https://youtu.be/8SNpFuyHH6c?si=EBnYTbV3G2BNuERW.

4. Groves, Mark, host. "#312 Change Yourself, Change the World." The Mark Groves Podcast (podcast). September 21, 2023. Accessed March 8, 2025. https://markgroves.com/episode/change-yourself-change-the-world-solo-episode/.

5. Strategy & Part of the PwC Network. "Our Research on the Connection Between Strategic Purpose and Motivation." Accessed August 29, 2025. https://www.strategyand.pwc.com/it/en/unique-solutions/capabilities-driven-strategy/approach/research-motivation.html.

6. American Psychological Association. "2023 Work in America™ Survey." Accessed August 28, 2025. https://www.apa.org/pubs/reports/work-in-america/2023-workplace-health-well-being.

7. Sustainable Brands. "More and More Talent Ready to Leave Companies Over Misalignment of Values." February 16, 2023. https://sustainablebrands.com/read/more-and-more-talent-ready-to-leave-companies-over-misalignment-of-values.

Brown, Stacy M. "Target Takes a Hit: $12.4 Billion in Value Lost After Boycott." *The Charlotte Post.* March 6, 2025. https://www.thecharlottepost.com/news/2025/03/06/business/target-takes-a-hit-12.4-billion-in-value-lost-after-boycott/.

8. Ibid.

9. Hill, David and Tim Zelina. "The Numbers Are In: Economic Blackout Dragged Down Retail Traffic." People's World. March 10, 2025. https://www.peoplesworld.org/article/the-numbers-are-in-economic-blackout-dragged-down-retail-traffic/.

10. The Culture Factor. "Country Comparison Tool." Accessed March 8, 2025. https://www.theculturefactor.com/country-comparison-tool?countries=ghana*%2Cunited+states.

11. Goff, Bob. *Catching Whimsy: 365 Days of Possibility*. Thomas Nelson, 2024.

12. Goff, Bob. *Dream Big: Know What You Want, Why You Want It, and What You're Going to Do About It*. Thomas Nelson, 2020.

Goff, Bob. "FW: It's Thursday." Facebook, February 21, 2013. https://www.facebook.com/bobgoffis/posts/fw-its-thursday-you-can-quit-anything-on-a-thursday-quit-believing-the-lie-that-/433709700037642/.

13. Catmull, Ed and Amy Wallace. *Creativity, Inc.: Overcoming the Unseen Forces That Stand in the Way of True Inspiration*. Random House, 2014.

McKee, Robert. *Story: Substance, Structure, Style, and the Principles of Screenwriting*. Dey Street Books, 2010.

Chapter Six: Feelings at the Table

1. Troyes, Chrétien de. *Perceval: The Story of the Grail*. Yale University Press, 2008. Note: Author's loose retelling of Perceval.

2. Raz, Guy, host. "Jewel: When I Was Poor, I Rejected $1M and Built a Plan for My Happiness." The Great Creators with Guy Raz (podcast). January 9, 2024. Accessed March 16, 2025. https://www.thegreatcreators.com/episodes/jewel.

3. eLearning Infographics. *Emotional Intelligence and Leadership* [infographic]. Accessed March 16, 2025. https://elearninginfographics.com/wp-content/uploads/Emotional-Intelligence-and-Leadership-Infographic.png.

4 Bradberry, Travis. "Why Emotional Intelligence Can Save Your Life?" TalentSmartEQ. June 20, 2022. https://www.talentsmarteq.com/emotional-intelligence-can-boost-your-career-and-save-your-life/.

5 TalentSmart. "The Business Case for Emotional Intelligence (EQ)." Last modified 2009. https://www.talentsmarteq.com/media/uploads/pdfs/The_Business_Case_For_EQ.pdf.

6 Dethmer, Jim, Diana Chapman, and Kaley Klemp. *15 Commitments of Conscious Leadership: A New Paradigm for Sustainable Success.*" Dethmer, Chapman & Klemp, 2015.

Miller, Michael. "Emotions, Feelings and Moods: What's the Difference?" Six Seconds. Accessed October 18, 2024. https://www.6seconds.org/2022/07/15/emotion-feeling-mood/.

Doucleff, Michaeleen. "Mapping Emotions On the Body: Love Makes Us Warm All Over." *NPR.* December 30, 2013. https://www.npr.org/sections/health-shots/2013/12/30/258313116/mapping-emotions-on-the-body-love-makes-us-warm-all-over.

Hamer, Ashley. "Scientists Have Mapped Where People Feel Emotions in Their Bodies." Discovery. August 1, 2019. https://www.discovery.com/science/scientists-have-mapped-where-people-feel-emotions-in-their-bodie.

7 Beck, Julie. "Hard Feelings: Science's Struggle to Define Emotions." *The Atlantic.* February 24, 2015. https://www.theatlantic.com/health/archive/2015/02/hard-feelings-sciences-struggle-to-define-emotions/385711/.

8 Blanning, Bill. "Sub Sinks Tugboat; Crewman Missing." UPI. June 14, 1989. https://www.upi.com/Archives/1989/06/14/Sub-sinks-tugboat-crewman-missing/1385613800000/.

Jones, Jack. "Sub's Sonar Failed to Detect Doomed Tug, Inquiry Finds." *Los Angeles Times.* June 22, 1989. https://www.latimes.com/archives/la-xpm-1989-06-22-mn-2845-story.html.

National Transportation Safety Board, Washington, D.C. Bureau of Accident Investigation. "Marine Accident Report – Sinking of the U.S. Tug BARCONA by the U.S. Navy Nuclear Attack Submarine USS HOUSTON (SSN 713), San Predro Channel, Near Santa Catalina Island, California, June 14, 1989." National Technical Reports Library. 1990. https://ntrl.ntis.gov/NTRL/dashboard/searchResults/titleDetail/PB90916406.xhtml.

9 Marr, Natalie S., Nur Hani Zainal, and Michelle G. Newman. "Focus on and Venting of Negative Emotion Mediates the 18-Year Bi-Directional Relations Between Major Depressive Disorder and Generalized Anxiety Disorder Diagnoses." *Journal of Affective Disorders* 303 (April 2022): 10–17. https://doi.org/10.1016/j.jad.2022.01.079.

Dethmer, Jim, Diana Chapman, and Kaley Klemp. *15 Commitments of Conscious Leadership: A New Paradigm for Sustainable Success.*" Dethmer, Chapman & Klemp, 2015.

10 American Academy of Child & Adolescent Psychiatry. "Physical Symptoms of Emotional Distress: Somatic Symptoms and Related Disorders." Last modified October 2023. https://www.aacap.org/AACAP/Families_and_Youth/Facts_for_Families/FFF-Guide/Physical_Symptoms_of_Emotional_Distress-Somatic_Symptoms_and_Related_Disorders-124.aspx.

WUSA9. "The 90 Second Life Cycle of an Emotion." YouTube video, 4:49. May 26, 2021. https://youtu.be/vxARXvljKBA?si=uTYWsBkL5Q9m2-kH.

11 Guan, Bichen and Denise M. Jepsen. "Burnout From Emotion Regulation at Work: The Moderating Role of Gratitude." *Personality and Individual Differences* 156 (April 2020): 109703. https://doi.org/10.1016/j.paid.2019.109703.

Dollard, Maureen F. and Arnold B. Bakker. "Psychosocial Safety Climate as a Precursor to Conducive Work Environments, Psychological Health Problems, and Employee Engagement." *Journal of Occupational and Organizational Psychology* 83, no. 3 (December 2010): 579-599. https://doi.org/10.1348/096317909X470690.

12 Torre, Jared B. and Matthew D. Lieberman. "Putting Feelings into Words: Affect Labeling as Implicit Emotion Regulation." *Emotion Review* 10, no. 2 (March 2018): 116–124. https://doi.org/10.1177/1754073917742706.

13 Miller, Michael. "Emotions, Feelings and Moods: What's the Difference?" Six Seconds. Accessed October 18, 2024. https://www.6seconds.org/2022/07/15/emotion-feeling-mood/.

Doucleff, Michaeleen. "Mapping Emotions On the Body: Love Makes Us Warm All Over." *NPR*. December 30, 2013. https://www.npr.org/sections/health-shots/2013/12/30/258313116/mapping-emotions-on-the-body-love-makes-us-warm-all-over.

Hamer, Ashley. "Scientists Have Mapped Where People Feel Emotions in Their Bodies." Discovery. August 1, 2019. https://www.discovery.com/science/scientists-have-mapped-where-people-feel-emotions-in-their-bodie.

WUSA9. "The 90 Second Life Cycle of an Emotion." YouTube video, 4:49. May 26, 2021. https://youtu.be/vxARXvljKBA?si=uTYWsBkL5Q9m2-kH.

14 Fosslien, Liz and Mollie West Duffy. *No Hard Feelings: The Secret Power of Embracing Emotions at Work*. Portfolio, 2019.

15 Kong, Yu. "Are Emotions Contagious? A Conceptual Review of Studies in Language Education." *Frontiers in Psychology* 13 (October 2022). https://doi.org/10.3389/fpsyg.2022.1048105.

16 Miguel Costa, Rui. "Projection (Defense Mechanism)." *Encyclopedia of Personality and Individual Differences* (January 2017): 1–3. https://link.springer.com/referencework/10.1007/978-3-319-28099-8.

17 Wallake, Braden. "This will be the most vulnerable thing I'll ever share." LinkedIn, 2021. https://www.linkedin.com/posts/bradenwallake_this-will-be-the-most-vulnerable-thing-ill-activity-6962886723617910784-_L4w?utm_source=share&utm_medium=member_desktop&rcm=ACoAACrb8T4BfExlW2vl1u8IP1dHaZq5Ui5tK2g.

Wallake, Braden. "Hey everyone, yes, I am the crying CEO." LinkedIn, 2021. https://www.linkedin.com/posts/bradenwallake_hey-everyone-yes-i-am-the-crying-ceo-no-activity-6963185324143390721-7pDH?utm_source=share&utm_medium=member_desktop&rcm=ACoAACrb8T4BfExlW2vl1u8IP1dHaZq5Ui5tK2g.

18 Husain, Shezray, Feroz Khan, and Waqas Mirza. "How Starbucks Pulled Itself Out of the 2008 Financial Meltdown." *Business Today Magazine*. September 28, 2014. https://www.businesstoday.in/magazine/lbs-case-study/story/how-starbucks-survived-the-financial-meltdown-of-2008-136126-2014-09-22.

CNN Money. "Coffee Break for Starbucks' 135,000 Baristas." February 26, 2008. https://money.cnn.com/2008/01/17/news/newsmakers/starbucks.fortune/.

Summit. "These Lessons Took Howard Schultz from Starbucks CEO to the Presidential Race." YouTube video, 50:40. January 29, 2019. https://youtu.be/pDPejlUxA_A?si=7vUHXCKSWYD8riMj.

O'Connor, Clare. "Starbucks Billionaire Howard Schultz to Oprah: It's OK for Men to Cry (Even CEOs)." *Forbes*. Last modified December 4, 2013. https://www.forbes.com/sites/clareoconnor/2013/12/04/starbucks-billionaire-howard-schultz-to-oprah-its-ok-for-men-to-cry-even-ceos/.

Chapter Seven: Clean It Up

1 Campbell, Kimberly Chrisman. 2015. "The Height of Fashion." *Iris Blog* (blog). *Getty*. July 26, 2015. https://blogs.getty.edu/iris/the-height-of-fashion/.

2 Shannon, C.E. "A Mathematical Theory of Communication." *The Bell System Technical Journal* 27, no. 3 (July 1948): 379–423. https://doi.org/10.1002/j.1538-7305.1948.tb01338.x.

3 Mazur, Caitlin. "40+ Worrisome Workplace Stress Statistics [2023]: Facts, Causes, and Trends." Zippia. February 11, 2023. https://www.zippia.com/advice/workplace-stress-statistics/.

4 Frizzell, Brian and Brock, hosts. "Communication – 3 Words That Create Barricades." Source Health (podcast). 2019. Accessed June 1, 2025. https://sourcehealth.org/calmmunication-3-words.

5 Brown, Brené. *Dare to Lead: Brave Work, Tough Conversations, Whole Hearts*. Random House, 2018.

6 Ibid.

7   Ibid.
8   Silva, André, José Ferreira-Alves, and Joana Arantes. "Book Review: We Are Unique When We Cry." *Evolutionary Psychology* 11, no. 1 (January 2013): 85-88. https://doi.org/10.1177/147470491301100108.

    Oaklander, Mandy. "The Science of Crying." *Time*. March 16, 2019. https://time.com/4254089/science-crying/.
9   WUSA9. "The 90 Second Life Cycle of an Emotion." YouTube video, 4:49. May 26, 2021. https://youtu.be/vxARXvljKBA?si=uTYWsBkL5Q9m2-kH.
10 Zak, Paul J. "Why Inspiring Stories Make Us React: The Neuroscience of Narrative." *Cerebrum* (February 2015). https://pubmed.ncbi.nlm.nih.gov/26034526/.
11 Storr, Will. *The Science of Storytelling: Why Stories Make Us Human and How to Tell Them Better*. Harry N. Abrams, 2020.
12 Zak, Paul J. "Why Inspiring Stories Make Us React: The Neuroscience of Narrative." *Cerebrum* (February 2015). https://pubmed.ncbi.nlm.nih.gov/26034526/.
13 Green, Melanie C. and Timothy C. Brock. "The Role of Transportation in the Persuasiveness of Public Narratives." *Journal of Personality and Social Psychology* 79, no. 5 (November 2000): 701–21. https://doi.org/10.1037/0022-3514.79.5.701.

    Zimney, Sally Koering. *Speaking Story: Using the Magic of Storytelling to Make Your Mark, Pitch Your Ideas, and Ignite Meaningful Change*." Wise Ink Creative Publishing, 2024.
14 Martinez-Conde, Susana, Robert G. Alexander, Deborah Blum, et al. "The Storytelling Brain: How Neuroscience Stories Help Bridge the Gap Between Research and Society." *Journal of Neuroscience* 39, no. 42 (October 2019): 8285–8290. https://doi.org/10.1523/JNEUROSCI.1180-19.2019.

    Pautrel, Amy. 2024. "Bolster Your Brain by Stimulating the Vagus Nerve." *Cedars-Sinai Blog* (blog). *Cedars-Sinai*. March 21, 2024. https://www.cedars-sinai.org/blog/stimulating-the-vagus-nerve.html.

    Harris III. *The Wonder Switch: The Difference Between Limiting Your Life and Living Your Dream*. Zondervan, 2020.
15 Dickerson, Kelly, Peter Gerhardstein, and Alecia Moser. "The Role of the Human Mirror Neuron System in Supporting Communication in a Digital World." *Frontiers in Psychology* 8 (May 2017): 698. https://doi.org/10.3389/fpsyg.2017.00698.
16 Mehrabian, Albert. *Nonverbal Communication*. Routledge, 1972.
17 Van Edwards, Vanessa. *Cues: Master the Secret Language of Charismatic Communication*. Portfolio, 2022.
18 Flynn, Jack. "25+ Critical Communication in the Workplace Statistics [2023]: How Effective is Good Communication?" Zippia. February 20, 2023. https://www.zippia.com/advice/communication-in-the-workplace-statistics/.

Chapter Eight: Conflict Is Opportunity

1   Canary, D. J., W.R. Cupach, and S.J. Messman. *Relationship Conflict: Conflict in Parent–Child, Friendship, and Romantic Relationships*. Sage Publications, Inc., 1995.
2   Syrtash, Andrea. "All Couples Fight: 11 Therapist-Approved Tips to Argue Fairly." *Glamour*. February 29, 2020. www.glamour.com/story/how-much-fighting-is-too-much-in-a-relationship.
3   Desilver, Drew. "The Polarization in Today's Congress Has Roots That Go Back Decades." Pew Research Center. March 10, 2022. https://www.pewresearch.org/short-reads/2022/03/10/the-polarization-in-todays-congress-has-roots-that-go-back-decades/.

    Davey, Liane. "The Case for More Conflict." Liane Davey. October 5, 2016. https://lianedavey.com/more-conflict-please/.

4   CPP Global. Huma Capital Report: Workplace Conflict and How Businesses Can Harness It to Thrive. The Myer Briggs, 2008. https://shop.themyersbriggs.com/pdfs/cpp_global_human_capital_report_workplace_conflict.pdf.

Salary.com. "Compensation Team Leader Salary in the United States." Accessed May 5, 2025. https://www.salary.com/research/salary/alternate/compensation-team-leader-salary.

5   Whitmer, Jenn. "Your Inner Story Can Make or Break Your Negotiation." YouTube video, 19:49. February 5, 2024. https://www.youtube.com/live/ooxWBdSgEkA?si=6eIpiCP9n2G-hUFOX.

Chapter Nine: The Wisdom of Tomatoes

1   Levine, Ilana, host. "Episode 143-Tommy Kail." Little Known Facts (podcast). May 12, 2019. Accessed August 30, 2025. https://www.littleknownfactspodcast.com/episodes-122151/2019/5/12/episode-143-tommy-kail.

2   Duke, Annie. *Thinking in Bets: Making Smarter Decisions When You Don't Have All the Facts.* Portfolio, 2019.

3   Ibid.

4   Lang, Susan S. "'Mindless Autopilot' Drives People to Dramatically Underestimate How Many Daily Food Decisions They Make, Cornell Study Finds." *Cornell Chronical.* December 22, 2006. https://news.cornell.edu/stories/2006/12/mindless-autopilot-drives-people-underestimate-food-decisions.

Pignatiello, Grant A., Richard J. Martin, and Ronald L. Hickman Jr. "Decision Fatigue: A Conceptual Analysis." *Journal of Health Psychology* 25, no. 1 (January 2020): 123-135. https://doi.org/10.1177/1359105318763510.

5   Zaltman, Gerald. 2003. "The Subconscious Mind of the Consumer (And How to Reach It)." *Working Knowledge* (blog). *Harvard Business School.* January 13, 2003. https://www.library.hbs.edu/working-knowledge/the-subconscious-mind-of-the-consumer-and-how-to-reach-it.

6   Dale Carnegie of Orange County. "Understanding How Your Employees Make Decisions." Accessed August 30, 2025. https://ocdalecarnegie.com/understanding-how-your-employees-make-decisions/.

7   Oracle. "Global Study: 70% of Business Leaders Would Prefer a Robot to Make Their Decisions." *PR Newswire.* April 19, 2023. https://www.prnewswire.com/news-releases/global-study-70-of-business-leaders-would-prefer-a-robot-to-make-their-decisions-301799591.html.

8   Fruit Trade Journal Co. "Virginia Truck Farms: How They Supply Food for The Great Cities." *Fruit Trade Journal and Produce Record* 56: 14. January 1916. https://books.google.com/books?id=xtlKAQAAMAAJ&vq=john+nix+fruit+commission&source=gbs_navlinks_s.

9   U.S. Supreme Court. "Nix v. Hedden, 149 U.S. 304 (1893)." Justia. May 10, 1893. https://supreme.justia.com/cases/federal/us/149/304/.

10 U.S. Supreme Court. "Nix v. Hedden, 149 U.S. 306 (1893)." Justia. May 10, 1893. https://supreme.justia.com/cases/federal/us/149/304/.

11 U.S. Supreme Court. "Nix v. Hedden, 149 U.S. 307 (1893)." Justia. May 10, 1893. https://supreme.justia.com/cases/federal/us/149/304/.

12 Some deep economic theory with historical consequences, the 1883 tariffs continued a protectionist model of economic policy that significantly contributed to World War I. Taussig, F. W. *The Tariff History of the United States.* Elibron Classics, 2005.

13 Donoghue, Kate. "Emotional Decision Making: Hardwired and Helpful. Template University Beasley School of Law. Accessed August 30, 2025. https://law.temple.edu/aer/2024/09/07/emotional-decision-making-hardwired-and-helpful/.

14 Ibid.

Okon-Singer, Hadas, Talma Hendler, Luiz Pessoa, and Alexander J. Shackman. "The Neurobiology of Emotion–Cognition Interactions: Fundamental Questions and Strategies for Future Research." *Frontiers in Human Neuroscience* 9 (February 2015). https://doi.org/10.3389/fnhum.2015.00058.

Cassidy, John. "Mind Games." *The New Yorker*. September 11, 2006. https://www.newyorker.com/magazine/2006/09/18/mind-games-3.

15. Lewis, Michael. *The Undoing Project*. W.W. Norton & Company, 2016.
16. Sullivan, Dan and Dr. Benjamin Hardy. *10x is Easier than 2x*. Hay House, 2023.
17. Ibid.
18. Love, Jessica. "Take 5: How Fear Influences Our Decisions." KelloggInsight. February 23, 2023. https://insight.kellogg.northwestern.edu/article/take-5-how-fear-influences-our-decisions.
19. Uzhga-Rebrov, Oleg and Peter Grabusts. "Decision Making Based on Possibility Theory." *63rd International Scientific Conference on Information Technology and Management Science of Riga Technical University* (2022): 1-7. https://doi.org/10.1109/ITMS56974.2022.9937090.
20. Duke, Annie. *Thinking in Bets: Making Smarter Decisions When You Don't Have All the Facts*. Portfolio, 2019.
21. Freeman, Emily P. *The Next Right Thing: A Simple, Soulful Practice for Making Life Decisions*. Revell, 2019.
22. Iyengar, Sheena Sethi and Mark Lepper. "When Choice is Demotivating: Can One Desire Too Much of a Good Thing?" *Journal of Personality and Social Psychology* 79, no. 6 (January 2001): 995-1006. http://dx.doi.org/10.1037/0022-3514.79.6.995.
23. Iyengar, Sheena. *The Art of Choosing*. Little, Brown, 2010.
24. Ibid.
25. Peterson, Eugene H. *The Message: The Bible in Contemporary Language*. NavPress, 2002.
26. Singer, Natasha. "When the Data Struts Its Stuff." *The New York Times*. April 2, 2011. www.nytimes.com/2011/04/03/business/03stream.html.
27. Johnson, Lukas, Shawn Ryan, and Matthew Quirk, writers. The Night Agent, season 2, episode 6, "A Good Agent." Directed by Ana Lily Amirpour, featuring Gabriel Basso, Luciane Buchanan, Arienne Mandi, et al. Aired January 23, 2025, on Netflix. www.netflix.com/title/81450827.
28. Iyengar, Sheena. *The Art of Choosing*. Little, Brown, 2010.

Part III: Experience

1. Associated Press. "Peirsol Gets Gold After All." ESPN. August 19, 2004. https://www.espn.com/olympics/summer04/swimming/news/story?id=1862948.

Roll, Rich, host. "Olympian Aaron Peirsol's Love Affair with Water." The Rich Roll Podcast (podcast). November 16, 2015. Accessed August 30, 2025. https://www.richroll.com/podcast/aaron-peirsol/.

Chapter Ten: Your Inbox Isn't a Hippo

1. Labour Bureau of India. "Wages Rate Data." August 2019. https://labourbureau.gov.in/assets/images/pdf/WRRI_August_2019.pdf.

Yeung, Jessie, Helen Regan, and Swati Gupta. "India's Sixth Biggest City is Almost Entirely Out of Water." CNN. Last modified June 20, 2019. https://www.cnn.com/2019/06/19/india/chennai-water-crisis-intl-hnk/index.html.

Palanichamy, Raj Bhagat. "How Does a Flood-prone City Run Out of Water? Inside Chennai's "Day Zero" Crisis." World Resources Institute. June 25, 2019. https://www.wri.org/insights/how-does-flood-prone-city-run-out-water-inside-chennais-day-zero-crisis.

2. Rubin, Rick. *The Creative Act: A Way of Being*. Penguin Press, 2023.
3. O'Hanarahan, Peter. Private Class, The Embodied Enneagram and the Narrative Enneagram. March 11, 2025.

4   The Commercial Appeal. "Bradford F. Baker." Legacy. August 7, 2016. https://www.legacy.com/us/obituaries/commercialappeal/name/bradford-baker-obituary?id=12098007.

    Brantley, Camille. Personal interviews with the author. May 21, 2021 and November 16, 2024.

5   Marsland, Anna L., Catherine Walsh, Kimberly Lockwood, and Neha A. John-Henderson. "The Effects of Acute Psychological Stress on Circulating and Stimulated Inflammatory Markers: A Systematic Review and Meta-Analysis." *Brain, Behavior, and Immunity* 46 (August 2017): 208-219. https://doi.org/10.1016/j.bbi.2017.01.011.

    Castaldo, Rossana, Paolo Melillo, Umberto Marcello Bracale, et al. "Acute Mental Stress Assessment via Short Term HRW Analysis in Healthy Adults: A Systematic Review with Meta-Analysis." *Biomedical Signal Processing and Control* 18 (April 2015): 370-377. https://doi.org/10.1016/j.bspc.2015.02.012.

6   Morey, Jennifer N., Ian A. Boggero, April B. Scott, and Suzanne C. Segerstrom. "Current Directions in Stress and Human Immune Function." *Current Opinion in Psychology* 5 (October 2015): 13-17. https://doi.org/10.1016/j.copsyc.2015.03.007.

7   Nagoski, Emily and Amelia Nagoski. *Burnout: The Secret to Unlocking the Stress Cycle.* Vermilion, 2019.

8   Kogler, Lydia, Veronika I. Müller, Amy Chang, et al. "Psychosocial Versus Physiological Stress — Meta-Analyses on Deactivations and Activations of the Neural Correlates of Stress Reactions." *NeuroImage* 119 (October 2015): 235-251. https://doi.org/10.1016/j.neuroimage.2015.06.059.

9   Nagoski, Emily and Amelia Nagoski. *Burnout: The Secret to Unlocking the Stress Cycle.* Vermilion, 2019.

10 Whitmer, Jenn. "Ep. 72 Purpose Unleashed: Successful Leadership with Jade Simmons." YouTube video, 25:00. January 15, 2025. https://youtu.be/GgtlQKm3ejo?si=X2Pf3Dv3zrLkwCKv.

11 Robbins, Mel, host. "The Body Reset: How Women Should Eat & Exercise for Health, Fat Loss, & Energy." The Mel Robbins Podcast (podcast). March 27, 2025. Accessed August 30, 2025. https://www.melrobbins.com/episode/episode-275/.

12 CDC. "Measuring Physical Activity Intensity." Last modified June 3, 2022. https://www.cdc.gov/physicalactivity/basics/measuring/index.html.

13 I think it was Shauna Niequist, but it was years ago, and searching found no sources!

14 Stone, Linda. "Just Breathe: Building the Case for Email Apnea." *Huffpost*. Last modified November 17, 2011. https://www.huffpost.com/entry/just-breathe-building-the_b_85651.

    Gupta, Alisha Haridasani. "What Is Screen Apnea? Why You May Breathe Less While Online." *The New York Times*. April 21, 2023. https://www.nytimes.com/2023/08/21/well/live/screen-apnea-breathing.html.

15 Ibid.

16 O'Hanrahan, Peter. *Embodied Enneagram Handbook.* Accessed February 15, 2025. https://theenneagramatwork.com/embodied-enneagram-handbook/.

17 Ross, Elizabeth M. "What Is Causing Our Epidemic of Loneliness and How Can We Fix It?" Harvard Graduate School of Education. October 25, 2024. https://www.gse.harvard.edu/ideas/usable-knowledge/24/10/what-causing-our-epidemic-loneliness-and-how-can-we-fix-it.

18 Sandstrom, Gillian M., Erica J. Boothby, and Gus Cooney. "Talking to Strangers: A Week-Long Intervention Reduces Psychological Barriers to Social Connection." *Journal of Experimental Social Psychology* 102 (September 2022): 104356. https://doi.org/10.1016/j.jesp.2022.104356.

19 Bazzini, Doris G., Elizabeth R. Stack, Penny D. Martincin, and Carmen P. Davis. "The Effect of Reminiscing about Laughter on Relationship Satisfaction." *Motivation and Emotion* 31, no. 1 (October 19, 2006): 25–34. https://doi.org/10.1007/s11031-006-9045-6.

20 NPR/Ted Staff. "Why Is Laughter Contagious?" Ted Radio Hour. March 4, 2016. https://www.npr.org/2016/03/04/468877928/why-is-laughter-contagious.
21 Dinesen, Isak. *Seven Gothic Tales*. Modern Library, 1939.
22 Payton, L'Oreal Thompson. "Eight Simple Ways to Close a Stress Cycle, According to Experts." Fortune Well. November 21, 2022. https://fortune.com/well/2022/11/21/how-to-close-a-stress-cycle/.
23 Bylsma, Lauren M., Asmir Gračanin, and Ad J.J.M. Vingerhoets. "The Neurobiology of Human Crying." *Clinical Autonomic Research* 29 (April 2018): 63–73. https://doi.org/10.1007/s10286-018-0526-y.
24 Eckstein, Monika, Ilshat Mamaev, Beate Ditzen, and Uta Sailer. "Calming Effects of Touch in Human, Animal, and Robotic Interaction—Scientific State-of-the-Art and Technical Advances." *Frontiers in Psychiatry* 11 (November 2020). https://doi.org/10.3389/fpsyt.2020.555058.
25 Friedman, Esther M., Arun S. Karlamangla, David M. Almeida, and Teresa E. Seeman. "Social Strain and Cortisol Regulation in Midlife in the US." *Social Science & Medicine* 74, no. 4 (February 2012): 607–615. https://doi.org/10.1016/j.socscimed.2011.11.003.
26 Grewen, Karen M., Bobbi J. Anderson, Susan S. Girdler, and Kathleen C. Light. "Warm Partner Contact Is Related to Lower Cardiovascular Reactivity." *Behavioral Medicine* 29, no. 3 (January 2003): 123–130. https://doi.org/10.1080/08964280309596065.
27 Gottman, John M. "How Couples Build Trust with Attunement." In *The Science of Trust: Emotional Attunement for Couples*. W. W. Norton & Company, 2011.
28 Pendry, Patricia and Jaymie L. Vandagriff. "Animal Visitation Program (AVP) Reduces Cortisol Levels of University Students: A Randomized Controlled Trial." *AERA Open* 5, no. 2 (April 2019). https://doi.org/10.1177/2332858419852592.
29 Fave, Antonella Delle, Ingrid Brdar, Dianne Vella-Brodrick, and Marie P. Wissing. "Religion, Spirituality, and Well-Being Across Nations: The Eudaemonic and Hedonic Happiness Investigation." *Well-Being and Cultures* (January 2012): 117-134. https://doi.org/10.1007/978-94-007-4611-4_8.
30 Balboni, Tracy A., Tyler J. VanderWeele, Stephanie D. Doan-Soares, et al. "Spirituality in Serious Illness and Health." *JAMA* 328, no. 2 (July 2022): 184. https://doi.org/10.1001/jama.2022.11086.
31 Conner, Tamlin S., Colin G. DeYoung, and Paul J. Silvia. "Everyday Creative Activity as a Path to Flourishing." *The Journal of Positive Psychology* 13, no. 2 (November 2016): 181–89. https://doi.org/10.1080/17439760.2016.1257049.
32 Caddy, L., F. Crawford, and A.C. Page. "'Painting a Path to Wellness': Correlations Between Participating in a Creative Activity Group and Improved Measured Mental Health Outcome." *Journal of Psychiatric and Mental Health Nursing* 19, no. 4 (August 2011): 327-333. https://doi.org/10.1111/j.1365-2850.2011.01785.x.
33 Vilhelmson, Bertil, Erik Elldér, and Eva Thulin. "What Did We Do When the Internet Wasn't around? Variation in Free-Time Activities among Three Young-Adult Cohorts from 1990/1991, 2000/2001, and 2010/2011." *New Media & Society* 20, no. 8 (November 2017): 2898–2916. https://doi.org/10.1177/1461444817737296.

Chapter Eleven: Wipe Out the Fuzz

1 Dent, Maggie. "Benefits of Silence and Stillness to Learning for Life." In *Saving Our Children From Our Chaotic World: Teaching Children the Magic of Silence and Stillness*. Pennington Publications, 2017. https://www.google.com/books/edition/_/zp9_DwAAQBAJ?hl=en&gbpv=0.

Donelli, Davide, Davide Lazzeroni, Matteo Rizzato, and Michele Antonelli. "Chapter 6 – Silence and Its Effects on the Autonomic Nervous System: A Systematic Review."

Progress in Brain Research 280 (September 2023): 103-144. https://doi.org/10.1016/bs.pbr.2023.08.001.

Stein, Samantha. "The Benefits of Quiet Solitude." *Psychology Today*. January 25, 2025. www.psychologytoday.com/us/blog/what-the-wild-things-are/202501/the-benefits-of-quiet-solitude.

Kirste, Imke, Zeina Nicola, Golo Kronenberg, Tara L. Walker, Robert C. Liu, and Gerd Kempermann. "Is Silence Golden? Effects of Auditory Stimuli and Their Absence on Adult Hippocampal Neurogenesis." *Brain Structure and Function* 220, no. 2 (December 2013): 1221–28. https://doi.org/10.1007/s00429-013-0679-3.

Bernardi, L., C. Porta, and P. Sleight. "Cardiovascular, Cerebrovascular, and Respiratory Changes Induced by Different Types of Music in Musicians and Non-Musicians: The Importance of Silence." *Heart* 92, no. 4 (December 2005): 445–52. https://doi.org/10.1136/hrt.2005.064600.

Cox, Janelle. "The Hidden Benefits of Silence." *Psych Central*. Last modified April 29, 2022. https://psychcentral.com/blog/the-hidden-benefits-of-silence.

2. Heuertz, Christopher L. *The Sacred Enneagram: Finding Your Unique Path to Spiritual Growth*. Zondervan, 2017.

3. Elon University. "Imagining the Digital Future." Accessed April 5, 2025. https://imaginingthedigitalfuture.org/wp-content/uploads/2024/02/AI2040-REPORT-Imagining-the-Digital-Future-PAGES-sm.pdf.

4. Heuertz, Christopher L. *The Sacred Enneagram: Finding Your Unique Path to Spiritual Growth*. Zondervan, 2017.

5. Galvez-Pol, Alejandro, Marcos Nadal, and James M. Kilner. "Emotional Representations of Space Vary as a Function of Peoples' Affect and Interoceptive Sensibility." *Scientific Reports* 11, no. 1 (August 2021). https://doi.org/10.1038/s41598-021-95081-9.

6. Niequist, Shauna. *I Guess I Haven't Learned that Yet*. Zondervan, 2022.

7. Down, Annie F., host. "Always Annie: Where Can I Grieve? – Episode 960." That Sounds Fun with Annie F. Down (podcast). February 20, 2025. Accessed August 20, 2025. https://podcasts.apple.com/us/podcast/always-annie-where-can-i-grieve-episode-960/id944925529?i=1000694287240.

8. Cloud, Henry, and John Sims Townsend. *Boundaries: When to Say Yes, When to Say No, to Take Control of Your Life*. Strand Publishing, 2002.

9. Bazen, Alexus. "Cell Phone Statistics 2025." Consumer Affairs. Last modified March 20, 2025. https://www.consumeraffairs.com/cell_phones/cell-phone-statistics.html.

10. Ibid.

11. Paulise, Luciana. "Here Is Why Batching Emails Beats Continuous Checking." *Forbes*. August 13, 2024. www.forbes.com/sites/lucianapaulise/2024/08/13/here-is-why-batching-emails-beats-continuous-checking/.

12. Brencher, Hannah. *The Unplugged Hours: Cultivating a Life of Presence in a Digitally Connected World*. Zondervan Books, 2024.

13. Ibid.

14. Rubin, Rick. *The Creative Act: A Way of Being*. Penguin Press, 2023.

15. Nowack, Kenneth. "Sleep, Emotional Intelligence, and Interpersonal Effectiveness: Natural Bedfellows." *Consulting Psychology Journal: Practice and Research* 69, no. 2 (June 2017): 66–79. https://doi.org/10.1037/cpb0000077.

16. Barnes, Christopher M., Eli Awtrey, Lorenzo Lucianetti, and Gretchen Spreitzer. "Leader Sleep Devaluation, Employee Sleep, and Unethical Behavior." *Sleep Health* 6, no. 3 (June 2020): 411-417. https://doi.org/10.1016/j.sleh.2019.12.001.

17. Shah, Parth, Shankar Vedantam, Tara Boyle, and Renee Klahr. "The 'Swiss Army Knife' of Health: A Good Night's Sleep." *NPR*. November 13, 2017. www.npr.org/2017/11/13/563831137/the-swiss-army-knife-of-health-a-good-nights-sleep.

Joyosity

18. Mayo Clinic. "Adult Health." February 1, 2025. https://www.mayoclinic.org/healthy-lifestyle/adult-health/expert-answers/how-many-hours-of-sleep-are-enough/faq-20057898.
19. Lovely, Rachel. "Make Your Day." TikTok video, 9:55. March 10, 2025. https://www.tiktok.com/@rachellovely5/video/7480346208972721451.
20. Berkman, Lisa F., Thomas Glass, Ian Brissette, and Teresa E. Seeman. "From Social Integration to Health: Durkheim in the New Millennium." *Social Science & Medicine* 51, no. 6 (September 2000): 843–57. https://doi.org/10.1016/s0277-9536(00)00065-4.
21. Duffy, Patricia. "26 Years Later: Would Kerri Strug's Famous Vault Have Happened Today?" Gymnastics Now. July 23, 2022. https://gymnastics-now.com/26-years-later-would-kerri-strugs-famous-vault-have-happened-today/.

    New York Daily News. "Kerri Stands Tall on Sprained Ankle." Last modified January 12, 2019. https://www.nydailynews.com/1996/07/24/kerri-stands-tall-on-sprained-ankle/.

    Olympics. "Kerri Strug: The Gymnast Who Battled Through Pain for a Taste of Olympic Glory." Accessed April 21, 2025. https://www.olympics.com/en/news/kerri-strug-the-gymnast-who-battled-through-pain-for-a-taste-of-olympic-glory.
22. Duffy, Patricia. "26 Years Later: Would Kerri Strug's Famous Vault Have Happened Today?" Gymnastics Now. July 23, 2022. https://gymnastics-now.com/26-years-later-would-kerri-strugs-famous-vault-have-happened-today/.
23. Olympics. "Kerri Strug: The Gymnast Who Battled Through Pain for a Taste of Olympic Glory." Accessed April 21, 2025. https://www.olympics.com/en/news/kerri-strug-the-gymnast-who-battled-through-pain-for-a-taste-of-olympic-glory.
24. Cooper, Alex, host. "Simon Biles: 'I Thought America Hated Me'." Call Her Daddy (podcast). April 17, 2024. Accessed August 30, 2025. https://open.spotify.com/episode/7h-01vlVxDCPsaIowobZMh7.
25. Ibid.
26. Ibid.
27. Kubota, Samantha. "Simone Biles Withdraws From Individual All-Around Final at Tokyo Olympics." Today. July 28, 2021. https://www.today.com/news/simone-biles-miss-individual-all-around-final-tokyo-olympics-t226681.

    IG Staff. "Russia Defeats the US Women Again, Claims Historic Team Gold." International Gymnast Media. July 27, 2021. https://www.intlgymnast.com/news/russia-defeats-the-us-women-again-claims-historic-team-gold/.
28. Martin, Jill, George Ramsey, and Homero De la Fuente. "Simone Biles Wins Her First Competitive Gymnastics Event Since 2021, Qualifies for US National Championships." CNN Sports. Last modified August 6, 2023. https://www.cnn.com/2023/08/05/sport/simone-biles-gymnastics-return-spt-intl.

Chapter Twelve: Three-Layer Biscuits

1. Gilbert, Elizabeth. "Your Elusive Creative Genius." TED video, 19:14. February 2009. https://www.ted.com/talks/elizabeth_gilbert_your_elusive_creative_genius.
2. Whitmer, Jenn. "Ep. 72 Purpose Unleashed: Successful Leadership with Jade Simmons." YouTube video, 25:00. January 15, 2025. https://youtu.be/GgtlQKm3ejo?si=s0LUm-9F1OASzFalm.
3. Whitmer, Jenn. "How Systems Support Your Success with Diana Fang." YouTube video, 23:39. March 8, 2023. https://youtu.be/fqy5Nm6CvSM?si=hDQqREoj6AOvFbrN.
4. Blake, Jenny. *Free Time: Lose the Busywork, Love Your Business*. Ideapress Publishing, 2022.
5. Ibid.
6. Porter, Michael E. and Nitin Nohria. "How CEOS Manage Time." *Harvard Business Review*. July 1, 2018. https://hbr.org/2018/07/how-ceos-manage-time.vv.
7. Adachi, Kendra, host. "#366 Twenty Helpful Decisions I Keep Repeating." The Genius Collective (podcast). August 1, 2024. Accessed March 1, 2025. https://www.thelazygeniuscollective.com/lazy/20decisions.

8   I've adapted this process from Michael Hyatt, Paul Graham, Dan Sullivan and Benjiman.
9   Graham, Paul. "Maker's Schedule, Manager's Schedule." Paul Graham. July 2009. https://paulgraham.com/makersschedule.html.
10 Freeman, Emily P., host. "73: Design Your Rhythm of Work – Theme Days." The Next Right Thing (podcast). May 12, 2021. Accessed August 30, 2025. https://emilypfreeman.com/podcast/73/.
11 Young, Kirsty, host. "Christopher Nolan." Desert Island Discs. February 23, 2018. Accessed May 3, 2025. https://www.bbc.co.uk/programmes/b09rwygm.
12 White, Martha C. "This Is the Easiest Productivity Hack in the History of Work." *Time*. December 16, 2014. https://time.com/3634542/productivity-hack/.

Seidl, Katharina N., Marius V. Peelen, and Sabine Kastner. "Neural Evidence for Distracter Suppression during Visual Search in Real-World Scenes." *Journal of Neuroscience* 32, no. 34 (August 2012): 11812–19. https://doi.org/10.1523/jneurosci.1693-12.2012.

13 Brooks, Alison Wood, Juliana Schroeder, Jane L. Risen, et al. " RETRACTED: Don't Stop Believing: Rituals Improve Performance by Decreasing Anxiety." *Organizational Behavior and Human Decision Processes* 137 (November 2016): 71–85. https://doi.org/10.1016/j.obhdp.2016.07.004.
14 Solodar, Jessica. "Sleep Hygiene: Simple Practices for Better Rest." Harvard Health. January 31, 2025. https://www.health.harvard.edu/staying-healthy/sleep-hygiene-simple-practices-for-better-rest.
15 Brown, Brené, host. "Austin Channing Brown on I'm Still Here: Black Dignity in a World Made for Whiteness." Unlocking Us with Brené Brown (podcast). June 10, 2020. Accessed August 31, 2025. https://brenebrown.com/podcast/brene-with-austin-channing-brown-on-im-still-here-black-dignity-in-a-world-made-for-whiteness/.
16 Radin, Dean, Nancy Lund, Masaru Emoto, and Takashige Kizu. "Effects of Distant Intention on Water Crystal Formation: A Triple-Blind Replication." *Journal of Scientific Exploration* 22, no. 4 (December 2008). https://www.researchgate.net/publication/255669110_Effects_of_Distant_Intention_on_Water_Crystal_Formation_A_Triple-Blind_Replication.

Whitworth, Damian. "Prince Was Right: Study Shows Talking to Plants Helps Them Grow." *The Sunday Times*. June 20, 2009. https://www.thetimes.com/comment/register/article/prince-was-right-study-shows-talking-to-plants-helps-them-grow-h2fhxkqfxjg?region=global.

Chapter Thirteen: The Serious Business of Play

1   Tignor, Steve. "Rewatch, French Open 2010: Djokovic's Career-Changing Loss to Melzer." Tennis. June 2, 2020. https://www.tennis.com/news/articles/rewatch-french-open-2010-djokovic-s-career-changing-loss-to-melzer.
2   Rothsch, Michael. "Djokovic: 'I Cried Uncontrollably after My Defeat against Melzer.'" TennisNet. March 7, 2021. https://www.tennisnet.com/en/news/novak-djokovic-i-cried-uncontrollably-after-my-defeat-against-melzer.
3   Tignor, Steve. "Rewatch, French Open 2010: Djokovic's Career-Changing Loss to Melzer." Tennis. June 2, 2020. https://www.tennis.com/news/articles/rewatch-french-open-2010-djokovic-s-career-changing-loss-to-melzer.
4   Howes, Lewis. "Novak Djokovic on Becoming #1 in the World and Overcoming the Odds with Lewis Howes." YouTube video, November 19, 2017. https://www.youtube.com/watch?v=ei_2LyVCWH4.
5   Scroll Staff. "Wanted to Quit Tennis after French Open Quarterfinal Defeat in 2010, Says Novak Djokovic." Scroll.in, May 1, 2020. https://scroll.in/field/960805/wanted-to-quit-tennis-after-french-open-quarterfinal-defeat-in-2010-says-novak-djokovic.
6   Wikipedia Contributors. "2011 Novak Djokovic Tennis Season." *Wikipedia, The Free Encyclopedia*. Last modified July 3, 2025. https://en.wikipedia.org/wiki/2011_Novak_Djokovic_tennis_season.

7   Howes, Lewis. "Novak Djokovic on Becoming #1 in the World and Overcoming the Odds with Lewis Howes." YouTube video, November 19, 2017. https://www.youtube.com/watch?v=ei_2LyVCWH4.

8   Brown, Stuart L. and Christopher C. Vaughan. *Play: How It Shapes the Brain, Opens the Imagination, and Invigorates the Soul*. Avery, 2010.

9   Ibid.

    Ferrabee, Gillian. "Play Creativity" (handout). Summer Poetics Retreat, New York, NY, July 12–15, 2023.

    Whitmer, Jenn. "Ep. 77 Tackling Toxic Work Environments with Play and Psychological Safety with Jeff Harry." YouTube video, 32:12. February 19, 2025. https://youtu.be/bm39gtlKO4U?si=NjyJkbUnHgX3nNzJ.

    Ware, Gary. *Playful Rebellion: Maximize Workplace Success Through the Power of Play*. Gary Ware, 2022.

    Eberle, Scott G. "The Elements of Play: Toward a Philosophy and a Definition of Play." *American Journal of Play* 6, no. 2 (2014): 214–233. https://www.museumofplay.org/app/uploads/2022/01/6-2-article-elements-of-play.pdf.

10 Csikszentmihalyi, Mihaly. *Flow: The psychology of optimal experience*. HarperPerennial, 2008.

11 Ferrabee, Gillian. "Play Creativity" (handout). Summer Poetics Retreat, New York, NY, July 12–15, 2023.

12 Freels, Timothy G., Daniel B. Gabriel, Deranda B. Lester, and Nicholas W. Simon. "Risky Decision-Making Predicts Dopamine Release Dynamics in Nucleus Accumbens Shell." *Neuropsychopharmacology* 45, no. 2 (September 2019): 266–75. https://doi.org/10.1038/s41386-019-0527-0.

13 Eberle, Scott G. "The Elements of Play: Toward a Philosophy and a Definition of Play." *American Journal of Play* 6, no. 2 (2014): 214–233. https://www.museumofplay.org/app/uploads/2022/01/6-2-article-elements-of-play.pdf.

14 McGraw, Seamus. "Essay: America's First Modern Mass Shooting Never Really Ended." *The Texas Tribune*. June 1, 2022. www.texastribune.org/2022/06/01/texas-tower-shooting-myth-good-guy-with-gun/.

15 Helmer, William. "The Madman on the Tower." *Texas Monthly*. August 1, 1986. www.texasmonthly.com/true-crime/the-madman-on-the-tower/.

    Brown, Stuart L. and Christopher C. Vaughan. *Play: How It Shapes the Brain, Opens the Imagination, and Invigorates the Soul*. Avery, 2010.

16 Ibid.

17 Brown, Dr. Stuart L. *Consequences of Play Deprivation*. National Institute for Play. February 2015. www.fa-sett.no/filer/Consequences_of_Play_Deprivation-Stuart_Brown_MD.pdf.

18 Brown, Stuart L. and Christopher C. Vaughan. *Play: How It Shapes the Brain, Opens the Imagination, and Invigorates the Soul*. Avery, 2010. p. 26.

19 BrightHR. *It Pays to Play*. 2015. p. 20. https://pages.brighthr.com/rs/217-MIC-854/images/itpaystoplay.pdf.

20 BrightHR. *It Pays to Play*. 2015. p. 19. https://pages.brighthr.com/rs/217-MIC-854/images/itpaystoplay.pdf.

21 Brown, Stuart. *Consequences of Play Deprivation*. National Institute for Play. February 2015. p. 8. www.fa-sett.no/filer/Consequences_of_Play_Deprivation-Stuart_Brown_MD.pdf.

22 Gray, Peter, David F. Lancy, and David F. Bjorklund. "Decline in Independent Activity as a Cause of Decline in Children's Mental Well-Being: Summary of the Evidence." *The Journal of Pediatrics* 260 (September 2023): 113352. https://doi.org/10.1016/j.jpeds.2023.02.004.

23 BrightHR. *It Pays to Play*. 2015. p. 12, 16. https://pages.brighthr.com/rs/217-MIC-854/images/itpaystoplay.pdf.

24 Lopushinsky, Paul. "Everything You Wanted to Know about Play at Work." Playficient. May 11, 2023. www.playficient.com/play-at-work/.
25 Eberle, Scott G. "The Elements of Play: Toward a Philosophy and a Definition of Play." *American Journal of Play* 6, no. 2 (2014): 36. https://www.museumofplay.org/app/uploads/2022/01/6-2-article-elements-of-play.pdf.
26 Brown, Stuart L. and Christopher C. Vaughan. *Play: How It Shapes the Brain, Opens the Imagination, and Invigorates the Soul.* Avery, 2010.

Whitmer, Jenn. "Ep. 72 Purpose Unleashed: Successful Leadership with Jade Simmons." YouTube video, 25:00. January 15, 2025. https://youtu.be/GgtlQKm3ej0?si=0BGCbIW-GORpAA6ux.
27 Whitmer, Jenn. "Ep. 76 Not Forced Fun: How Play Powers Productivity with Jeff Harry." YouTube video, 31:17. February 12, 2025. https://youtu.be/EtDJHs46hTw?si=nFS6_hLgap-WAe709.
28 Van Vleet, Meredith and Brooke C. Feeney. "Young at Heart." *Perspectives on Psychological Science* 10, no. 5 (September 2015): 639–45. https://doi.org/10.1177/1745691615596789.
29 Palagi, Elisabetta. "Adult Play and the Evolution of Tolerant and Cooperative Societies." *Neuroscience & Biobehavioral Reviews* 148 (May 2023): 105124. https://doi.org/10.1016/j.neubiorev.2023.105124.
30 Fluegge-Woolf, Erin R. "Play Hard, Work Hard." *Management Research Review* 37, no. 8 (July 2014): 682–705. https://doi.org/10.1108/mrr-11-2012-0252.

National Institute for Play. "Why We Play." Accessed April 26, 2025. https://nifplay.org/what-is-play/biological-drive-to-play/.
31 Csikszentmihalyi, Mihaly. *Flow: The psychology of optimal experience.* HarperPerennial, 2008.
32 Brown, Stuart L. and Christopher C. Vaughan. *Play: How It Shapes the Brain, Opens the Imagination, and Invigorates the Soul.* Avery, 2010.
33 Ibid.
34 Gray, Peter. "Play Makes Us Human. Commentary on Adult and Juvenile Play in Humans and Other Primates." *Neuroscience & Biobehavioral Reviews* 169 (February 2025): 105981. https://doi.org/10.1016/j.neubiorev.2024.105981.
35 Bekoff, Marc. "Wild Justice and Fair Play: Cooperation, Forgiveness, and Morality in Animals." *Biology & Philosophy* 19, no. 4 (September 2004): 489–520. https://doi.org/10.1007/sbiph-004-0539-x.
36 Fluegge-Woolf, Erin R. "Play Hard, Work Hard." *Management Research Review* 37, no. 8 (July 2014): 682–705. https://doi.org/10.1108/mrr-11-2012-0252.
37 Xiang, Nina. "SHRM Report: Workplace Culture Fosters Employee Retention Worldwide." SHRM Business. December 12, 2024. www.shrm.org/executive-network/insights/shrm-report-workplace-culture-fosters-employee-retention.
38 Glynn, Mary Ann and Jane Webster. "The Adult Playfulness Scale: An Initial Assessment." *Psychological Reports* 71, no. 1 (August 1992): 83–103. https://doi.org/10.2466/pro.1992.71.1.83.
39 Kotler, Steven. "Is the Secret to Ultimate Human Performance the F-Word?" *Forbes.* Last modified February 8, 2014. https://www.forbes.com/sites/stevenkotler/2014/01/08/the-research-is-in-a-four-letter-word-that-starts-with-f-is-the-real-secret-to-ultimate-human-performance/.

Csikszentmihalyi, Mihaly. *Flow: The psychology of optimal experience.* HarperPerennial, 2008.
40 Karyn Purvis Institute of Child Development. "Introduction to TBRI®." YouTube video, 1:06:38. September 29, 2015. https://youtu.be/7vjVpRffgHQ?si=cZwH1TrD-kXUyWNX.

Note: There is some dispute about this claim because of Purvis' untimely death, and her notes are missing the source.

41 McKenzie, Aaron. "After Working for John Surtees and Founding the Long Beach Grand Prix, Nate Jones Is Teaching Kids How to Work on Cars." Hagerty Media. July 11, 2016. www.hagerty.com/media/archived/nate-jones/.

42 Cranston, Susie and Scott Keller. "Increasing the 'Meaning Quotient' of Work." McKinsey & Company. January 1, 2013. www.mckinsey.com/capabilities/people-and-organizational-performance/our-insights/increasing-the-meaning-quotient-of-work.

Brown, Stuart L. and Christopher C. Vaughan. *Play: How It Shapes the Brain, Opens the Imagination, and Invigorates the Soul.* Avery, 2010.

43 Brown, Stuart L. and Christopher C. Vaughan. *Play: How It Shapes the Brain, Opens the Imagination, and Invigorates the Soul.* Avery, 2010.

44 Ware, Gary. *Playful Rebellion: Maximize Workplace Success Through the Power of Play.* Gary Ware, 2022.

45 Morgan, Jessica. Personal interviews with the author. November 2021, May 21, 2025, June 16, 2025.

46 Teitelbaum, Daniel. "Dr. Stuart Bown Was Born to Play." Dumbo Feather. August 12, 2019. https://www.dumbofeather.com/conversations/dr-stuart-brown-believes-we-were-born-to-play/.

47 Davey, Liane. "How to Work for a Childish Leader." Liane Davey. April 23, 2014. https://lianedavey.com/childish-leader/.

48 Swinn, Emma and Steven Campbell-Harris. "The Myth of Growing Up: How Childlike Traits Benefit Adults." *Think* 23, no. 68 (Autumn 2024): 29-35. https://doi.org/10.1017/S1477175624000071.

49 Ibid.

50 Mohr Lone, Jana. *Seen and Not Heard: Why Children's Voices Matter.* Rowman & Littlefield, 2021.

51 Ware, Gary. *Playful Rebellion: Maximize Workplace Success Through the Power of Play.* Gary Ware, 2022.

52 Buck, Pearl S. The Joy of Children. Bookworld Enterprises, 1974.

53 Whitmer, Jenn. "Ep. 72 Purpose Unleashed: Successful Leadership with Jade Simmons." YouTube video, 25:00. January 15, 2025. https://youtu.be/GgtlQKm3ej0?si=gZrJkCBfHOZ-pJWTX.

54 Taylor, Kate. "Chick-Fil-A's Mobile Sales Are Skyrocketing as Execs Say the Chicken Chain Is Entering a New Tech-Obsessed Era." Business Insider. May 21, 2019. www.businessinsider.com/chick-fil-a-mobile-sales-skyrocket-2019-5.

55 Csikszentmihalyi, Mihaly. Flow: The psychology of optimal experience. HarperPerennial, 2008.

56 Oprescu, Florin, Christian Jones, and Mary Katsikitis. "I Play at Work—Ten Principles for Transforming Work Processes through Gamification." Frontiers in Psychology 5 (2014). https://doi.org/10.3389/fpsyg.2014.00014.

57 Ferrabee, Gillian. "Play Creativity" (handout). Summer Poetics Retreat, New York, NY, July 12–15, 2023.

58 Marshmallow Challenge. "Marshmallow Challenge." *Marshmallow Challenge* (blog). *Marshmallow Challenge.* Accessed January 5, 2025. https://www.marshmallowchallenge.com.

Wujec, Tom. "Tom Wujec: Build a Tower, Build a Team." TED video, 07:44. February 2010. https://www.ted.com/talks/tom_wujec_build_a_tower_build_a_team.

Schnuck, Matt. "You Don't Need to Even Like Basketball to LOVE This Play." X, April 20, 2024. https://x.com/mattschnuck/status/1781738109081944251.

59 Perlovsky, Leonid and Roman Ilin. "Brain. Conscious and Unconscious Mechanisms of Cognition, Emotions, and Language." Brain Sciences 2, no. 4 (December 2012): 790–834. https://doi.org/10.3390/brainsci2040790.

60 Morgan, Jessica. Personal interviews with the author. November 2021, May 21, 2025, June 16, 2025.

Your RSVP to Joyosity

1   Whitmer, Jenn. "Ep. 85 The Leadership Trap: What's Distracting You from Real Impact? With Ron Tite." Youtube video, 26:07. April 16, 2025. https://youtu.be/Exwp1dh6U-cA?si=huMDiIoF0o_JOYpO.

2   WorkLife with Adam Grant. "Building an Anti-Racist Workplace Transcript." TED. April 20, 2021. https://www.ted.com/podcasts/worklife/building-an-anti-racist-workplace-transcript.

3   Zokovitch, Grace. "That's the Ticket! Fenway Concerts Brought in $125M in 2024." Boston Herald. June 2, 2025. https://www.bostonherald.com/2025/06/02/thats-the-ticket-fenway-concerts-brought-in-125m-in-2024.

4   Campbell, Carrie. Personal interviews with the author. January 2024. September 2024. April 18, 2025.

5   Hasse, Dr. John Edward. "Jazz." Smithsonian Music. March 2016. https://music.si.edu/story/jazz.

6   Gladwell, Malcolm. *Revenge of the Tipping Point: Overstories, Superspreaders, and the Rise of Social Engineering*. Little, Brown and Company, 2024. p. 121–132. Author Note: *Italics* and phrasings Gladwell's.

7   Kerr, Dr. Jacqueline. Personal interview with the author. March 14, 2025.

Stories That Didn't Fit

1   Whitmer, Jenn. "How to Build Better Systems." YouTube video, 22:19. August 3, 2023. https://youtu.be/Dgf8Hs5HDik?si=mTyIbCH6En345Ee1.

2   Steele, J. Dorman. *Manual of Science for Teachers*. A.S. Barnes & Company, 1888. p. 5. https://ia800102.us.archive.org/32/items/ERIC_ED620657/ED620657.pdf.

3   The Pew Charitable Trusts. "Pursuing the American Dream: Economic Mobility Across Generations." Pew. July 2012. p. 2. https://www.pew.org/~/media/legacy/uploadedfiles/pcs_assets/2012/pursuingamericandreampdf.pdf.

4   Abrams, Stacey. *Minority Leader*. Henry Holt. 2018.

High-Fives, Hugs, and Hallelujahs

Leadership is a team sport. Turns out, so is writing a book. And I am overwhelmed with gratitude for this championship crew of coaches, coffee-bringers, and cheerleaders.

You, the Joy-Wanting Reader

I'm genuinely proud of you. Because joy is vulnerable, intense, and skepticism-inducing, it's incredibly tempting to leave cultivating joy behind. Thank you for reading and, even more, thank you for doing the work that will change the world. One joy-bringer at a time.

Joyosity Works VIP, Podcast Listeners, and Online Friends

I wouldn't be here without you, your stories, and your engagement with me. I'm so grateful you're along for the ride for my weighted vest walks, #MutliBeverage stories, and the *Joyosity* podcast journey. I love when you send me reels of musicals, Disneyland jokes, and anything about joy at work. But more, I'm so grateful when you share yourself with me.

Mentors from Afar and Kind of Close

I absolutely stand on the shoulders of the amazing leaders who have cultivated joy before me. These wonderful humans have inspired, challenged, and encouraged me along this journey. I've observed their brilliant, beautiful work of making this complex world better. Some have sat with me, and others have no idea of their legacy in my work: Austin Channing Brown, Brené Brown, Kwame Christian, Henry Cloud, Viola Davis, Liane Davey, Annie F. Downs, Jess Ekstrom, Emily P. Freeman, Seth Godin, Adam Grant, Bob Goff, Will Guidara, Kindra Hall, Justin Jones-Fosu, Kim Kaupe, Patrick Lencioni, Shannon Matson, Jo Saxton, Stephen "Shed" Shedletzky, Jade Simmons, Stephen Sondheim, Suzanne Stabile, Reese Witherspoon, and the *Ted Lasso* writers and cast.

Keynote Audiences and Coaching Clients

Every time I stand before you, we have a new experience. We all walk away as different people. I'm impressed and moved by you. And you let me know what works and what doesn't—I'm enormously grateful for that. Thank you for being the Magic Third of my Joy Ratio.

Ariel Curry, Aileen Weintraub, and Christina Caruccio

I am often a fireworks display of ideas and exciting words. Ariel, thank you for helping me arrange my explosions into a logical flow. Aileen, thank you for helping me harness the fireworks into fire so readers can fuel change. Christina, thank you for getting my voice immediately and adding the claps. Editors, you are treasures.

Ideapress

First, thank you for showing me I can do this, and that the world needs the message of *Joyosity*. And then thank you for being the business end of publishing. I just want to deliver keynotes, write, and coach people. You took on my Toil's Tiny Ten and my Messy Middle and made it magic. Thank you, Rohit Bhargava, Kameron Bryant-Sergejev, Allison Griffith, Lynnette McCurdy, Marnie McMahon, Athena Potkovic, and Megan Wheeler.

Coverdell Cove, Sarah's Sunporch, and Libraries

This book would not exist without the places of safety that let me focus on the deep work of creativity. Jeff, Christina, and Sarah, thank you for generously sharing your spaces with me. I spent hours writing at the Boston Public Library on Boylston and the St. Louis County Library Mid-County and Clark Family branches. For both the space and the thousands of books I've checked out over the decades, thank you.

Sunshine Lane, We Make Systems Sexy, and Robinson Management

You already know I'm not the best at details. This book would not exist without the work of my team. Thank you to Shelby Merryweather and the Merryweather Sisters-in-Law for doing the work of producing the podcast, sending the emails, designing the graphics, managing the admin work, and generally being amazing humans. I just adore you. Ashley Weigl and We Make Systems Sexy, thank you for seamlessly picking up and taking me onto the next stage. Daniel Robinson and Maddison Wilcox, your business management gave me the freedom to make this happen.

Movers and Poetics

Thank you to Harris III and the Poetics. Your coaching and community shaped my business, the book, and me as a human. I would never have dreamed this book was possible, let alone build a business, without you. The Movers Collective has walked this road from my first keynote, my TEDx, and the shaping of this book. The Collective has cheered and suggested and laughed with me for the last six years.

Sally Z.: The words to express how much I love you and what you've built seem so pale compared to the impact you have had on me. Joyosity would *hundo p* not exist without you.

Marco Polo Disney Crew

A day at Disney birthed so many things. Thank you for responding to the panicked Polos, the daisy-chaining, and the "I'm damn good at this" revelations with wise compassion and enthusiastic *yeses* and earmuff warnings. Thank you for being the first people to buy this book the moment it had a preorder link. You embody that a healthy, joyful business isn't separate from, and actually requires, living one, whole life. *Kloveyabye!*

March Girls

Camille, Ferg, Linds, and Sarah, we fill me with so much joy. Thank you for the best adventures, the needed prayers, the amazing encouragement, the endless laughter, and the healing tears. Thank you for continuing to lobby for Disney and for the continuous stream of messages and Polos. I'm so grateful that you sing back to me more than "Cardinal is her color . . . " Let's do this for another thirty-one years.

Family

To my parents: Even when they didn't really get what I was doing, they kept making sure I was liking it, every speakerphone call we had. Darlene, thank you for commiserating about the ones who give us gray hairs and for being my little sis who towers over me. Mark and Barbara, thank you for cheering me on like your own. Melissa, you have celebrated and cried with me for decades. Thank you for being the sister who keeps our family's poop in a group.

Annalise, Sabrina, Stuart, and Chase, you have served and cheered and let me share your stories. Thank you for being excited at every turn, for persevering with me, and for quoting *Penguins*. You are my heart on the outside. I'm always after your best.

Michael, there are not enough words to convey my undying gratitude for who you are as a man, a father, a partner, a creator, a collaborator, and a servant. I know you cheer the loudest and the hardest, but even more, you work for my success more than anyone else. I'm so grateful we've shared this life since pre-K Sunday school. I love you.

The Lord

Praise and glory to God, who has placed me in the Kingdom of Light and called me to be a repairer of the breach and to make community livable again. You are the bedrock of my joy.

About Jenn
Your Joy-Bringing Host

Jenn Whitmer helps leaders with Joyosity, creating positive culture with complex people. Through solving conflict, cultivating communication, and capitalizing on the uniqueness of each person, Jenn helps you create empowered teams full of engaged humans who want to stay and create great work.

As an international keynote, TEDx, and Vistage speaker, and Enneagram specialist, Jenn helps organizations retain employees, increase efficiency, and develop healthy culture so that work is a joy, people are whole, and organizations flourish. (Usually, that means a lot of laughter!)

She also has the credentials you're looking for: Jenn holds graduate certificates in music education, theology, and leadership, along with a master of arts in communication and culture from Webster University and certification as an Enneagram coach. And she's been in the trenches of leading people. She spent twenty years as an educator and school leader, wrangling students, mobilizing volunteers, managing projects, and leading professionals.

Through her work on event stages, in conference rooms, and at workshop tables, Jenn has stood in front of thousands of people, helping them develop the skills to improve their teams. She also sits behind the mic as the host of the *Joyosity* podcast, interviewing leaders and experts to help you restore the joy of work, creating a healthy workplace culture that is people-first and purpose-driven.

Working with Jenn, you and your team improve communication, resolve conflict, and develop deep respect for the unique skills and gifts each person brings to their work—all so you can live an integrated, peaceful life where you bring all of yourself to work without sacrificing your productivity, your profits, or your life.

When she's not helping leaders, she's probably walking through TSA PreCheck with her Frownies on, not-at-all-secretly wanting her life to just be a musical (Favorite? *Newsies*—because who doesn't love a good underdog story?), and quoting *Ted Lasso* gems like, "Don't you dare settle for fine," to anyone who will listen. Jenn lives in St. Louis, Missouri, with her high school sweetheart and husband of nearly thirty years, Michael. They have young kids in their twenties and teenage years, as well as a surly Russian Blue cat who judges their life choices from the armrest of the couch.